Withdrawn

The Fifth Season

BOOKS BY DONALD HONIG

Baseball When the Grass Was Real
Baseball Between the Lines
The Man in the Dugout
The October Heroes
The Image of Their Greatness
    (with Lawrence Ritter)
The 100 Greatest Baseball Players of All Time
    (with Lawrence Ritter)
Baseball's 10 Greatest Teams
Baseball America
The All-Star Game: An Illustrated History
Baseball: The Illustrated History of America's Game
Shadows of Summer

The Fifth Season

TALES OF MY LIFE IN BASEBALL

Donald Honig

Ivan R. Dee   Chicago   2009

www.ivanrdee.com

Library of Congress Cataloging-in-Publication Data:
Honig, Donald.
    The fifth season : tales of my life in baseball / Donald Honig.
        p. cm.
    ISBN-13: 978-1-56663-810-4 (cloth : alk. paper)
    ISBN-10: 1-56663-810-0 (cloth : alk. paper)
    1. Honig, Donald. 2. Sportswriters—United States—Biography.
3. Baseball. I. Title.
GV742.42.H66A3 2009
070.4'49796357092—dc22
    [B]   2008036471

For Stanley

The Fifth Season

One

⨠ IT ISN'T how profound or impressive your mind is, it's knowing in detail some ludicrously obscure fact at precisely the right moment that can earn you the reputation as an "authority." And once conferred, this secular canonization is hard to shake off, not that you really would want to do that. In fact the opposite happens; you strive not only to beguile people with what you know but occasionally to astonish them. There's nothing like it. But there's something even better: now and then you are able to transcend yourself by stupefying them with some scrap of knowledge that should be so remote to human memory no normal person should have been capable of possessing it or have rational reason to. Anyway, I'll tell you exactly what happened.

In the summer of 2005, Mitchell Scherr, producer of television documentaries for Major League Baseball, called and asked if he and some colleagues might come up from New York to where I lived in central Connecticut and interview me for a show they were preparing. The subject matter would include the 1951 National League pennant race, with emphasis on the Branca-Thomson version of *High Noon*; the

3

sale of Babe Ruth to the New York Yankees; some Ebbets Field memories; and, because of the digressive ways of these conversations, whatever else might come flapping out of the past. Being an old Brooklyn Dodgers fan, for me 1951 was not an especially pleasant time to revisit (accounts of it read like baseball's *Journal of the Plague Year*), but I thought that at least I would be able to achieve some balance by tormenting Red Sox fans with a detailed account of Ruth's sale to the Yankees.

We agreed on time and place, the latter being a rather large and splendid motel about two miles from my home. Arriving there at the appointed time, I went to the registration desk and asked the tall young man standing behind it where I might find the representatives of Major League Baseball. His face brightened.

"Major League Baseball," he said with some feeling, as if announcing the title of a poem he was about to recite.

"That's right," I said.

"Major League Baseball," he said, "is in the Presidential Suite." He then gave me directions to that august quarter.

When I walked into the suite I found its tasteful accommodations occupied by five gentlemen and a setup of inquisitorial technology. Wires and power cables were strewn across the carpeting, and there were several elevated, soul-searching, and truth-demanding key lights focused on a leathery armchair where I was to sit and dispense baseball lore. It was a scene set for either a suspect or an authority; fortunately I was the latter.

The crew consisted of the lighting man; the sound man, who sat and watched a boxed dashboard of dials and little colored lights; an apprentice, whose sole function, as far as

I could determine, was to stare at me while I spoke; and two representatives of Major League Baseball. These latter were Scherr, the series producer, who sat silently throughout with an evaluating face, and Roger Schlueter, the production assistant, whose job it was to sit off-camera and feed me topics and questions.

For a little more than two hours I sat under the audio cable and boom mike in that fixed flash of light and prattled away, trying to make the oft-told tales fresh and vivid. Thomson once more stroked his sempiternal home run, the deity Ruth once more was sold away to the sidewalks of Sodom, and the charm of Ebbets Field was revisited. It went smoothly, I thought, and everyone seemed satisfied.

After they packed up I accompanied them downstairs to the lobby where the MLB reps went to the desk to check out. As he watched Mitchell Scherr attend to these details, the tall young gentleman behind the desk said in an admiring voice, "Major League Baseball."

"That's right," Mitchell said.

"My great-uncle was a pitcher," the clerk said.

I was off to a side talking to Roger Schlueter when I heard a name mentioned.

"Kemp Wicker," the clerk said.

In the back of my mind some memory chimes rustled slightly. I turned to him.

"Left-handed pitcher," I said.

He smiled appreciatively. "That's right," he said with an upbeat of surprise.

"Pitched for the Dodgers in 1941," I said.

With a trace of uncertainty now: "I believe so."

"He won just one game."

"Did he?"

"Early in May," I said. "It was against the Cardinals at Ebbets Field. He came on in relief and got the win. He pitched very well, as a matter of fact."

"He did?" the clerk asked. He was staring at me. They were all staring at me.

"It went twelve innings," I said. "In the bottom of the twelfth, Cookie Lavagetto singled through the left side, scoring Joe Medwick from second, and that was the game. Five-four, Brooklyn."

They continued to stare at me, in a way that made me feel as if I'd just materialized from another galaxy.

"How do you know that?" Roger asked. I think he was having some difficulty keeping the skepticism out of his voice.

"It's a baseball fact," I said. "Check it out."

"Oh, no," he said. "We believe you."

A day or two later he called. We spoke about the interview for a few minutes, how satisfied they'd been with it, and then he got around to it.

"About that Kemp Wicker thing," he said. "We were talking about it on the way home. We figured you had to be joking around with that guy. You couldn't have remembered that."

"Did you check it out?"

He laughed. "Well, yes, as a matter of fact. Just for the hell of it. You had it exactly right. Twelve innings, the Lavagetto hit, Medwick scoring."

"And Wicker got the win."

"That's right."

"Well," I said, "that's what happened."

"Listen," he said, "how did you remember that? Those details?"

"It was only sixty-four years ago."

"But—"

"I don't see anything remarkable about it," I said. "I'm supposed to be the big authority, right?"

"I guess so," he said.

You often find yourself being asked, *How did you know that?*, a question that can be insulting or flattering, depending on where the emphasis is placed. You needn't feel the compulsion to answer; the line between the authority and the charlatan is best left blurred. There is a hocus-pocus aura about arcane knowledge and no good reason to disturb it.

But the fact is, a head filled with esoteric minutiae is no accident. In my case it was what some people might call—and indeed some did—a misspent childhood, though if you trace the headspring you will see it wasn't that at all. If you were much of a boy growing up in the Maspeth section of Queens in the late 1930s and 1940s, you had the baseball fever. It seemed contagious, but it struck mostly from within. The malady had various strains and was curable if the remedy was desired. The affliction was generally benign, unless your supposedly contending team took a nosedive through the standings; when that happened, depression was apt to set in. Further manifestations were the memorization of endless statistics (past and present), friendships ruptured on the basis of partisanship, offense taken at the demeaning of a favorite player, and digestive tracts impaired by the loss of a close game. This was serious business.

For some youngsters the disorder was seasonal, assured to drop away with the autumn leaves, but for the more gravely infected it was year-round. If you were unable to play the game (a blizzard was capable of inflicting this upon you, and sometimes a mere cloudburst was known to do it), you talked about it, sagely with fellow partisans, loudly and irrationally with the other damn fools. With professional football and basketball mostly still waiting for an as yet embryonic television miracle to display their virtues, the single compelling sport was baseball, played in Maspeth on the slush of melting March snows and on until the onset of late November's bladed winds, at which point it became passionate conversation.

If baseball permeated its young acolytes like a theology, then in 1941, that last great season before the war, its doctrine was embodied by three young demigods who were building careers destined to become luminous in the game's annals. Like the note-by-note construction of a mighty symphony, they were methodically compiling statistics for the ages. In 1941 they were baseball's hierarchy: Cleveland pitcher Bob Feller, Boston Red Sox outfielder Ted Williams, and New York Yankees outfielder Joe DiMaggio, who was already and who would remain to the end of his long life a revered icon, a veritable flesh-and-blood *objet d'art*.

That these three players should have been at peak performance in that summer of menacing shades gave the 1941 season a sunlit perpetuity, with Williams's season-ending leap across the .400 barrier a fortissimo send-off. Feller was merely his normal blazing self, rising to twenty-five victories (after a season of twenty-seven) and then not to be seen again in all his manifest command for five years. Williams and DiMaggio— with his fifty-six-game hit streak that summer—piled achievements so high as to leave them seemingly forever snowcapped and beyond reach. When the two outfielders were to remain enlarged beyond their careers and prevail in the imagination to the end of their days, each living within the contours of Ruthian celebrity, it was 1941 that always radiated most brilliantly from them.

And if you went to Yankee Stadium when Boston was in town, you could, for the price of a single bleacher ticket, see them both in performance. You watched the motionless bat-cocked DiMaggio at the plate suddenly explode his lethal right-handed swing; you studied him in center field in his splendid isolation, bent at the waist, hands on knees, waiting to metamorphose into "the sleekest ship of state ever to cross the green grass of America."

And—for the price of that single ticket—the lanky Williams at bat, agitated with quivering tension, impatient to uncoil that meter of baseball poetry, that *swing*, and rifle the ball with crackling authority; swing by flawless swing on his way to fulfilling that grandiose boyhood obsession—"to have people say, 'There goes Ted Williams, the greatest hitter who ever lived.'"

You were ten years old and so you stared down at them from your bleacher seat with blessed awe and wonderment. You stared at them and tried to imagine what they might be thinking, what it felt like to be them. They were there to show you your game at its best, before disappearing back into whence they had come, into whatever mysterious sheath they had been drawn from. They were ideal for a ripening ten-year-old imagination that was already stirring air currents under its fledgling wings. A ten-year-old boy knew his entitlements; he knew he could spangle his private sky with whatever gleams of light he chose, sure that as one stage of life followed another they would never dim and the old man would hold them fast.

And if you were one of nearly 53,000 who sat in that Grand Canyon of a ballpark on July 1, 1941, you got double your money's worth when the Red Sox invaded for a double-header. You sat there transfixed in a cauldron of mid-nineties heat watching Joseph whack hits in both games to raise his streak to forty-four and tie an old Willie Keeler mark set in 1897, while Theodore hovered at just .400.

When we arrived home, my older brother Stanley and I, clutching our rolled-up scorecards, drenched with perspiration and excitement, my mother had one look and said, "Go take a shower and don't use up all the hot water."

"DiMaggio hit in both games," I told her.

"I know," she said. "I heard it on the radio."

"He tied Willie Keeler's record," Stanley, ever the scholar, informed her.

"I only know Ruby Keeler," she said, referring to the famous Broadway tap dancer.

The baseball fever was only enhanced by the multiple choices then available—Ebbets Field, Yankee Stadium, the Polo Grounds, each with its ghosts and its histories. When you sat in one of those American coliseums of such varying configurations, you could with but slight draw on your imagination feel yourself more than mere spectator. You were a student and there was vicarious participation; you had played those same nine innings and by those same rules. You were knowing about what DiMaggio and Williams were doing: you had faced pitched balls yourself, you had tried to outrace a fly ball before gravity forced it to earth. You watched, you studied, you learned, and the next day you believed you were a better player as you cocked your bat like Joe or fidgeted in the box like Ted.

An obsession modifies as one matures, or anyway should. Other things come to besiege you, psychic energy is siphoned away. But the ten-year-old would not allow himself to be entirely repudiated, lest he had never been. So the obsession remained, growing proportionate with one's maturity. The mind proved itself an accommodating mansion, allowing DiMaggio, Williams, and Feller to coexist with the likes of Shakespeare, Dostoevsky, and Tolstoy.

Often, in later years, when I was writing a long series of books on the game (on my way to becoming that shameless "authority"), some well-intended philistine would ask to have explained to him the fascination with baseball. I offered my stock answer: "If you have to ask the question, you'll never understand the answer." Facile, perhaps, but probably true enough. Of course a plethora of explanations have been advanced for the game's sway over people. Some of these theories have been rather erudite, suggesting reasons anthropological or psychological; still others cite a national ethos embracing democratic principles and atavistic rural yearnings. A game that attracts the passions and loyalties of people by the hundreds of millions, which has indeed spread across the oceans like some giant amoeba, cannot escape the scrutiny of theorists. The answer, if there is one, probably lies within the individual who swore himself to the game at an early age, when one is most serious and vulnerable to all permeations, who found some primal satisfaction in stroking a pitched ball over an infielder's head or chasing a fly ball with heart and glove, and then learning there were men who could do these same things masterfully enough to set thousands roaring. How the gurus of other professions accomplished their feats was usually shrouded in mystery; what a DiMaggio did was open to all, magical in its simplicity.

In Maspeth the aspirers, the would-be crown princes, played the game in the streets with broomsticks and pink rubber balls (the "spaldeens," a part of urban lore), wary of the wide-mouthed sewers in depressions at every corner waiting to make the ultimate putout. And with grapefruit-sized softballs it was played on the two concrete diamonds of Junior High School 73, where occasionally some fervent player would send himself sliding into one of the painted bases, an incipient Ty Cobb who would go home in trousers looking like Maypole streamers. And with a grand baseball itself the game was played on empty lots and onetime cow pastures with rickety backstops, potholed infields, unfenced outfields that sprouted occasional tufts of grass, and cut-up squares of cardboard for bases (who can forget the day when a kid named Pickles showed up with an empty liquor store carton and announced, "Here's the bases"?). An umpire, usually dragooned into the thankless job, called balls and strikes from behind the pitcher. And of course there were no foul lines. Nor were we always completely equipped, a deficiency that one day led an intrepid lad to volunteer to go behind the plate without a mask, resulting in a foul-tip mashing too indelicate to report. Rudimentary, yes, but there were still ninety feet between bases (more or less), and the rules were observed. It was baseball, played no less intensely than DiMaggio and Williams played theirs. And when the game was over there was a further ritual—invading Pete's candy store and spinning on the stools while swallowing sodas and egg creams and replaying the game. Athletes after a hard day's work.

We lived on Grand Avenue, Maspeth's trolley-lined main thoroughfare. The small four-room apartment was upstairs from a German delicatessen, whose Teutonic proprietor was known, before the war, to wear a swastika armband from time to time. "It's a free country," my father said, "but he should drop dead anyway."

Just around the corner was Junior High School 73, known formally as William Cowper Junior High. Who William Cowper was was a mystery, even to some of the English teachers. The school was four large and sturdily red-brick stories high, fairly new then and well equipped and maintained. But little of its classrooms or printing or woodworking shops or biology lab or music room meant much to me. The only component of this academic center I found to be of much use was the large schoolyard with its two ballplayers' diamonds, which I would stare longingly at whenever near a window.

Being situated around the corner from the school, my brother and I were able to come home for lunch. Three years older, serious and mature beyond his years (and always remarkably aware of the responsibilities of an older brother), Stanley always hurried home to his peanut butter sandwich and returned on time; I was wont to straggle, seeing no advantage in hurrying only to have to turn around and go back.

One day in early May 1941, however, it was different. When we climbed the stairs and walked into the small kitchen with its linoleum-covered floor, oilcloth-covered table, icebox, and hot-water boiler next to the stove, my father was sitting at the table with a roguish smile while my aproned mother was hovering by with the sulky expression of one who has just lost a debate to inferior logic.

My father, who seemed to have a lot of spare time in those days, was a large and brawny man with a big belly who never minded when we called him "Chubby," probably because he had been slender as a boy, the weight packed on after his psyche had determined what he physically was. The rogue's expression set in his broad fleshy face looked like the smile of a man of no vices but perhaps a hive of dubious virtues. He was smoking one of his inevitable Chesterfields, one of the many that would eventually sabotage his heart and lungs and take him from us much too early.

"What would you rather do," he asked when we came in, "go back to school or go to Ebbets Field?"

My mother was a welter of contradictions. She was strict about school and study and homework and all those other banes that interfere with childhood; yet she knew how profoundly her two little darlings were looking forward to their first big-league game, particularly if it was at Ebbets Field, that Brooklyn cathedral where those virtual family members, the hallowed Dodgers, could be seen, those Dodgers who so far existed only through the radio and in the pages of the *Daily News*. Was there a real choice for a mother between scholarship and euphoria?

Where he got the tickets is a fact lost to history. But he had them. Even if he had managed a fourth, my mother wouldn't have come along; she was an island of resistance among the roiling baseball waters around her, maintaining an attitude if not of disdain then of tolerant superiority. The question had been settled before our arrival—the sandwiches were on the table, in waxed paper, an apple alongside each.

"Can we really go?" asked my bewitched brother.

"Sure," my father said nonchalantly, as though the occasion were an everyday one. "So you'll become president a day later."

School or Ebbets Field. That day was a harbinger for the rest of my life, as my true textbooks were to become *Who's Who in Baseball*, *The Baseball Guide*, and *The Baseball Register*, my newspaper of record *The Sporting News* (in those years sworn to baseball and only baseball, its pages unsullied by accounts of games played with oversized balls, hard rubber pucks, or misshapen pieces of inflated pigskin).

Games started later then, and we were there in plenty of time. My father parked our boxy old Ford on a nearby lot, and we headed for this marvelous, looming edifice which hitherto had come cheering and shouting only through the radio, given graphic life by announcer Red Barber's Southern-mellow accounts laced with winsome cracker-barrel similes and metaphors.

Properly awed, we passed through the turnstiles and walked across the ornate rotunda on a floor of Italian marble (given my frame of mind, I probably would have felt easier walking barefoot). We bought our obligatory scorecards from a bellowing hawker (he really did say, "You can't tell the players without 'em") and were directed to a ramp that led Stanley and me to our first view of Ebbets Field. Emerging into the bright spring sunshine we found ourselves for the moment directly behind the St. Louis Cardinals dugout, and there standing, unmistakably, was the imposing, broad-shouldered person of slugging first baseman (and future Hall of Famer) Johnny Mize, already with batting and home run championships to his name, his large, narrow-eyed moonface gazing impassively directly at us.

"Johnny Mize!" I whispered breathlessly, taking hold of my brother's arm.

"I know," he said as we gaped at our first big leaguer.

(Years later, when I was interviewing him for a book called *Baseball When the Grass Was Real*, I recounted for Mize this landmark moment. He merely stared at me, patently unmoved, as impassive as that first time, waiting for me to say something more interesting.)

We went on, climbing low concrete steps, finally settling into our seats in the upper left-field grandstand. The view was like a natural wonder, down the right-field line, the wall with its high screen, the scoreboard, the rooftops of Brooklyn going off into the blue sky, the outfield bleachers bellying down toward the field. And that green grass—it looked freshly painted. And an infield without rocks or potholes, with pillowy white bases strapped into place. And a real mound; you could see the swell.

"It all looks so smooth," I said to Stanley.

"It's the big leagues," he said.

I asked my father if he had ever sat in the box seats.

"Sure," he said cavalierly. (I came to realize in later years that when he said "Sure" like that, there was usually a bit of blarney in it.)

We watched batting practice, long drives sailing insouciantly higher and farther than seemed possible; and infield practice, watching pegs snapped from base to base with a zest and alacrity that was eye-popping. By itself worth the price of admission, it was a terrific exhibition of skill, an entertainment, better than acrobats or jugglers ever could have been.

And then the field emptied—a most dramatic departure, creating the tension of a held breath—and the ground crew came out for a final watering down and raking of the infield. And then they were gone too and the field lay springtime bright under the eyes of the murmurous crowd. My own gaze never left the field as I slowly chewed my sandwich; I didn't want to miss anything, even if nothing was happening.

A spacious voice of celestial resonance greeted us and like a tolling bell began reading out the lineups. And then to whoops and cheers the Dodgers dashed from their dugout and scattered to their positions across the field. We rose for the National Anthem, which sounded so appropriate sung out across the green field.

Who were the Dodgers on that long-ago and precious spring day? We had Mickey Owen behind the plate, a fine catcher who unfortunately would be charged with a fatal passed ball in the World Series that year. Dolph Camilli, the league's Most Valuable Player that year, was on first base. Billy Herman, newly acquired from the Cubs and a future Hall of Famer, played second. At shortstop was young, baby-faced Pee Wee Reese, also to go into the Hall of Fame. The steady Cookie Lavagetto was the third baseman. The surly, hard-hitting Joe Medwick was in left field. In center field was my soon-to-be favorite player, the youthful Pete Reiser, that year's league batting champion, whose incredible run of injuries aborted what would surely have been a Hall of Fame career (that day, in fact, he ran into an outfield gate and had to leave the game a few innings later). The popular Dixie Walker was in right field. Right-hander Luke Hamlin was the starting pitcher. In the dugout sat the abrasive, megaphone-voiced Leo Durocher, who that year would skipper the team to its first pennant in twenty-one years.

It was a fine game. It was tied four-all when lefty Kemp Wicker came in to relieve Hamlin in the sixth inning. Wicker pitched airtight relief through the twelfth. In the bottom of that inning Joe Medwick got to second with two outs, to be driven home with the winning run (with the help of my shout-ing voice) by Cookie Lavagetto's ground-ball single through the left side, for which Cardinals third baseman Jimmy Brown made a diving, futile attempt, which I can see to this day. Yes, that's exactly how it happened, and it ingrained itself upon my memory like a gallery of snapshots.

Kemp Wicker won just that one game for the Dodgers, against the Cardinals, in twelve innings, on May 8, 1941, at Ebbets Field. It was my first major league game, the one game you never forget. If I'd told them about it, the gentlemen from Major League Baseball would have understood how such obscure things from sixty-four years ago were remembered. If I'd told them.

Two

☈ I'VE ALWAYS thought it impolite to ask people how they came to be fans of a certain team; the question has an air of disapproval or condescension about it. But, since this is a tale of revelations, I'll tell you how I became a Dodgers fan and how it all could have been otherwise. The story of my baseball allegiance is a remarkably uncomplicated and of course very familiar one: my father was a Dodgers fan. The origin of that fact, however, intrigued me.

Preceded by his parents and seven siblings, he arrived at Ellis Island on October 12, 1920. "Me and Columbus arrived the same day," was his standard quip. Why he was the last of his family to arrive is an interesting story, but first let's find out how a young immigrant from a patch of land in a tiny village fifty miles west of Cracow became a Dodgers fan.

"Did you hear of the Dodgers in Poland?" I asked. To my passionately baseball-Dodgers mind, the question seemed reasonable.

"We never even heard of baseball," he said.

That was too deplorable for comment.

"Then what made you a Dodgers fan? Was your father a Dodgers fan?"

He smiled with affectionate tolerance at me across the kitchen table, where in those years most conversations of significance took place.

"You knew him," he said. "Did he look like a Dodgers fan?"

My callow mind rolled back to grandpa, now two years under the soil of his adopted land. Almost entirely sedentary in his later years, he had spent most of his time sitting in a high-backed chair, his thick-fingered hand resting atop the curved handle of a timeworn cane carved from the wood of the Polish forest. The cane was a vital adjunct when he walked, which I seldom saw him do. He had a long, black snarl of rabbinical beard and was never without a black silk yarmulke. His name was Elias. He seemed remote, spoke not a word of English. But he was a kindly man, always greeting me with a kiss to the forehead. So—no, I guess he hadn't looked like a Dodgers fan.

So I knew why *I* was a Dodgers fan; it was for the same reason I was a Democrat—because my father was. There was no question that my children would follow in these same patrician footsteps, and their children after. But how, I wanted to know, had the dynasty begun?

Patiently explained, it seemed that the parents and seven siblings who had preceded him to the land of Freedom, Opportunity, and Baseball had all checked in at the Ellis Island landfall and from there gone directly to a cousin (who was the family's actual Columbus) who lived on Myrtle Avenue. In Brooklyn. So when he arrived, my father made the migration from Ellis Island (where he had Anglicized Gustav into George) to Myrtle Avenue. ("How old did you make yourself?" one of his older brothers asked when he arrived. "Twenty," the freshly named George replied. "No good," the brother said. "I made myself five years younger. In the long run it's better.")

In the long run this fellow had to wait until he was seventy to start collecting Social Security.)

He took a job as a grocery clerk—the grocery business became the family trade—began learning English, and made friends. He was a good-looking rogue, well liked, and had a bit of style. He didn't start ballooning up until he married my mother in 1927. In later years she admitted ruefully that giving him all those chocolate pudding and whipped-cream desserts had been a mistake.

"Everybody I knew liked the Dodgers," he said, "so I liked the Dodgers. There didn't seem to be any other team. Some guys took me to a game at Ebbets Field . . ."

"When?" the future historian eagerly asked.

"Who the hell knows? Nineteen twenty-two, maybe later."

"Were you excited?"

"I didn't know what was going on. Guys running around, people yelling. I think they must have won."

"Who pitched?" I asked. "Was it Dazzy Vance?"

"I don't know."

"Burleigh Grimes?"

"Who remembers? It was twenty years ago. All I remember is on the way home somebody was drunk and threw up all over the trolley car. It smelled so much we got off and waited for the next one."

That's what he remembered of that historic day, some bozo shooting his cookies on the trolley car, not whether it had been Vance or Grimes on the mound, or who won, or anything, whereas his son would remember Kemp Wicker sixty-four years later, not to mention Lavagetto's hit and Jimmy Brown's futile full-length dive for the ball. I can see them yet. But never mind.

"So you became a Dodgers fan because your friends were," I said.

"Yep."

So it had been as prosaic as that, as simple as being born a Jew or a Catholic or a Protestant. My birth certificate should have read, *Donald Martin Honig, Dodgers fan.* I had been stamped with a permanent, unequivocal mark.

There were times, usually during those long-time-till-dawn nights after an extra-inning loss, when I had matured enough to cogitate things like Destiny and Fate, I thought that if that first pioneering cousin (whose name I don't think I ever knew) had turned in another direction and headed north to the Bronx, to be followed later by my grandparents, the seven children, and eventually my father, I would probably have been born a Yankees fan. Privately, sharing the heresy with no one, I wondered what might have been, how much angst I would have been spared. The Dodgers had the torturous habit of winning or losing pennants on the last day of the season (1946, 1949, 1950, 1951, 1956) while the Yankees usually sailed like luxury liners through the placid waters of the long campaign. Every Dodgers loss could be fatal; Yankee fans took their occasional losses with benign smiles, as though having made a donation to charity.

In the Bronx my father's friends would have been Yankee fans, and he would have been taken to that sacramental Stadium, where he would have been indoctrinated and I would have been scion to Babe Ruth and Lou Gehrig, and Joe DiMaggio would have been *my* pride instead of a Lord of the Flies and Home Runs I had no true claim on. I would have inherited all those pennants and world championships. I could have been one of those smug, secure, patronizing Yankee fans, immune to paranoia, my obsession more like a leisurely avocation. I would have been one of baseball's materialists and probably far less spiritual. Bobby Thomson's unendingly tragic home run would have been good, entertaining baseball.

And so when I read Robert Frost's "The Road Not Taken," I try to avoid personal interpretation.

Three

﹥ IT WAS PART of family lore that my father had fought in the War. In those years there was only one war—the one that was supposed to end them all, as if the mayhem had been unsurpassable and there was no point in having any more. The catch to my father's military experience was that he had gained it in the Austrian army, which not only was not on the western front (from the American perspective, where else was there?) but wasn't even an ally.

"Never mind the war," my Uncle Jack, youngest of the brothers, told me years later. "There was a time when he was only about fifteen when he took his life in his hands, and I mean literally."

My grandmother (who once told my mother that from marriage to menopause she was either carrying or miscarrying and barely knew what a period was) had gone off to visit relatives in another village, and a pogrom had broken out.

"You just never knew when it would happen," my uncle said. "It was like an epidemic, it happened, killed people, and then stopped. Nobody could stop it because nobody gave a damn. So we found out that one had started and that my mother was caught up in the middle of it. When your father

24

heard about it he hitched up a horse and wagon, took a rifle, and set off to bring her back. Not alone, of course; alone he wouldn't survive. He rounded up a bunch of his friends, tough Polish kids who he knew would back him up. They all had rifles."

"Why did he go?" I asked. "Why not his father or the older boys?"

"Because the Polish kids wouldn't have gone with anybody else. They respected your father."

I'd heard the story before, of course, and now again, a few days after the Old Man had died and could no longer bask in the light for having "pulled a Wyatt Earp" (as I used to tease him). Those were the days of the *shivah* sitting, when friends and family came to share the grief and to tell the best, the most interesting, the most amusing and praiseworthy tales they knew of the deceased, trying through the balms of good memory to assuage the pain of loss.

"He got her out," Uncle Jack said, "and they brought her back. He said his mother sat with her eyes closed the whole time, because there were dead Jews lying in the road. But he said his friends had their rifles leveled on all sides. He said they would have killed anybody who tried to get in the way."

How did a Jewish kid manage to evoke such loyalty in a group of boys whose instincts were probably little different from those conducting the slaughter?

"He had that way about him," my uncle said. "He wasn't afraid of anything." Then he repeated it: "They respected him."

And what about the War? The Austrian army? My uncle laughed: it had been fought right across their modest farm (twelve or fifteen more or less arable acres). The Honigs (*honey* in German) simply hunkered down, Austrian infantry on one side, Russian infantry and Cossacks on the other. The family lay down on the floor and waited it out. Except for one. Sometimes I would get my father to ratchet up the stories.

"There was one Austrian sharpshooter," he said, "who used to climb up on our roof, hide behind the chimney, and pick them off. One time he said, 'See that one on the white horse?' He was pointing to an officer wearing a big white fur hat. He picked him right off, with one shot. Then he turned around and winked at me."

"You mean you were there?" I asked.

"Sure," he said. "I'd climb up and sit behind him."

"What'd your parents say?"

"What could they say?" he asked mildly.

I suppose they did have seven others to worry about.

He was seventeen when the Austrian army drafted him and labeled him another bit of cannon fodder for the Serbians to the west or the Russians on the Carpathian front. In our school library there was an illustrated history of the war. On one page marched a sludgy-looking file of Austrian troops in their round hats, overcoats, and black boots, with shouldered rifles. I tried to pick out my father, but they all looked alike, men marching to some unchronicled nowhere.

"They didn't give a damn about the men," he used to say, not with bitterness but with a worldly acceptance of what had been in another time and in another world far away. "We slept on the ground, never had enough to eat, and what there was tasted like dirt. And a Jew was less than dirt."

When they went to the line, he said, he didn't know if he'd get shot in the front or the back. Exacerbating his situation were a couple of fistfights he'd had with a few of his fellow soldiers who had been bullying a Jewish youngster too weak to defend himself.

"He could knock you out with one punch," Uncle Jack said. "So he wasn't too popular, and there was no doubt some of them would be gunning for him. He said that some nights he wouldn't sleep. He was afraid of having a bayonet stuck into him."

When he heard that his unit was moving up to the front, young Gustav realized that his chances of having grandchildren were being reduced to just about zero. So he stole off into the night.

"He walked into the house one day," Uncle Jack said, "and we were petrified because we knew he wasn't supposed to be there."

A radical idea of self-preservation during wartime has never been highly rated among a soldier's merits, something my unlearned grandparents didn't need textbooks to know.

They insisted he return before it was too late, not realizing it was already too late, that somewhere papers had been stamped and a firing squad was warming up. My father, who seldom took bad advice, took it this time. My grandmother gave him a paper bag filled with provisions, topped off by a protruding loaf of black bread, and sent him off.

Then he was on a train crowded with sullen, heavy-lidded soldiers, clutching his bag of provisions with that chimney loaf of bread, watching a wintry war-gloomed countryside in flight beyond the window when he saw in the car ahead a brace of military policemen moving through on an inspection of papers.

"I didn't have any papers," my father said. "They would have taken me off the train at the next stop and shot me."

"Just like that?" I asked.

He stared at me with that big, fleshy poker face and said, "They worked on commission."

He got up and began retreating, car by car, as the two golems advanced, until he was at the last. When he saw the military policemen enter that final refuge, jostling men awake to examine their papers (men headed for Serbian bullets that would at least catch them in the front), he opened that last door and stepped out onto the platform, he and his bag of provisions with that protruding loaf of bread baked by his mother's loving hands, and stood in the cold wind, the train grinding away the Polish countryside beneath him.

"He jumped off a running train," Uncle Jack said, retelling the story at the *shivah* sitting when I was twenty-eight and still not beyond enthrallment. Not only had my father once been seventeen years old, but he had done these things and never once had displayed any bitterness but only his simple narrative and then a mild smile at my enthrallment, as if it had all been merely concomitant with the world he had grown up in, alien to a boy for whom calamity had been a Dodgers loss.

He jumped, clutching that bag of food with its chimney of bread like some talisman.

"I can still see that loaf of bread flying away when I jumped," my father would say, always attendant to those details that depict. That was always the keynote of his leap for his life from a running train—not his hitting what must have felt like a violently moving earth, not the pain of impact or rolling or banging into whatever he rolled or banged into. The jump into thin and flying air and that loaf of bread sailing away.

There were other near misses and harrowing escapes as the story became an odyssey through Poland and Germany until he finally crossed the frontier into Denmark where, by that time, he had been told of a lifeline established by a wealthy Jewish banker to aid and abet those adamant life-seekers like himself.

He worked for some time in Copenhagen waiting tables until he had earned his passage to America, where by now through grit and what strikes one today as preternatural foresight his family had arrived. Some years after the war (the Big One), we were attending a wedding, sitting at a table with some people we didn't know. Someone mentioned, in one context or another, Denmark.

"I was in Denmark," George, nee Gustav, said.

"Really?" he was asked. "What were you doing there?"

"Buying sardines for the A&P," he said.

My mother looked across the table at me with a helpless shake of her head. You never could be sure of what he was going to say. For instance, what we heard in December 1941, a few days after Pearl Harbor.

My brother and I had come running up the stairs for lunch and found them sitting at the kitchen table, my father with his chin resting on his clasped hands, cigarette in mouth, serenity in his face. He was looking up in the air, as if to avoid the frown he was receiving from my mother across the table. When we came in she directed the frown at us.

"He wants to enlist," my mother said.

"In what?" my brother asked.

"The army. Did you ever hear of such a thing?"

"He's too old," my brother said.

"He's too fat," I said, more helpfully than disrespectfully.

"I can shoot a rifle," my father said. "I have a very sharp eye."

"Then go to Coney Island," my exasperated mother said, "and win a teddy bear."

He soon forgot about lending himself to the armed forces and instead became an air-raid warden, replete with tin helmet and thin leather chin strap, armband, and whistle, which he now blew every time he arrived home and began climbing the stairs. His job was to put on that inverted-soupbowl tin hat whenever there was a blackout drill. These drills, called for by the Civilian Defense Agency, began with a vast bedlam scream from the large siren that revolved slowly on the school roof, where it was manned twenty-four hours a day by a New York City fireman.

The blackouts melted every light into darkness and compelled every automobile to the curb, creating an eerie, phantasmal aura, which in an urban setting was distinctly unnatural. Darkness could absorb tree and leaf; brick and glass did not so easily yield. Stanley and I would stand at the window gazing out at the Stygian breathlessness that was in its way a spectacle, a symbolic panoramic tribute to where the action really was.

One night I yielded to this seductive scene and slipped out of the house. With all traffic sidelined and people huddled in stores or doorways, I had the world to myself. I treated myself to the middle of Grand Avenue, walking along the cobblestones between the imbedded trolley tracks. It was a heady feeling.

My father's post was around what was called "The Square," a small circular area consisting of wooden benches, a flagpole, and a modest three-sided marble monument dedicated to the neighborhood's World War I dead, whose names were incised on the sides. As I neared his post I heard his manly baritone bark out, "Put out that goddam light!"

I followed that vibrant sound and found him standing not far from the monument, tin helmet strapped under his chin, adamantly at his civic duty.

"What are you doing?" he asked. "You're not supposed to be out."

"I know," I said, figuring the admission would cover the sin.

I walked behind him for a few moments, and then he barked it out again: "Put out that goddam light!" The refrain issued every few minutes, and each time I looked around for the offending bit of illumination and saw nothing. Finally, after the fourth or fifth such outburst, I said, "Pop, there are no lights on."

"I know," he said.

"Then why are you yelling?"

"What the hell am I supposed to do," he said, "just stand out here like a dope?"

Soon the siren geared up and, slowly revolving to all points of the compass, hurled out a vibrating, ear-filling "All Clear."

When we got home I told my mother what he had been doing.

"I know," she said. "He likes to stand out in the street and yell."

"Why?"

"You're asking me why?"

"Is that why he became an air-raid warden?"

She shook her head in puzzlement. "I don't know why he became an air-raid warden."

I think I knew why: he was a joiner. If it was there, he joined it. Masons, Kiwanis, Lions, Knights of Pythias. It was his natural good fellowship. Sign up, shake hands with everybody, then soon forget about it. From firsthand testimony, however, we know he did attend at least one convening of the Knights of Pythias. The witness was my Uncle Herman, second youngest of the five brothers, my father being in the middle (all of them lived in Maspeth, the three sisters in Brooklyn, like some Hasidic gender segregation).

"He said to me once," Uncle Herman related—again a tale for the *shivah* sitting—"I should come over to the Knights of Pythias with him. I asked him what for. 'You'll see,' he said. Well, they had hired a belly dancer. She was putting on some show when all of a sudden the door comes crashing down and the cops are charging in yelling and all hell breaks loose. George grabs me by the arm and we go running and jump out a back window and run like hell."

(No flying loaf of bread this time, but still a vivid image: one's father jumping out of a window because of a police raid.)

"We were lucky," Uncle Herman said. "They collared everybody else, put them in a couple of paddy wagons, and drove them out to Brooklyn someplace and let them go."

"I never heard that story," my unamused mother said.

Uncle Herman also enlivened that unhappy time with the tale of how his late, deeply beloved older brother once came close to snuffing him out. He said it was his first memory (and almost his last).

"I was about three years old, which makes your father about seven. We were all sitting at the dinner table. His job was to feed me. He was feeding me mashed-up beets, and I think he must have got bored. So he dipped the spoon into a dish of red horseradish my mother made. Only the adults could stand it—it was pure fire. I swallowed the spoonful and began going crazy. I was choking and gagging and God knows what. My mother said she thought I was going to die. Your father got some licking for that."

"We had about five or six geese," my Aunt Sylvia said. "One day I walked out of the house and they were all lying on the ground. I ran to my father and told him the geese were dead. By the time we got back the geese were on their feet, staggering around. My father looked at me as if I had played a joke on him. Then he went to the big wooden trough they drank from and ladled out some water. He tasted it and spit it out. There was wine in it. He asked me who had put that in there. I told him I didn't know."

"But you had a good guess," I said.

"It wasn't a guess," she said.

But I choose to believe there was an innocence to his mischief, which I think is borne out by an episode he often told me about. When he was about eleven years old he had a pet pony named Franz Joseph (after the Austrian emperor). One day he brought it into the house ("It was raining," he explained), into the living room, and there it stood.

"My father came in, and when he saw the pony he let out a scream. The pony got frightened and jumped right through the window. My mother had a row of flower pots on the sill, and the pony's hind legs kicked them over as he jumped out. I can still see those flower pots going over." Those details. He could still see them, as he could still see the flying bread, and so can I, these hundred years later. He always finished this tale on a note of bemusement. "I don't know why he screamed like that," he would say. "The pony wasn't doing anything." Ergo, it is acceptable to bring a pony into the living room as long as it conducts itself with decorum.

My mother seemed to feel the need to maintain some balance of parental propriety; nevertheless she was not beyond some antics of her own, the most frequent being hiding when she heard my father coming up the stairs. Since it wasn't exactly

Blenheim Castle we were living in, her choices of concealment were few.

"Don't say anything," she instructed us as she hurried out of the kitchen.

In he would come. And ask where she was, to be answered by a pair of slender shrugging shoulders. But he usually sensed what was afoot and went on the prowl. Finding her was no problem—she was always under the bed.

One evening I was sitting alone with her in the kitchen when we heard the downstairs door sweep shut and then the slow, heavy-man ascent. My mother brightened with an inspiration.

"I'm going to hide in the closet," she said, getting up and going off.

He came in, closed the door, looked at me, and asked where she was.

Impulsively deciding to enter into the spirit of things, I told him she was out shopping. He poured himself a glass of raspberry soda, sat down, and flamed up a cigarette. We began a learned discussion about our multi-talented center fielder Pete Reiser, whether the burgeoning young star would blossom into another DiMaggio. I said I thought that Pee Wee Reese made too many errors at shortstop. He said it didn't matter (this sounded like sublime wisdom, a pearl from a Himalayan ashram, to pass unquestioned). I asked if he liked that favorite tactic of Durocher's, the squeeze play. Only when it worked, he said.

It might have been as long as twenty minutes before she appeared, looking more than a little annoyed.

"Where the hell were you?" my surprised father asked.

"I've been standing in the closet half the night," she said. "I felt like a damned fool."

"Who asked you to stand in the closet?"

"You were supposed to look for me."

"He said you were out," Pop said with an accusing finger in my direction.

With a shake of her head she looked at me and said, "You're such a jackass."

Ruefully my father said to me, "You should've said something."

Four

▤ WE DIDN'T have to deal with pogroms, only with the people who would have liked to indulge in this edifying recreation. You could feel the toxic clouds brooding and sense those frustrated and unreconciled instincts in many of the Eastern Europeans—mostly Poles and Ukrainians— who lived in the neighborhood, sequestered mainly in a section known inelegantly as "Polack Alley." The Polish peasant, those with firsthand knowledge claimed, was one step above a wild animal, while descriptions of Ukrainians made the Poles sound like Boston Brahmins.

They had a penchant for standing on street corners in small groups, men with fat, high-boned faces, with porcine eyes that could turn repellently scrutinous, wearing cloth caps, suit jackets, work pants, tieless white shirts buttoned to the top. Generally they wore expressions of unrelieved moroseness, as though never having gotten over the disappointment of pogroms not being a recognized team sport in this country. Many of their sons were no better.

The fact of walking through what was sometimes the hostile environment of my own neighborhood did little to deflect my predilection for mischief (I'll tell you about it in a moment; it was infamous). "You get it from him," my mother would say reprovingly of this genetic bane, the "it" being the mischief, the "him" being my father. (Though I found the comparison flattering, I would have preferred being known as an original.)

In those early, pre–bar mitzvah years, Hebrew school was like a punishment for something I hadn't done. We, my brother and I, came home after school, had a glass of milk (a glass of milk was like a passport to leave the house), and walked down Grand Avenue to the synagogue. There we climbed the high flight of stone steps (apparently nobody gave thought to the *alte* when designing the building), went inside, walked on the red carpet between the long rows of smooth wooden benches, turned right at the end, and entered the small room where the future bar mitzvah boys sat for one hour every weekday. There were about a dozen chair-desks, writing surfaces extended on the right-hand side (the left-handed kids were out of luck). Our bearded rabbi, who seemed no happier than we were for the hour, taught us Hebrew, discussed the less racy passages of the Old Testament, and generally prepared us for a hostile world.

One day we had a substitute rabbi, a splendid Old World specimen, with an enormous thicket of black beard that was rather intimidating. His large, drooping eyes gazed at us from under the brim of his round, high-crowned black hat, and from inside that beard his moist red lips said little. Obviously he had rather been elsewhere. He assigned us a reading lesson and sat at his desk writing letters.

Why is this day worthy of remembrance? For two reasons, in my catalogue of memories one minor and one major. First the minor. The rabbi had finished and addressed a letter and was attempting to moisten a stamp when it slipped from his fingers. He tipped to the side and looked down at the floor; not immediately finding it, he abandoned it and took another and adhered it to the envelope. The errant stamp, however, had dropped into his beard and there hung. For most of that hour we sat in mute fascination, staring at the postage stamp in his beard, a three-cent issue showing a profile of Thomas Jefferson, who seemed looking for a way out.

("Why didn't you tell him?" my sweet mother asked later. I can't imagine how she could have asked that.)

This was the minor thing that happened that day, soon to be overshadowed by one of the occasions that enabled my mother to say that I got "it" from "him."

We wore in that little room in the synagogue the obligatory yarmulke. Synagogue property, these were of black paper and sat like little pillboxes on the head; we removed them and dropped them into a cardboard box as we left the building. One day my sometimes absentminded brother (actually an inaccurate depiction: his mind was always vigorously and cogently present; what was absent was banality and hokum) forgot to slip off his paper head cover. I took note of the oversight and thought it a fine thing not to mention it.

And so we walked home, through that neighborhood of lurking anti-Semites, Stanley quiet and serious as ever, his head piously covered, unwitting recipient of sullen stares, curled-lip smirks, sneers. The friends we passed nodded to him with puzzled frowns. I suggested we stop in the candy store, where I bought a five-cent pack of baseball cards, each packaged with its powdery square of pink gum that was as chewable as the cards. The usual hangers-on, sitting on stools at the small fountain, stared at my brother.

Then we went on, walking slowly home along Grand Avenue's busy early-evening sidewalks, unwrapping the cards to see whom we might have acquired that we didn't already have. I remember only Yankees left fielder Charlie Keller. Stanley was pleased; so was I, more than he knew. While he stopped to read the text on the back of the card, I stared at the black paper pillbox sitting on top of his head, as did whoever passed by.

When we arrived home we found my mother at her usual post at the stove, where pots and pans were simmering. She gave my brother a perplexed look.

"Why are you wearing your yarmulke?" she asked.

"He wore it all the way home," I said, sidling up to her.

Stanley's hand shot up to his head, found his covering, and whipped it away, a shot of anger crossing his face as I huddled closer to momma's apron.

"He didn't tell me," he said irately.

My mother, straining for Solomonic wisdom, said to him, "What's the matter—are you ashamed of wearing a yarmulke?" And then to me, sternly, "Why didn't you tell him?"

"I don't know," I said. It was the best I could do.

Henry James once said that he had been blessed in having the "perfect older brother" in his sibling William. Henry could have been speaking for me.

It is an important thing, I think, for older brothers to be born wise, patient, and tolerant. I have known many who didn't possess any of these virtues and as a consequence saw younger brothers lead lives of dissolution that might have been otherwise. If this seems to place unfair burdens on the older brothers, so be it; the good ones are capable of managing.

Stanley was three years my senior, a difference that allowed him at times to legitimately detach himself from me when he had more interesting matters to attend to, as well as to be a close companion. He taught me to play chess, and we played together Monopoly, card games, and of course baseball, even in the house. That marvelous pastime adapted to any environment, from stately Yankee Stadium to schoolyards to empty lots to your own living room. If the ball was round and you had to run to a base, it was the National Pastime, duly sanctioned by statistics. In our living room it was known as "Tap Ball," a distant but nonetheless legitimate variant on Abner Doubleday's invention (I had only recently been disabused of Santa Claus and was not yet ready to surrender Abner).

Tap Ball involved looping a rubber ball on one bounce to the "batter" who tapped it with an open hand and dashed for a base—sometimes a floored copy of my mother's beloved *Anna Karenina*—and reaching it before the ball was fielded. If the ball rolled into the next room, where second base was set (*Jane Eyre* or perhaps an Edna Ferber), the batter could keep running. Sometimes there were close plays; I can still see my brother sliding across the linoleum-covered floor and clear under my parents' bed. These games came to a halt when one day the ball crashed through the glass door of the living room secretary. After that we were reduced to sitting cross-legged on the floor and rolling the ball back and forth. But this wasn't baseball; it was penance.

Stanley was a first baseman. This destiny was assured him when one day, in 1939 or so, my mother's uncle gave him that position's glove. It was a ratty-looking thing, with flimsy webbing and a worn-out pocket. When he appeared in the schoolyard with this sorry caricature he was naturally assigned first base. Like everything else he ever attended to, he took this responsibility with high seriousness.

With that glove in possession he became a connoisseur of first basemen. He could tell you about Rudy York of the Detroit Tigers, Babe Dahlgren of the Yankees, Joe Kuhel of the Chicago White Sox, George McQuinn of the St. Louis Browns, Johnny Mize of the St. Louis Cardinals, Babe Young of the Giants, Phil Cavaretta of the Chicago Cubs, Zeke Bonura of the Washington Senators, Frank McCormick of the Cincinnati Reds. Stanley saw himself as a member of this fraternity. But for some reason the man he adopted as personal hero was not Brooklyn's own Dolph Camilli but Pittsburgh's Elbie Fletcher. I think he liked the name, in addition to his best friend being named Fletcher.

Elbie was not a star. He had a flashy glove around first base, was a lifetime .270 hitter, and stroked a modest handful of home runs. But he was one of those baseball backbones, one of the oblivion-fated majority who play the game at an acceptable level and provide the moderate standards by which stars like DiMaggio and Williams are measured.

That Elbie was left-handed all the way and my brother the opposite was of no matter: he had that glove, and he needed an identity. So Elbie's was the name he would bark out whenever scooping up a low throw: "Elbie does it again!" These conjurations connected him to the big-league diamonds. Mine was the more lavish dream: I was Bob Feller, wide-swinging windup, high-kicking delivery and all. Only the fastball was missing. (A studious and studiously nonbaseball friend of mine once asked me, "Who is Bob Fellow?")

Passionate baseball fan though he was, Stanley's youthful interests were already beginning to diversify. The world beyond the outfield fences was rising into view. He was a boy of strong intellect and inquiring mind, qualities he tried to awaken in me. One day he took me into Manhattan with him to investigate the Museum of Natural History. I was about ten years old (again, it was that hot, shimmering summer of 1941, when so much was coming to unwitting end and so much more to explosive beginning).

Not counting the home of a dour maiden aunt, I had never been in a museum before. And when we got to the Museum of Natural History I was sorry there had to be a first time for everything. This place was no Ebbets Field. It was quiet, reverential; people spoke in whispers.

Stanley was fascinated by the collections of stuffed birds, baboons, and other distant relatives, and by glass cases of plants and insects, all of which grasped at his interest and curiosity.

I, who preferred my primates active and gibbering, was less enthralled, especially with baseball sunshine burning beyond those cultured walls. I was bored, and there are few people of less use to society than bored children. Their adaptability is zero, and what entertainment they are forced to contrive for themselves seldom adds much to the world's pleasures. As, for instance, stubbing the toes of one's sneakers abruptly against a marble floor so that a quick screech is produced. For some minutes I followed my engrossed brother about like a vehicle testing its brakes. He, wrapped in the wonders around him, paid me no attention, though annoyed faces were beginning to turn in my direction.

A museum employee appeared, wearing a sort of uniform, his face set in the querulous expression of one assigned to stand on his feet all day. He raised one thumb like a hitchhiker.

"Get out," he quietly told me. When Stanley looked around, he heard, "You too. Out."

We left meekly, the guard glowering at me as, hands in pockets, I slouched past him. When we were back outside in the baseball sunshine, away from that macabre taxidermy, Stanley said, "I don't know why he kicked us out."

He really didn't, that nice boy.

Built between two residential streets, J.H.S. 73 had to adapt its schoolyard configurations to the bordering two-family houses, calling for certain sacrifices, namely in right field. What there was of right field consisted of about thirty feet beyond the infield before breaking out to deeper regions. Closing off that truncated field was a fifteen-foot-high wire fence and beyond that the backyards and houses that front on Sixty-ninth Place. Over the right field fence was "out," and whoever did pop one into the forbidden area was charged with retrieving it, either by climbing the fence or going around to the yard.

And sometimes the ball was not retrieved; this was because it had cleared the fence and flown through someone's imprudently unscreened back window. For any boy who ever played America's game in an urban setting, the crackling bang of a shattering window is ever familiar. This dissonant shriek ended the game and usually emptied the schoolyard in a hurry.

The most memorable game-ending occasion occurred in the summer of 1940; not only did it end a game but a whole day's activities as well. It was another world then, whether for better or worse is best left to individual evaluation. How different was it all? Well, you could buy from someone a car for five dollars, drive the life out of it for a weekend, and when the gas ran out, leave it right there. You weren't going to go far, just around the neighborhood, up one side street and down the other, blowing the horn, waving to people. You stayed away from Grand Avenue, which was not only sensible but necessary because you really didn't know how to drive that well and to prove it had no license, in fact were too young to have one, since the proprietors of these cars were usually around fifteen years old. Those days seem numinous now, carefree and un-aged, as though every twenty-four hours was not a chapter in time but a book complete unto itself.

Adam Kelly was one of three boys who had chipped in and purchased the five-dollar car, and he alone was at the wheel that afternoon when it came rolling through the open back gate into the schoolyard. The make, year, even color of the car are lost to memory; remembered only is that it had a rather high roof, a rumble seat that was half open, wide run-ning boards, and frequent sputters.

The ballplayers scattered, though with delight at the intrusion. We whooped and yelled at the grinning Adam as he maneuvered his old nag of a vehicle around the yard and blew the horn. Some of the more intrepid jumped onto the running boards, secured themselves with one hand and waved with the other, then jumped back off, some tumbling to the ground. "Five cents a ride!" Adam called out gleefully.

His favorite exercise was to circle the bases, then drive through the outfield to the other diamond at the far end of the yard, wheel around the bases there and return, cheered all the way by a platoon of youngsters who took vicarious thrill in chasing after him.

Then something happened, or rather didn't happen. Try-ing to stop, he found he couldn't. His five dollars' worth of brakes no longer functioned. A look of perplexity and then panic in his face told us something was wrong. Then his shout made it clear: "I can't stop it!" He shouted for advice from a group of nine- and ten-year-olds, most of whose fathers didn't even own cars. (None of us, nor Adam himself, knew enough merely to switch off the ignition.) So on he rode, stamping frantically at the unresponsive brakes.

And on he rode, in circle after circle, the accelerator frozen at around fifteen or so miles an hour, down to one end of the yard and turning and coming back, the car moving now with a self-mesmerized idiocy, obeying the turns of the wheel but otherwise free and independent in its robotic rebellion. Someone told him to crash it, but this well-meant sidelines advice was not helpful—there was no soft place for him to do that, the school being brick, the base of the fence concrete. He was doomed, the Flying Dutchman of the J.H.S. 73 school-yard.

We drew back and sat down at the base of the fence, watching with a strange, almost spiritual fascination. He went on and on, circling, turning, coming here, going there, going nowhere, captive to a smooth, unswallowing vortex. When he neared us he looked at us with a blank helplessness, reiterating his single and by now obvious plight: "I can't stop it!" and again stamping at the brakes as he rolled on to the other side of the yard, our heads turning with his passage.

The indefatigable journey to nowhere went on and on in its countless repetitions. At times Adam seemed heroic behind the wheel, at other times mindlessly lunatic, as if at some abstruse ritual. Other boys drifted into the schoolyard seeking a game of ball, asked what was happening, were informed, and sat down to watch, engrossed by the seemingly choreographed turns and circles, watching the approaching and departing Adam Kelly, who after a while had turned stoic and had stopped looking at us.

Several times someone had shouted to him to jump, but each time he looked down at the concrete skimming alongside him and wisely thought better of it. Once, when he came near, someone asked how much gas he had left. He didn't know, Adam shouted back as he rolled on. The gauge was broken.

The evening shadows were falling and no one had stirred when the car began sputtering, loudly and continuously. Then it began to slow. We rose as one to watch this turn of events. The car finally rolled to a halt in short left-center field. We watched as though there were a possibility of something else happening. But it didn't. Adam got out, tentatively at first, one foot on the running board and then both on the ground, with all the drama of a Lindbergh arrival. He did a deep knee bend, his joints crackling like snapping twigs. He hurried to a corner and urinated, splashing away for what seemed minutes. Then, buttoning up his fly, he began walking away, calling out to us, "Don't say anything," leaving the car in short left-center field. The next day some men appeared from a garage and towed it away. And we played ball again.

Five

    >> I ASKED my brother, "Do you think Reiser is as good as Williams or DiMaggio?"

This would have had to be in 1942, when our Dodgers center fielder had already the year before become the youngest batting champion ever and on his way to repeating. I had raised the names of two reigning demigods, but the question was not without validity. Going into mid-July Reiser was well beyond his .343 championship mark of 1941, but he was also a young (twenty-three) player of speed and power, flavored with intangibles that gave him a thunderbolt excitement on the field. He didn't play his center field with the sovereign artistry of DiMaggio but rather with his own élan, with surges of hellbent ardor that seemed at times reckless.

My brother did not think the question was out of order.

"I think he will be," he said. "He's only a kid; he's going to keep getting better and better."

"A ball in the air," Reiser once said, "is supposed to be caught." It was a creed with him, and to its observance you might say he was fanatical. He played baseball as though every day were the first of its invention, when it was still primal, and he was determined to establish a standard. But he was playing in front of concrete walls; a baseball could strike these walls and bound insouciantly away, whereas a man in collision with one at top speed (Reiser's sole gear) was putting himself in the gravest danger. Sometimes Pete Reiser looked as though he were alone on the field and only God was watching.

"Watch him run if he hits a grounder," my father said. "He's down the line like a rabbit. Watch him going from first to third; when he comes around second he gets faster."

"I wonder how he does that," I said.

"Excitement," my father said. He always had an answer, even when he hadn't been asked a question.

I saw Reiser steal home in 1942, during a doubleheader with the Cubs. There he was, inching down the line in a half-crouch, watching the pitcher like a famished predator, and then—a roar from the crowd—he became a flash, a stitch of uniformed lightning, an eruptive burst of dust, sliding around home plate with gritted teeth, one hand thrown back to brush across the surface as the crouched umpire swung palms down over him.

So what do you do? You're eleven years old, intoxicated with this handsome young dynamo, you're standing on third base in the middle of a game on one of Maspeth's lumpy ball fields. So what do you do? What *did* I do? I edged down the line. I crouched slightly, a voyeur's eye upon the pitcher. As he swung into his windup, I ran, propelled by the spirit of my hero. I ran. Never had ninety feet seemed so distant. I was running down the wrong end of the telescope. Grimacing, chest out, arms pumping, I ran, preparing for the home-plate collision, the stirring cloud of dust, the hurrahs of my team-mates. But it didn't happen. None of it occurred. By the time those ninety interminable feet had been accomplished, the catcher was standing up, ball in hand, waiting for me. Politely I was tagged out.

"What the hell did you do that for?" I was asked by more than one teammate.

He thinks he's Pete Reiser. Blessedly, no one said it.

Of course I thought I was Pete Reiser. Who else was I supposed to be? DiMaggio wasn't mine to impersonate, Williams was from Boston, and I could be Feller only occasionally, when they would let me pitch. Pete Reiser was ours, just two bus rides and a fifty-five-cent bleacher seat away. He was the best ballplayer I have ever seen.

Mays? By near-unanimous consent the best since DiMaggio, and perhaps the best ever? In his noisily outspoken autobiography, *Nice Guys Finish Last* (written with Ed Linn), Leo Durocher, the most vocal of Willie's admirers, has this to say (the italics are Leo's):

> ... Pete Reiser, who was every bit as good as Mays. *Might have been better.* Pete Reiser might just have been the best ballplayer I ever saw. He could throw as good as Willie—as least as good—and he could throw right-handed and left-handed. You think Willie Mays could run in his heyday? You think Mickey Mantle could run? Name whoever you want to, and Pete Reiser was faster. . . . He ran down to first base consistently in 3.6 and 3.7 and, believe me, there has never been anybody before or since who could do that.

Durocher's encomium ends: "Pete Reiser had everything but luck."

The luck began to turn sour in July 1942 when Pete and his .380 batting average crashed into the wall in St. Louis, causing a deep concussion. He should have sat out the rest of the season, but Durocher, in a pennant race with the Cardinals, and enamored of his electrifying star, soon had him back in the lineup.

"He asked me if I wanted to play," Reiser said years later. "Not if I could. I couldn't, but I wanted to." And so he did, to his and the team's detriment both. He had headaches, dizziness, he couldn't always see the ball, but that insentient engine inside him would not relent. He sank to .310, and the Dodgers fell two games short at the end. "I cost us the pennant," he said.

"Of course we wanted to see him in there," Dodgers ace Kirby Higbe said in a 1975 interview. "Twenty-five percent of Pete Reiser was still better than anybody else." Even though an errant pitch or another wall collision might have proved fatal, as it came near to being in Ebbets Field in 1947. "It was like a hand grenade went off inside my head," he said. He was carried off the field and given last rites in the clubhouse. He came back, but for all intents and purposes it was over, the might-have-beens off into the night like a fading train whistle.

The Dodgers let him go at the end of the '48 season, and he drifted, from the Braves to the Pirates and finally, in 1952, to the Cleveland Indians, where Al Lopez was managing. Catching for the Pirates in 1941–1942, Reiser's dream years in Brooklyn, Lopez had marveled. "He was as naturally gifted a ballplayer as I ever saw," Lopez said. "I won't say he was better than Mays or Mantle, but neither will I say they were better than he was. With everything else, he also had a drive and a spirit like few others. He played right down to his every ounce and inch."

But what Lopez had was a ghost, the ounces flattened and the inches ground to nubs by a wholesale catalogue of injuries: concussions, broken ankles and elbow, cartilage tears in his knee, torn leg muscles, dislocated shoulder. Pistol Pete went home after thirty-four games with a .136 batting average.

As those injuries mounted I sometimes found myself becoming exasperated with my hero.

"Why does he have to play like that?" I demanded of my brother. "He's always getting hurt."

Stanley's explanation was trite but true: "It's the only way he knows how to play. It's all or nothing."

It turned out to be both.

We had been denied. Our scintillating young idol had left behind a glittering sample and then a blank page. Reiser now occupies nostalgia-sweet corners in the memories of those able to make the long regression to other days, and with our overflowing cups of memory we are a diminishing breed. The eyes of evidence are closing, and soon it will all have to be taken on faith, as are the tales of Tris Speaker in center field, or Wagner at short, Cobb on the bases, Walter on the mound.

Reiser belongs to a particular caste, one which the ultra-romantics will tell you never aged. They are the athletes whose lifelines to glory were prematurely severed, leaving them arrested in full animation and forever undefeated. The poignance of what they did not do is drawn from the man-child excitement of what they did. Their exceptional talents seemed designed for long and standard-setting achievement; truncated, these losses raise a melancholy baseball-mythic hierarchy. Stellar among them are Boston Red Sox right-hander Smoky Joe Wood, Cleveland left-hander Herb Score, and Pete Reiser.

Joe Wood, aged twenty-two, was said to have thrown a baseball as hard as Walter Johnson. In 1912 he was 34-5, then won three more in Boston's World Series victory over the New York Giants and the totemic Christy Mathewson. The following spring he injured his arm, and that fastball ceased to pop. Herb Score came to Cleveland in 1955 at the age of twenty-one. In his first two years he won thirty-six games and struck out more than five hundred. Bob Feller, who had just retired, had, it seemed, alchemized into young Master Score. But early in 1957 a line drive back to the mound struck him in the eye, and he was never the same.

And so this special category. The logic of making declarative assertions about unfulfilled careers and uncompiled statistics may seem reductive to any but the baseball romantic. Through the wistful computers of his imagination, this unreconstructed dreamer runs his numbers and starts the old clocks to ticking again. He heals Wood's arm, Score's eye, Reiser's hurts. A dreamer's truths are as good as anyone else's. We are free to uncork our genie bottles and let swoosh forth what we want, and in our countermarch we become as knowledgeable about what never happened as we are about what did.

For two years at Ebbets Field, 1941 and 1942, we had the reality. It was powerful. It even made me try to steal home once.

Six

≪ TODAY it probably isn't that common, but in those years—1930s, 1940s—it seemed a Jewish family was not complete without an aberrant, harmless bachelor uncle who without great detail served to represent the family's *shtetl* roots in Eastern Europe. Their childhoods were misted in vague memories that sometimes seemed deliberately set adrift or suppressed. To a child their blood kinship was obscure, derived through this or that unknown or unremembered uncle or aunt. Like most people who turned up for a meal (invited or not, they knew they would be fed), they had a facile and hard-striving charm, like a snare being laid for the next visit. They were like objects fallen from an assembly line, left to wander on their own, regarded by their more settled kinsmen with dutiful affection, and when the time came peremptorily mourned and filed away like an old studio portrait.

Our member of this inside-outside subspecies was Uncle Fendel. Unmarried, in his sixties (that was a guess; my mother said he himself didn't know exactly how old he was), with a large, round, nearly bald head, a friendly smile that showed several gold teeth, a self-pleasing line of chatter that touched here and there and landed nowhere—this was Uncle Fendel. He was a man of unfixed place in the world, with tenuous relationships; he beamed with delight whenever anyone indulged him. It became a fact of family life that every third or fourth Friday Uncle Fendel would ring the downstairs bell and come grinning up the stairs for dinner, carrying several small bottles of cream soda as his contribution to the repast. "I was passing by," he would say, a ploy no one ever questioned. He had the unwelcome custom of greeting Stanley and me by pinching our cheeks and telling us how big we were getting.

"He's a pain in the ass," my father said mildly of this unaccountable relative, though always maintaining a cordial relationship. My mother, of course, loyally defended her uncle, saying he was lonely and had no one. Uncle Fendel had washed up on these shores ahead of any of them, some time around 1890, a boy in his teens, alone.

"He worked as a furrier," my mother said. "When he wasn't working he would come and hang around. He'd sit outside on the stoop talking to everybody, come up for a meal, then go back downstairs again. Sometimes he would disappear, for months at a time, and then one day the door would open and there he was again. Once he told my father he had a girlfriend in the Bronx. But we never asked him any questions."

Once, she said, she asked her mother who he was. "She said she didn't know," my mother said, "and told me to ask my father. When I did, he said that Fendel was from my mother's side. I think by that time they really didn't know anymore. But it didn't make any difference; he was a relative, somehow. Everybody had an uncle like that."

I think we were just about the only ones in the family who offered Uncle Fendel any hospitality, a state of affairs that may have derived from an incident years before. He had been invited to a family dinner of rather lavish proportions. When the table had been loaded with food and the dozen or so guests were about to dig in, someone spoke admiringly of all the gleaming culinary treats, to which Uncle Fendel whimsically whispered to his neighbor, "In twenty-four hours it's all going to be a pile of shit." Unfortunately his forecast was heard by several others, including the hostess, and he was scratched off.

Now, in that summer of 1941, he was living in a small walk-up apartment in the East Twenties and spent much of his time sitting in a cafeteria on Lexington Avenue with cronies, whom he seemed to enjoy annoying.

"They sit and yell about socialism and communism and the workers and revolution," he told us one evening, "while I sit there reading the sports pages. They ask me how I can read that stuff while the world is exploding. I tell them there is more truth in the sports pages than anywhere else in the paper. There you find out exactly what happened and how it happened. Right to the point and no baloney. And then I tell them that Joe DiMaggio is a greater man than Stalin or Trotsky. That really gets them."

If Uncle Fendel seemed somewhat eccentric, it was made even more so because, unlike most of his *landsleit*, he was a baseball fan. It was this anomalous uncle who had had style enough to give my brother that worn-down first base-man's glove that had transmuted the boy into Elbie Fletcher. Baseball fan though he was, Uncle Fendel had a serious flaw: he was a Giants fan. (This may have been the chief reason my father disapproved of him. He had little tolerance for this particular breed, continually arguing with a pair of Polo Grounders, the Feldman brothers, of whom he said, "One of them doesn't know a damned thing and the other one knows twice as little." Once you sort it out you get the point.)

"What made you a Giants fan?" I asked Uncle Fendel with the most serious curiosity, as if probing for the source of some illness.

"Christy Mathewson," he said.

Christy Mathewson. I just about breathed the name aloud. If there is a New York baseball lineage leading high to Olympus, its progenitor, sire to latter-day saints Ruth, DiMaggio, Gehrig, Mantle, Mays, Seaver, was the nonpareil New York Giants right-hander who arrived at the Polo Grounds with precise chronological punctilio in 1900, athletic herald of the American century, come to seed the iconic line. He was tall, he was handsome, cultured, dignified, regally aloof—and, most important, four times a thirty-game winner, sealing it and leaving it forever untouchable by dying in 1925 at the age of forty-seven, from tuberculosis.

Once, sitting in the kitchen in my usual baseball haze, I asked my mother (born 1899 on Ludlow Street in the abounding ethnic thickets of the Lower East Side) if as a child she had known anything about baseball. She looked at me as if I'd gone flatulent.

"Baseball?" she said. "In my house? Are you crazy?" Then, after a thoughtful moment, she said, "Well, of course everybody knew Christy Mathewson."

Even there, in that alien enclave of striving and struggling Yiddish-speaking immigrants, that densely packed ghetto of bearded zaydes and harassed bubbehs and payessed Hasidim; into that tiny Ludlow Street apartment with its communal toilet, with parents that never spoke a word of English, where baseball was as remote as Easter Island, the name had filtered. *Everybody knew Christy Mathewson.*

"You saw him pitch?" I asked Uncle Fendel.

"Of course I saw him pitch," he said. "A hundred times if once."

"Was he better than Walter Johnson?"

"Walter Johnson was no slouch, but Mathewson was better."

"What was he like?" I asked.

"He stood out on that mound like a champion. You couldn't beat him."

I knew that at that moment Uncle Fendel was visualizing Mathewson in his mind, and I stared into his eyes, trying to see beyond them the conjured memory, to see for myself—Christy Mathewson in those layered summers of long ago, winding up on the mound, kicking forward and delivering from out of what had been the most lethal arsenal of pitches any pitcher had ever possessed: fastball, curve, and that mystery pitch he alone could throw and no one could hit.

"The fadeaway," Uncle Fendel said.

"What did it do?"

"It faded away."

"How did he throw it?" I asked.

"I can tell you that. I used to watch him like a hawk, and I saw how he did it. I'll show you one day."

"You will?"

"Sure," he said. "We'll get gloves and a ball and I'll show you."

In the late 1970s I traveled to New Haven to see Smoky Joe Wood, the young lightning bolt of 1912 who had fired his Johnsonian fastball to a 34-5 record and then three World Series victories, the final one over Mathewson.

"It was a thrill to face him," the eighty-eight-year-old Smoky Joe said. "They called him the King of all Pitchers, and maybe he was," the loyal American Leaguer said, "though I'd still take Walter. Matty wasn't as fast as he'd once been. When I saw him his greatest asset was control and a beautiful curveball that he'd start over your head and bring right down. I'd never seen a curveball like it. He also threw what they called the fadeaway, which is the same as a screwball. As far as I know, he was the only one who threw it at that time, and it was damned hard to get the bat on it. You didn't like to see him on the mound, I can tell you that. Just the way he stood there, like a winner."

There is a picture of the two aces taken during the Series. They are squatting, like two men over a campfire, each with a bat in hand. Showing him the picture, I said to Mr. Wood, "It looks like he's talking to you."

"Might have been," he said, squinting at the picture.

"What was he saying? Do you remember?"

He laughed. "Hell," he said, "that's—how many years ago? Sixty-five?"

(Don't snicker—I've gotten some very good answers from some very foolish questions.)

For Joe Wood, who would ruin that magical arm the following spring and become a frieze on baseball's wall of what-might-have-beens, the Mathewson aura, almost seven decades later, was still seductive. More than that, it was a mystique that went on traveling across the baseball dreamland.

"He was my hero," Tom Seaver said as we sat in a noisy, pregame Mets clubhouse. "Right from the time I was a kid in California. I read everything I could about him."

In certain photographs you can find a facial resemblance between New York's two greatest right-handers, and Seaver too had a keen intelligence and commanding mound presence. (He didn't have Christy's fadeaway, but neither did Christy have Tom's slider.) And, rare among big-league players, Seaver took an interest in the game's history.

"You spoke to Joe Wood?" he said with some surprise. "God, how old is he?"

"Pushing ninety," I said.

"Is he still competent?"

"Very much so."

"Did you ask him how he hurt his arm?"

"He said he came in to field a ball, the grass was wet, and he took a tumble."

"Just like that?" Seaver said quizzically, as if unnerved by how tenuous it all could be.

"He broke his thumb. When he came back he said he had some pain in his shoulder, but they put him back in the rotation and kept pitching him until he blew it out."

"They pitched a thirty-game winner with a sore shoulder?" Seaver was incredulous.

"It was a different world."

"I guess so."

"They only carried about six pitchers."

"The good old days," Seaver said whimsically.

"It was pitch or perish, I guess."

"More like pitch *and* perish."

"He talked about you," I said. "He watches you on television every chance he gets. He compared you to Mathewson, very favorably."

"Joe Wood said that?"

A young pitcher, whose name I cannot recall, was sitting at the next locker, listening. Seaver laughed and rapped him lightly on the shoulder, and said, "You hear that? Joe Wood compares me to Mathewson."

"And," I said, "he's seen them all since Cy Young."

"You know a guy who saw Cy Young pitch?" the young man said.

"They were teammates in 1911."

"The guy was Cy Young's teammate?" the young man said, impressed by this further drench of history.

Then Seaver looked at me and asked, "What did he tell you about Mathewson?"

The interest was clinical. He listened intently as I repeated Joe Wood's words, putting Seaver in as close contact with his boyhood hero as I could. Seaver looked at me as though trying to see past me into Joe Wood, whose related memories came down through the decades on invisible wires: Matty in the mists, as dominant in his world as Seaver was then in his. That big beautiful curveball, the inscrutable fadeaway that only he held the secret to, the masterful control that enabled him, in the words of a contemporary, "to throw strikes with his eyes shut." Christy Mathewson, of whom *everybody* had heard, alive once more, on the mound and in that locker room.

"He was my hero," Seaver said again.

One day, early in 1942, Uncle Fendel came up the stairs for his dinner and announced he was getting married. She was a widow, a very "refined" person. They were going to live in Florida. We toasted him and wished him luck.

"She must be rich," my mother said later.

"She must be crazy," my father said.

We received the occasional postcard showing white beaches and blue water. One day my mother mentioned that we hadn't heard from Uncle Fendel in years, nor did we ever again.

I never did find out how Mathewson threw the fadeaway.

Seven

⧖ BASEBALL was neutered by the war, and not just because most of the stars had, as the sportswriters liked to say, "exchanged one uniform for another," or "swapped his bat for a rifle." (I never saw it written that a pitcher might have swapped baseballs for hand grenades. There was indeed a story that came out of the war about a Cardinals pitcher named Bill Reeder, who had helped get himself and his buddies out of a difficult situation by hurling hand grenades for considerable distances with precise accuracy. When asked later if he'd been concerned about hurting his arm, he replied, "I'd rather have a dead arm on a live body than the other way around.") Parents were sobered by what the world was turning into, and children were confused. Even though the initial, seal-breaking blow at Pearl Harbor had been sudden, the thing itself, the gathering plague, had been hardening its reality and gesturing toward us for several years, so that when finally it did strike it had that tsunami momentum. The impact was colossal and nation-sweeping.

The past summers suddenly seemed wrapped in wistful memory; there was the feeling that what had given them their quality of endless sunlit childhood had broken away, not to return, or if returning would be the province of other youngsters. Baseball's grip on the imagination was not quite as it had been before. Memory tells me we didn't go to a game after 1942 and not again until 1946.

There were pictures in the papers of those familiar faces in unfamiliar uniforms, duffel bags thrown over their shoulders, waving, smiling (a celebrity going off to war had to show how blithe he felt about it). By the opening of the 1943 season the great stars and many of the lesser were gone, leaving behind an unfillable void which was handled the only way it could be, with ever-descending standards, the nadir being reached in 1945 when the St. Louis Browns introduced a tough, gritty one-armed outfielder named Pete Gray.

Hank Greenberg saw dangerous service with the air force in India and China. Bob Feller requested combat duty and got plenty of it in the Pacific. Joe DiMaggio was in Hawaii, assigned to entertaining the troops with exhibitions of his unique talents. Ted Williams was an instructor with the air force in Florida.

And Pete Reiser? The army had him and was so enamored of his talent it kept him in the States, playing on service teams (the interservice rivalries were taken quite seriously by the brass). The uniform swap didn't do much for his luck, however. Launching himself after a fly ball on a Fort Riley, Kansas, field, he crashed through the outfield fence, rolled down an embankment, and knocked himself cold. He awoke to find a two-star general standing over him saying, "Son, that was one of the bravest things I've ever seen."

The war had a unifying impact on the country. I think every person felt the same thing at the time—that every effort had a positive effect somewhere, and that they could make a difference. War wasn't fought with just bullets, we were told; and so we made our contributions, collecting scrap iron, tin foil, rubber; we became urban farmers and planted and watered victory gardens and then crouched down and waited for tomatoes and radishes to spring into the sunshine. There were shortages of meats, butter, coffee, canned goods; sugar was rationed and so was gasoline, and new tires were virtually impossible to come by. The five-dollar weekend joyride car was gone forever.

When my mother graduated from public school she had been awarded a volume of Tennyson, inscribed to "Mildred Elson, for general excellence." Next to her two darlings, that book was probably the thing she was proudest of; it was tangible evidence that scholastic effort went neither unnoticed nor unrewarded. So it was with chagrin that she read my report cards (polar opposites of my brother's, for whom it all seemed to come so easily). She even tried using the national crisis as a scholastic incentive.

"You have to study harder," she said. "There's a war on."

But here my rampant patriotism faltered. What classroom praise I did receive was for my knowledge of current events. But this, like most things commendable about me, was owed to my brother, who knew where Dnepropetrovsk was, that Guadalcanal was not an artificial waterway, and how important the El Alamein victory was.

"They teach too many things that aren't interesting," I told my mother.

"Like what?"

"Science. Art. Woodworking. Math. Geography. English."

"What *do* you like?"

"History," I said. "Sometimes."

In the eighth grade I was further demoralized when they introduced a new subject: Spanish. After months of this torment, all I could manage was the ability to count to ten. My usually sympathetic brother's observation on this achievement was that if I ever moved to Spain I could become a referee.

Several times, when I was in the eighth grade, I carried home with me for delivery to my mother sealed brown envelopes addressed to her. I didn't have to steam them open to know what was inside—they were invitations from this teacher or that to come around the corner for a chat, and it wasn't going to be about recipes or foreign policy. When my mother confronted me with the gist of these councils, it always followed a pattern.

"They think you're very smart but don't show it."

I found that perplexing: how could they tell if I didn't show it?

My mother, however, never lost faith. I think she must have felt that if one son was such a bright bulb, it was unreasonable that the other could be of so drastically reduced wattage. Her ears perked up, however, when she was called in one day to confer with my English teacher. The cause this time was paradoxical—it seemed I had done something so laudable as to suggest I couldn't have done it.

"He has been handing in short stories," my mother was told. The stories were of a quality that apparently belied their author. What the teacher wanted to know was if my brother had written them. (Stanley had since graduated, but his presence had left an afterglow.) My mother confirmed for the teacher my authorship, but whether she was believed was doubtful, for none of the stories appeared in the school magazine. (This tender-age experience at having my work rejected for asinine reasons proved a valuable apprenticeship.)

But the meeting with the English teacher was to have a bigger and better consequence. My mother's reasoning was that if the stories were good enough to cast doubt on their author, perhaps her twelve-year-old enigma possessed an unsuspected talent.

This was the genesis of my first typewriter. It was an Underwood, whose provenance probably traced back to Joe Wood's heyday, if not before. We bought it for twelve dollars from a woman who said it had belonged to a maiden aunt who had used it only for occasional letters (the way people selling a used car say grandpa drove it just once a month).

For about six months the Underwood obeyed every tapped command. Then it stopped. Pressing the space bar accomplished nothing; in addition, the ribbon spools got tired of turning. I was devastated. I had become married to the thing, writing my stories with a great mindless joy (though no longer deigning to show them at school). It was like a first glimpse of the end of the world.

My father, who fancied himself an all-around handyman (he had once fixed our recalcitrant toilet, after which no one would shake hands with him for a week), said he would "look it over." That evening he sat himself down in front of the intransigent beast with a screwdriver, a tweezer, and some toothpicks, like some sort of shaman, minus only the chicken bones and goat's lips. Piece by piece he began dismantling the thing, scattering my typewriter across the table. I couldn't bear it; it was like watching surgery on your pet dog.

My brother and I left and took a long walk around the neighborhood, he trying to cheer me with the thought of the world's unlimited supply of pencils, an instrument, he reminded me, of no complications and unfailing fidelity. I was not consoled.

When we returned some time later, we were greeted by my mother's amazed smile.

"He fixed it," she said.

We went inside and there he was, sitting in front of the Underwood in all the pride of an Edison, his ink-stained fingers punching at the keyboard of a most obediently responding typewriter, whose carriage was hiccupping nicely along. He was adding further lines of gibberish to a page already filled with it.

Filled with a Christmas-morning delight, I asked him what he'd done.

"I fixed it," he said.

"What was wrong?" I asked.

"It wasn't working right," he said.

Perfectly logical, but maddening. (Once, staring at our windup alarm clock which hadn't been wound for a while, he said, "When it slows down it goes fast.")

I took over and began rattling away at the keyboard, and all was fine. Then I noticed three or four tiny screws and a couple of round metal nuts lying to a side.

"What are these?" I asked.

"I didn't know where the hell they went," he said.

The Underwood performed like a champion for years.

Unlike my mother, my father never showed much interest in how his heirs were doing in school. He had us pegged as grocers, the family trade, and as long as we could manage the basics in arithmetic, the rest didn't matter. In the fall of 1945 he bought a grocery store in the Ridgewood section of Queens. I used to watch him at the end of each day sitting at his little desk in the back room, filling in three different ledgers. When I asked him why he had three sets of books he said that one was for him, one was for the government, and one for whomever he sold the store to. Everybody did it that way, he said, even General Motors.

Before he became a tactical mathematician, he worked as a clerk in my Uncle Herman's grocery, which was located right there on our corner. When we walked home from school there he would be, standing outside, a big man in a long white apron.

"How'd it go?" he'd ask, as if we'd been playing ball.

I would give him a shrug, but Stanley always paused to give an account of the day's education. Then Pop would look at me.

"Did you learn anything today?" he'd ask.

"No."

"Did you forget anything?"

"No."

"All right," he'd say, "then you broke even."

Evenings, when I'd be sitting at the kitchen table scowling over that gratuitous torture known as homework, he'd duck in and tell me to hurry, that the game was on. One night, drenched after trying to add up two and two, I went inside and found him placidly beside the radio, hands folded on his big belly, listening to the game.

"What's the score?" I asked.

"They're losing," he said, "one-two."

I needed a moment to take this in.

"That's not how you say it," I told him.

"No?"

"You don't say 'one-two.' You always put the higher number first. You say 'two-one.'"

"What's the difference?"

"There's a difference."

"All right," he conceded. "Two-one. But they're still losing."

The war had settled upon everyone and everything a permanent, unchanging tension. Along with the rationing, the shortages, the disappearing young men, the radio carried news accounts every thirty minutes. And the heart-stopping *We interrupt this program for a special bulletin*—from Europe, North Africa, the Pacific. Air raids over Germany, naval battles, the titanic Russian front. And those names: Roosevelt, Churchill, Stalin, Hitler, Mussolini, Tojo, Chiang Kai-shek ("The Chink in our armor," one clever clod said in the candy store one day). And of course our invincibles—Eisenhower, Patton, MacArthur.

Living on the East Coast, as we were, the war, though thousands of ocean miles away, could become tangibly evident. Allied merchantmen, convoying supplies to Britain, were being torpedoed off the coasts of Long Island and New Jersey, so that even the broad Atlantic could turn ominous.

In the summer of 1943 my mother took my brother and me to Rockaway Beach to spend a few seaside days with relatives. Walking along the shoreline early one morning, Stanley and I came upon some desolate items that had washed up—long spars of wood, tin cans, the remains of a life preserver that showed "H.M.S.," the name of the dead ship gone, as whoever had reached for the device was probably gone. The explosion, the screams, the terror behind this sunbaked, sand-crusted artifact lying on the beach numbed our minds. We didn't touch it, merely stared at it as we might into an open grave.

At six o'clock, the beach-clearing curfew hour, a young Coast Guardsman appeared (the year before, eight would-be German saboteurs had been landed by submarine on a Long Island beach, hence the patrolling). He was a tall lad, sailor-capped, with a blue uniform and yellow leggings. He couldn't have been more than eighteen or nineteen, but the rifle hanging from his shoulder was fearsomely real and made him all man.

"Time to clear off, fellas," he said. He put a cigarette between his lips and expertly lit it in the sea wind, match cupped in hand. "Better not come out here tonight," he said, the cigarette batting in his mouth, "or I'll have to shoot you."

Soberly we withdrew, leaving him standing there on the sands at the edge of America, cigarette in mouth, gazing out to sea.

By 1943 the older boys—the "big guys"—for so long so familiar about the neighborhood, were gone. These high teenagers, who had played vociferous dollar-a-man softball games in the schoolyard, who had crouched around noisy crap games in the yard's corners, who had carried packs of cigarettes in the folds of their rolled-up sleeves, were gone, recast as sailors, Marines, soldiers, airmen. From younger siblings we heard about them. Youngsters who had seldom strayed far from Maspeth were in North Africa, Italy, New Guinea. Sometimes, home on furlough, they would sentimentally visit the school, and in uniform, sometimes wearing battle ribbons, stand before the class and answer questions. One boy (I call him a boy now), home from the Pacific with healing wounds, was ingenuously asked if he had killed anybody. We watched the boy-man face ponder the question, the teacher staring at him with deep curiosity.

"You try to stay alive," he finally said.

It ended first in Europe, in May 1945, to a binge of national celebration. And in the Pacific it ended with the same sudden explosiveness as it had begun, with what in today's sports-page vernacular might be described as a "walk-off A-Bomb" over Nagasaki.

Eight

❦ YOU MIGHT SAY that it was the Dutch
Reformed Church that stopped me from getting through high
school.

Junior High School 73 was right around the corner and
thus inescapable. Newtown High School in neighboring Elmhurst, however, where I enrolled in the fall of 1945, was a
mile and a half away. A lot of things could happen in a mile
and a half, especially when I generally forwent the trolley car
and chose to walk to school. A boy with an innate distaste
for school is not as a rule in a rush to get there. At my slow,
dreamy pace, distractions and diversions abounded. The
slower I walked, the more adept I became at seeing things
that weren't there.

The Dutch Reformed Church was on the other side of
Queens Boulevard, where the trolley tracks turned, just a few
blocks from my ostensible destination. What stopped me there
was not some burst of piety but rather the small, fenced-in,
rustically simple graveyard. Here some stillness of prevailing
mood would catch and hold me.

I would lean on the fence and gaze at the two dozen or
so tenuously poised tombstones and begin drifting out of the

moment, oblivious to the clamors of 1945, taken up by visions that were never mine to see. The tombstones of the old country churchyard, set by hands themselves long merged with the bottom earth, were worn thin by wind and storm and time itself, some run through with jagged arterial cracks, some tilted one way or another, some no longer whole. A few of the nearer ones bore still intelligible epitaphs, the crowning years being in the late 1700s or early in the next century. I wondered who they had been, if any had been at Valley Forge, known George Washington. Knowing nothing, I was free to invent at will.

By the time my meandering mind had resettled in 1945, it was too late to make the first bell at Newtown High. Believing that never was better than late, I began retracing my steps, entertaining new abstractions. The rest of the day always took care of itself.

My ragged attendance record soon caught the school's eye. One day, having survived the lure of the graveyard and made it to school on time, I was summoned from my home room to the office of the assistant principal, one Mr. Baker. He sat me down before him and began informing me of things I already knew, showing curiosity more than sternness. I tried as best I could to explain my disinclination for sitting in classrooms, though I must say that it is not easy to express a preference for doing something that is against the law, especially to someone whose job it is to maintain and uphold that law. I didn't feel rebellious or confrontational; I was simply one who was going to follow the luted airs as he heard them. Perhaps sensing that not all boys were mixed from the same can of powder, Mr. Baker seemed if not sympathetic then at least concerned. He reminded me again that by law I had to remain in school until I was sixteen. An eternity of two more years. I think he realized, as I did, that that might be beyond reach.

He asked me what I wanted to do with myself. The question was probably tactical, pointing toward the world's vagaries, its rough handling of the unschooled. I had two answers: to be a baseball player and to be a writer (which sounded like two vocations without an apparent connecting point). But I told him about neither. I felt self-conscious about the first and reluctant to state the latter, perhaps knowing the lecture on the vital importance of education that would follow.

When I had no answer for him, he got to the immediate: what would I do if I stopped going to school?

"Work in my father's store," I said.

"And what kind of a store does your father have?" he asked.

"A grocery."

"Your father has a grocery store?" The interest was unmistakable. He stared at me now as if I had changed identities.

Let me now declare on behalf of Mr. Baker—who seemed to have been taking a concerned interest in my life and destiny—that these were the immediate postwar days, when shortages still prevailed and rationing of certain items was still in effect, with precious government-issued stamps needed to obtain some of them. Like sugar.

"Do you think," Mr. Baker said, "you could bring me five pounds of sugar?"

No mention was made of a stamp; we were that quickly in collusion, and colluding people have mutual instincts, no matter how wide apart might be their stations in life.

I appeared the next day with a double-bagged five pounds of sugar. My father, for whom these sorts of transactions had a certain appeal, said to make a gift of it, but Mr. Baker insisted on paying (the word "stamp" never passed our lips).

I don't know if it was a quid pro quo or an act of sympathetic understanding, but there was in Long Island City (a modest bus ride from Maspeth) an Industrial School that took in "certain" wayward scholars whose obligation it was to attend classes one day a week. These classes were limited to woodworking, printing, and electrical wiring (they seem to have left out plumbing). Upon attaining the age of sixteen the students were released to go out, get their working papers, and begin the climb to the top.

Arriving at this school I joined a group of slouching, moody time-servers. My first question to one of my new colleagues was about how scrupulous the place was in marking attendance. "Show up once in a while," I was told. I spent my first day in woodworking, planing down a chunk of wood locked into a vise. The teacher had drawn a straight line across the center of the wood, and I was to plane down until I was even with it. It turned out to be more complicated than it sounds—for me, anyway. My second day was spent in electrical wiring, learning how to splice wires. I don't know what they had planned for me in printing because I didn't get that far. I never went back.

I waited for repercussions. But there were none. And so my academic career came to a quiet close.

My mother sighed her acceptance. My Gandhi-like insurrection had been effective. My father had raised no opposition; he was satisfied to have a full-time, unpaid clerk where he believed all Honigs belonged anyway—behind the counter of a grocery store. It was a job hardly to my liking, my day beginning at 6 A.M. and going tediously on. But this time there was no recourse. My father had all the sugar he needed.

Nine

≫   THE CITY of San Pedro de Macoris lies
in the southeastern part of the Dominican Republic. Situated
on the Caribbean Sea at the mouth of the Higuamo River,
this modest urban setting of some ninety thousand or so is a
leading port. Textiles and alcohol are produced and shipped
from here. But the city's most notable—and to many most
baffling—production and export is baseball players. Including such first-rank stars as Sammy Sosa, George Bell, Tony
Fernandez, Robinson Cano, and many others, what has risen
from the spike-marked soil of this Dominican city presents for
baseball's insatiable talent hunters a pleasant if inexplicable
riddle. The city has become the baseball equivalent of those
streets of gold that Cortez and his teammates came here looking for some five hundred years ago.

This is what happens, people say, when youngsters tal-
ented and willing are encouraged to play the game they love.
Accordingly, major league teams, moving to exploit what may
be the triumph of desire or mere coincidence or the manifestation of something beyond understanding, have crowded into
San Pedro de Macoris and its environs, distributing equipment, building facilities, establishing baseball academies,

and otherwise colonizing in the name of Abner Doubleday while any scout with at least one good eye prowls the landscape looking for that level swing, those intuitive moves of the natural-born infielder, that limber young arm that can blur a ball in the yellow sunshine. Baseball is indeed avidly played on that Caribbean island, and not just because the game is loved but because it can be an avenue out of tropical poverty. But San Pedro de Macoris continues to mystify. All of that rich talent simply defies the law of probabilities.

Sadly, Maspeth, where baseball was played with no less fervor than it is in San Pedro de Macoris, to this day has produced but one bona fide big leaguer (we did turn out a few who slipped in for the proverbial "cup of coffee," the major league beverage of brief acquaintance). This was James Joseph Ring, neighborly proof that what we dreamed of did exist and was attainable.

Jimmy Ring was a rugged, heavyset man of gruff exterior, but he had kindly understanding for a youngster who wanted to know what it had been like. If he seemed at times unsentimental about his career, that was the veneer; the pride was never far from the surface.

Ring had been a tough, highly respected fastballer who had worked the National League mounds with Cincinnati, Philadelphia, New York, and St. Louis from 1917 to 1928, coming home at the age of thirty-three with a record of 118–149. The record is deceptive, for Ring spent most of his prime years laboring for relentlessly woeful Phillies teams, for whose last-place edition he won an impressive eighteen games in 1923, the most of any Phillies pitcher in that decade.

"Did you know that, Mr. Ring?" I asked him. "That no Phillies pitcher topped you in that decade?"

"I didn't know that," he said.

75

This proved a common thread with every major league player I ever spoke with: a claimed unfamiliarity with their own statistical histories. I could never tell whether this was affectation or not; if it was genuine, it was one more thing that separated them from the true believers. But this tough professional did have his hero. Mr. Ring would raise his hands and hold his forefingers in parallel lines a few inches apart, then move them farther away from each other until showing a gap of nearly two feet. It was a demonstration of how many different curveballs Grover Cleveland Alexander could throw.

"He was the best," he said.

"Better than Mathewson?" I asked.

"Just as good."

He spoke of Rogers Hornsby and Paul Waner and John McGraw (for whose Giants he pitched in 1926). And what about the infamous 1919 World Series, when he shut out that band of Chicago "Black Sox" renegades on three hits in Game Four? Did he think they were playing honest ball that afternoon?

"It wouldn't have made any difference," he said gruffly. "They weren't going to hit me that day. Nobody was."

In the 1940s Mr. Ring worked nights in a liquor store a few blocks from my home, leaving him a sitting duck for a baseball-obsessed youngster thirsty for tales of the old days and all within them. Several nights a week I came through the door and, between customers, we sat on wooden folding chairs behind the counter and talked.

It was my first opportunity to sit with a big leaguer and ask questions. I was to learn later that Mr. Ring's kindness, patience, and willingness to respond were typical of the breed. It has often been said that baseball is a storyteller's game, which is absolutely true; and the players—who are the stories—tell them better than anyone else. Mr. Ring, who had lived the life, ridden the trains that crisscrossed the trails of baseball America, fired his smoke from Ebbets Field to Sportsman's Park in St. Louis, was the harbinger of so much that was to come my way later.

He joined the Reds in 1917 at the age of twenty-two. Young Jimmy had won an eye-catching twenty-five games for Utica the year before and was considered a hot prospect.

"Didn't make any difference," he said. "When I joined the Reds I was about the same as a batboy. That's the way it was for rookies then. You're there to take somebody's job, and they didn't make it easy for you. Mathewson was the manager then. He was a perfect gentleman but he hardly spoke to me. Did he teach me anything? No; I learned more from watching Alexander. But I'll tell you one thing: the day I showed up, a couple of the veterans pulled me aside and warned me to stay away from Hal Chase."

Hal Chase. Baseball's "Benedict Arnold," by that time a man of sinister and unsavory reputation, but a first baseman of such scintillating skills that teams in that raggedly ethical era were willing to put up with his occasional doctoring of games.

"I was starting a game one time," Mr. Ring said, "when he came up to me and asked me if I wanted to make some money. I said to him, 'You ever say that to me again and I'll punch the shit out of you.' And he knew I could do it. So he walked away."

The Reds jettisoned Chase the following year and John McGraw signed him for the Giants, no doubt assuming Chase wouldn't try any monkey business with him. But Chase was incorrigible and finally, late in the season, McGraw booted him out, and with John McGraw's footprints on his rear end Chase never returned to organized ball.

And what about that 1919 World Series that came close to disillusioning the country about its national game?

"Some of the games they put out and some they didn't," Mr. Ring said. "We knew something fishy was going on. They cut off relays, screwed up some plays. You could see it. But they weren't going to beat us, no matter." He was adamant about that. "We had the pitching."

Rogers Hornsby and his .400 bat? "Well," Mr. Ring said laconically, "he could hit. He could talk too. If he didn't like you, he told you so. If he didn't think you could play, he told you that too. I didn't know Cobb, but they said he could be a real bastard too. Four-hundred hitters," he muttered, as if aside to himself, expressing a pitcher's grudging judgment on this regal fraternity.

In 1920 the lively ball was introduced and batting averages soared, taking earned run averages, Mr. Ring's among them, with them. The spitball and other doctored deliveries were banned; scuffed balls, heretofore kept in play, were now quickly discarded; the new ball was smooth and shiny and hard to grip (they underwent no pregame rub-up as yet). And men who had learned their game as choke-up contact hitters in the dead-ball era were whacking sharp line drives and shooting hard skippers through the infield. A decade of ferocious hitting that would vandalize the record book had begun. (From 1920 through 1925 the diplomatic Mr. Hornsby *averaged .397.*)

One day I found in one of my record books the box score of what is the totemic game of that hitter's decade. It was played on August 25, 1922, at Chicago's Wrigley Field. The final score was Cubs 26, Mr. Ring's Phillies 23. When I handed him the box score he studied it impassively, nodding his head a few times. Philadelphia's starting pitcher that day, who was sitting next to me, had given up twelve hits and five walks in three and one-third frisky innings. At the end of the fourth inning the score was 25-6, Chicago. But in those resounding years you never counted yourself out. The Phillies scored three in the fifth, eight in the eighth, and then six in the ninth, falling short by three.

"We should have won that game," Mr. Ring said in quiet understatement. "We had the bases loaded when it ended."

That afternoon's merriment in the late summer of 1922 remains in the record book: most runs game, both clubs, 49; most hits by both clubs, nine-inning game, 51. Throw in 9 errors and 21 walks and you have entertainment enough for sadist and masochist both.

"You remember it?" I asked.

"Sure," he said. "One or two more hits would have done it." Then the tough old pitcher gave me one of his rare smiles. "It doesn't matter how many runs are scored," he said. "A close game is still a close game."

Mr. Ring had mentioned Paul Waner, who for years played alongside younger brother Lloyd in the Pittsburgh outfield, each building a Hall of Fame career. Thinking of them gave rise to an extravagant double dream—Stanley (with his Elbie Fletcher glove) and me wearing the uniform of the Brooklyn Dodgers. I would be on the mound, and he would be flashing his leather around the bag. Stanley, however, with his firmer grip on reality, had begun looking to the wider world. He was reading poetry, serious fiction, and history, bringing home classical music on those fragile old 78s, and talking to my blank face about somebody named Picasso. One day my father found a book about architecture on the kitchen table. Bemused, he looked at me and said, "Everything is his business."

In those years baseball didn't seem the family trade that it is today. There were some brother acts—the DiMaggios and Waners most prominently—but almost none of the multi-generation talents we have now, when the game seems almost an inherited profession, with examples of genetically infused aptitudes appearing regularly—the Boones and the Bells (three generations each), the Griffeys, the Bondses, and so many more.

So with Stanley as a baseball dropout, I was going to have to carry the family's big-league banner alone. I saw myself hitting the top in 1952 and playing until around 1970, retiring after achieving all the glory a rising imagination could conjure. I even looked far beyond retirement, to when I would be a geriatric big-league veteran at peace in the pools of yesterday, telling my own eager auditors what it had been like, as Mr. Ring had told me. Urban lad that I was, I nevertheless always saw these years of old remembrance being spent in a bucolic setting, sitting on a rocking chair on my front porch. (In baseball it seems impossible to imagine one thing without recalling another. When asked what it was like working for Billy Martin, one of his Yankees coaches replied, "I'll tell you one thing—when I'm out of all this and sittin' on my front porch, ain't *nobody* ever callin' me 'cocksucker' again.")

Get an old ballplayer talking and you never knew where or how far he would go. But no matter how far afield it might stray, the story always found its way back to baseball, as in the strange tale told by Bucky Walters. This outstanding Cincinnati Reds pitcher of the late 1930s and early '40s (league MVP in 1939) had been part of a morale-building tour of the European battlefronts in late 1944.

"I was there along with Frankie Frisch, Dutch Leonard, Mel Ott, and a few others," Walters said, sitting in his suburban

Philadelphia home and telling the story some thirty years later. "We couldn't play any baseball—it was freezing cold—but we went around and talked to the soldiers, told stories, answered questions. It really impressed me how hungry those guys were for that sort of thing. Frisch was a great storyteller. He'd stand up in front of the guys and say, 'I'm going to tell you some terrific stories, and some of them will even be true.'

"We were pretty close to the front, but it was quiet. Then all of a sudden all hell broke loose. There was a lot of shooting and cannon fire and explosions, and everybody starts running around like crazy. You know what it was? It was the Battle of the Bulge, ripping off right in front of us. The Germans were coming through, taking the whole line by surprise. Some officer comes running up to us and says we've got to get the hell out of there, that this looks like it's for real."

The ballplayers were hustled into a truck that roared off along the rutted, solidly frozen roads into a falling twilight. They were told to lie down in the back and cradle their heads with their arms, the latter piece of advice Walters described as unnecessary, with all the explosions going on around them.

"All except Frisch," Walters said. "That crazy Dutchman insisted on sitting up front with the driver. We're flattened out there in the back cradling our heads, and Frisch is sitting up front like a tour guide, yelling about everything he's seeing. Explosions, artillery flashes, God knows what. 'Keerist!' he's yelling. 'Look at that! What a sight!' We're afraid to raise our heads an inch, so we start cursing him and telling him to shut up. Dutch Leonard says, 'Don't listen to the crazy son of a bitch, he'll get us all killed. Keep your head down.' And believe me, that's just what I was doing."

Some time later, Walters said, they pulled into a tiny Belgian village.

"It had quieted down by then," he said, "and we were told we'd stay there till morning. They billeted us around to this house and that. I was put into a small house that belonged to a farmer, who'd agreed to put me up for the night, though I don't know how much he had to say about it. But he seemed an all-right guy, a little guy with a mustache who never stopped smoking his pipe. I don't know if he had a family or not, but there was nobody else there. I guess he'd seen it all by now because his face never changed expression. He had a few words of English, not a hell of a lot; and whatever language he spoke, I didn't have a syllable. He gave me some bread and cheese and wine, and it tasted good. I was too nervous to sleep, so we sat in this little living room, lit by a candle, and stared at each other. He must have been wondering who the hell I was.

"Then it started again. Artillery shells started banging around. Whose they were and where they were coming from, I had no idea. Suddenly the whole place started to shake. Dirt was coming down from the ceiling timbers. He yipped something, jumped up waving at me, and I followed him down to the cellar. He lit a candle there and we sat on the floor, listening to the explosions. Some seemed pretty close, some far away. Sometimes it quieted down, and then boom!, it started up again.

"Then he started talking. 'American?' he asked. I nodded. Then he got through to me that he was a farmer. I pointed to myself and said, 'Baseball player.' He seemed confused, probably wondering what the hell a baseball player was doing there. But he'd heard of baseball. He made a motion like throwing a ball, showing he understood. Then he made a few more gestures. He wanted me to show him how it was played.

"I got some bits of paper and laid out an infield design on the floor. Bases and all. 'Batter,' I told him, pointing to the plate area. I held up an imaginary bat, swung it, and ran my fingers along to first base. Then I swung again and ran my fingers around the bases back to home plate. 'A run,' I told him. How much he got, I don't know, but he was watching with great interest. So there I was, in the middle of an artillery barrage, sitting by candlelight in the cellar of a house somewhere in Belgium, trying to explain baseball to a farmer who had about six words of English.

"When I told Frisch about it the next day he had his usual wisecrack. 'Pitchers don't know anything,' he said. 'I should have been there. The guy would be a fan by now.'"

Sometimes the memories had raw, bitter edges, but even these could, at long distance, come forward with a kind of leavening.

The memories of James (Cool Papa) Bell were entitled to the corrosions of bitterness. Because of his skin color this incomparable outfield star of the 1930s Negro Leagues had been denied the opportunity that rightfully should have been his. But in recounting those dark and dismal times Bell showed a high-minded tranquility. It had all happened, yes—the insults, the degradation—but the world had gone on, correcting itself as it went, and for this gentle man that was what mattered. In *Baseball When the Grass Was Real*, Bell ends his recollections with these words:

> But I'm not looking back at the past; I'm looking ahead to the future. I'm not angry at Mississippi or anyplace else. That's the way it was in those days. I pray that we can all live in peace together.

One summer's night a few years ago I was sitting home watching a Red Sox game on television when suddenly there was a power outage and all went dark. After the usual muttered curses and a futile wait for Fenway Park to reilluminate on my television set, I lit a candle and turned to the consoling comfort of one of my own books, one which I had not looked at in years. Opening it at random I found myself at Bell's chapter and by the flickering candlelight began reading.

He was telling a story that occurred in 1937, when he was a star in the Negro Leagues. He and Satchel Paige and some of the elite players were asked by Rafael Trujillo, the iron-fisted dictator of the Dominican Republic, to come to the island and play for his team in the Caribbean championship series. So Bell, Paige, and an array of stellar talents decamped to the island nation.

"When we got to the Dominican Republic," Bell said, "we went to San Pedro de Macoris, which is the little town they kept the ball club in."

They were young, vibrant athletes, a constellation of stars—some of the brightest ever—instant heroes in a culture already baseball obsessed. One supposes they didn't sit in their hotel playing cards all night.

Ten

❯ I DIDN'T KNOW what time it was; it felt like two or three in the morning. The world beyond the train window had that settled, self-possessed quiet about it, though not the quiet of prairie or desert where it is inscrutably spatial, but the poised, temporal quiet that abides over steel and concrete and is always ready for imminent fissure.

The train stopping was what woke me, and it certainly wasn't anything seen from my coach window that lured me to my feet and led me down the aisle of soundly sleeping passengers. At the end of the car I pulled aside the heavy door, went down the iron steps into the cool moistened air, and stood on the platform, feeling the muted excitement of a cautious alien. Getting off the train felt like an adventurous thing to do at two or maybe three o'clock in the morning, in a place where I had never been (I was beginning that part of my life where no matter where I was, it was a place I had never been).

The platform was deserted except for the lone figure of a becapped and frock-coated conductor who was standing several car lengths away, in the pose of a man whose employment for these silent minutes was superfluous but obligatory.

The platform benches were empty, the waiting room dark, the ticket window closed. From farther along the track a mist of engine steam blew out with an insistent hiss, making a brief, sibilant incursion on the quiet, which quickly resettled.

On the wall above the unoccupied benches a painted sign-board told me where I was. The very name of this place was a soft exotic breath in my mind. I had never been in Savannah before, just as I had never been in Philadelphia, or Baltimore, or Richmond. In fact, except for a few brief migrations to New Jersey, I had never been out of New York, never been more than two hours from home. Unusual travel had been riding the Third Avenue El and glancing into the windows of strangers. I had never been to the Statue of Liberty or to the summit of the Empire State Building (though whenever on Thirty-fourth Street I always leaned back and gazed high, like somebody from Ohio). I was the very model of a sixteen-year-old Maspeth bumpkin.

Nor, as I began my steady washing away of "nevers," had I ever been on a train before, or set foot in Pennsylvania Station, or felt so edified as when I took my seat, settled in by my father, who had mightily raised my brand-new suitcase into the overhead rack, then introduced me to my seatmate, a shy youngster named Frank Malzone.

And then my father was standing outside on the platform and it looked like he was moving, performing some lateral glide with his hand in the air and a large hopeful, maybe wistful smile, as though seeing me suddenly from a different angle; but then I realized it was not he but we who were moving. With barely enough motion to wrinkle a pond, the East Coast Champion was leaving the station, padded wheels on velvet tracks it seemed, all of those sleek silvery wide-windowed cars rolling in tandem through the black tunnel and then under the seaward Hudson waves and then suddenly out into a burst of eye-bruising sunshine like the symbolic flash of a new world. Maintaining the same fluid momentum we ran past North Jersey's industrial eyesores and along the grey early-spring flatlands. I had now and then lent an ear during my truncated scholastic experience, most often during History, and I knew that through the window of the frictionless East Coast Champion I was seeing the ground where General Washington had marched his ragtag Continentals. I tried to imagine them out there, ghost-filing in a Revolutionary mist with their shouldered muskets and tricorn hats, the meditations of the callow writer mingling with those of the equally callow baseball player.

I had listened enough in History to know, too, that standing on that empty platform in Savannah I was on the soil of what had been the old Confederacy, and I felt a keen awareness of the long ago, imagining gaunt grey shadows within the Georgia night.

Removing myself from Confederate soil, I reboarded the train and walked back through the sleeping-coach car and sat back down, resting my head against the white cloth covering the seat's upper padding, and closed my eyes. Georgia. Atlanta. Sherman. The Civil War. And of course, Ty Cobb had been born here, a man who had averaged .367 for twenty-four big-league seasons. I thought of that too as I went dreaming away into all the many reveries.

This was in early April 1948. My journey south had begun in November of the preceding year when a Boston Red Sox scout named Charles Niebergall climbed the stairs over the delicatessen on Grand Avenue with a contract in his pocket.

Mr. Niebergall, a congenial, solidly built man in his early fifties, with the thick, knotty handshake of an old catcher, had indeed been just that, catching briefly for the St. Louis Cardinals for parts of three seasons in the early 1920s. Now he was bird-dogging the New York City sandlots, where I had been pitching, this time on city-maintained fields, with teammates who all wore the same uniform.

We sat in the living room, Mr. Niebergall in the place of honor, our lone comfortable armchair. He sat with his legs crossed, talking to us. He was holding the contract in his hand; folded, it was slender, dun-colored, about the size of a long mailing envelope. He tapped it absently into the palm of his hand as he spoke. He told us of the interest the Red Sox organization took in its personnel, not just as players but as young men, how everyone, from the highest (Ted Williams) to the lowest (soon to be me), was considered important. But I was barely listening. My eyes, my entire being, were fixed on that slender document he continued to tap casually in his hand. I was afraid it might crumble into dust before I could sign it, or that it might somehow turn into a paper airplane and sail away through an open window.

Mr. Niebergall began talking about spring training and Florida, and at the sound of that my mother (who was happy for me, but nevertheless) stared at the contract as she might have at enlistment papers for the Egyptian army. I should have been paying attention, but my eyes remained rapt upon and my mind frozen upon that Magna Carta the man kept tapping into his hand, a magical document endowed with the power to turn festooned fantasy into vivid reality.

My father's exuberance had built into runaway momentum as he turned to me and said, "Listen, if you work hard and use all your talent and believe in yourself, you can make it to Cooperstown."

Mr. Niebergall, no doubt considering the odds, smiled benignly.

I was far from being a fledgling Bob Feller, but I had received offers from the Philadelphia Phillies, Cincinnati Reds, Chicago Cubs, New York Yankees, and New York Giants (I looked in vain for a beckoning finger from my Dodgers). The Yankees and Giants I rejected on the grounds of anathema, while the other clubs held no enchantments. The Red Sox had a certain cachet, not to mention having Ted Williams as teammate. The idea of playing on the same team as the man I had seen whaling baseballs into the Yankee Stadium bleachers was intoxicating. (My choice had an unexpected bonus when twenty-five years later I settled in a central Connecticut town that was a fervent enclave of the Red Sox Empire, where I was looked upon as one who had been lightly dusted with the true glory.)

The suspense finally ended and I was at last handed the contract. On its cover it read:

CLASS D

National Association

PLAYER'S CONTRACT

Eastern Shore League

OF

The National Association

of

Professional Baseball

Leagues

Milford Base Ball Club

with

Donald Honig   Player

We went into the family's Oval Office, the kitchen, and there I signed my name. Then, because I was not of legal age, my father, with a flourish, signed his Consent as Parent or Guardian, and it was done. (The salary, incidentally, was $150 per month.)

Mr. Niebergall asked if I had any questions.

"Did you ever face Grover Cleveland Alxeander?" I asked.

So the dream, which is an unborn memory, had become a reality. That evening the small Maspeth apartment felt like the site of a coronation. Signing the contract in November gave me all winter to expand and embroider the dream. I shot so far ahead into my sunlit future, and with such conviction, that I was able to be thankful for not having to pitch to Williams, who would be a teammate. But there was still the mighty DiMaggio, and I was going to have to work out a way to deal with that menace, especially with the game on the line. When the windows were frosted shields of ice and the streets lay snow-stacked from the great December blizzard, I found it easy to bedazzle the fearsome Joseph.

The night before I was to entrain and head through the old Confederacy I went to say goodbye to Mr. Ring. He shook my hand and wished me luck. Then he squinted one eye, looked me over, and asked how much I weighed.

"I'm up to one-forty," I said.

He nodded. The look in his eye said, "I'll see you in a couple of weeks."

Eleven

≫ NO ONE, I told myself, not my grand-
parents, not my father or any of his brigade of Polish-born
siblings, not Uncle Fendel, none of them, could possibly have
imagined the extent of the golden offerings of the land they
had struggled to reach. Arriving at last in New York harbor
and gazing up at the exalted Statue guarding these portals,
who could have thought, even in this wide and bountiful
America, that if you were skilled with bat and ball you could
play baseball and be paid to do it? Who would have thought
that youngsters who spent their summer days playing a mere
game would be wooed and flattered by prosperous organiza-
tions and seated on sleek trains and sped away to Florida
sunshine? There you and your peers are settled into a small
and rather elegant seaside hotel (the Bahama Beach Club),
where the only thing between you and the coast of Morocco
is the Atlantic Ocean. A team bus transports you here and
there. You are fed generously, given genuine Boston Red Sox
uniforms to wear, supplied with bats and balls, turned loose
on immaculate diamonds, and told to do the one thing you
love to do more than anything else.

Nevertheless there exists no perfect Eden. The first serpent to slither through the grass was calisthenics. I never knew what was so wonderful about being able to touch your toes without bending your knees, and then, after having proved you could do it, be asked to do it another thirty or forty times. Or lying on your back in the hot sun and pretending you're riding a bicycle. And then running. A baseball gospel is that pitchers must run. Someone, probably back in the days when Abner Doubleday was diagramming the first hit-and-run play, must have said, "Look, they can't hit and they can't field. You can't just let them hang around and clutter things up, so make them run. It will keep them busy." I guess running gives the impression of something important happening. You run to save your life, to catch a train, to set a track record. Running is action. Running is good. So turn them loose, otherwise you're paying a bunch of guys to work for a few hours two or three times a week.

So we ran. Lined up at one outfield line, we were dispatched one at a time across deep center field to the opposite line, then sent back again. To keep our legs in shape, we were told. A pitcher's legs were vital. (I had always thought that a particular upper limb was the vital one.)

But then the most insidious serpent of all made its presence known. This was the disturbing revelation that this game wasn't quite as easy to play as it had been on the sandlots, where the opposing team might have one or two players of reasonable ability. In Florida, on the green grass of Melbourne's spring training diamonds, I found myself surrounded by gifted young ballplayers; no, not the kind of talent you see in a big-league camp, but youngsters who had taken the game to its next level, who had been in their venues all-city or all-state and who were soon showing evidence of the reasons why.

Bruisers were entering the batting cage and hitting baseballs that took flight into the blue sky and seemed to stay there forever. Others, slimmer but no less deadly, were snap-wristing crackling line drives in all directions. Asking my Maspeth fastball to speed past these lively swatters was going to be a challenge. I had not at that time heard of Samuel Johnson's observation about the prospect of being hanged concentrating a man's mind, but I was certainly beginning to concentrate.

I didn't immediately realize it, but at that grassroots level your teammates are also your competition. The Milford, Delaware, club, like most Class D teams, carried around seventeen players, not more than six of them pitchers. At a guess, I would say there were between fifteen and twenty pitchers in camp, a couple of them back from last year's club, which tightened the odds even more. Since those contracts we had all signed seemed to us like certificates of achievement, we had all arrived with bright and impermeable confidence. It took a short while for that confidence to turn slightly porous and to realize we had a lot of arms for oblivion.

My education amidst these unsentimental Darwinian strivings began early. In one of our first intersquad games I threw a curve that had always stunned them back home to a big lefty-swinging kid who shot it loud and high out to straight center. I turned around, hands on hips, to watch. There were no fences bordering the several diamonds, and the center fielder wheeled around and began turning smaller and smaller. I had never seen anyone playing behind me become so small in such a hurry. That ball was on a trip to eternity.

When I got back to the bench (there were no dugouts), one of my buddies said, "That was a nice one."

"Hell," I told him, "I've given up longer ones than that."

"Really?" He sounded impressed.

Sometimes they worked the pitchers out in teams of three on the sidelines, firing into three squatting catchers. I thought I was doing well one morning when I took note of the tall rangy right-hander next to me. Big, easy motion and then that white baseball in the air like an orb of exclamation mark and the shotgun sound in the catcher's mitt. A coach was standing to one side watching us, arms folded, back slightly on his heels, the way evaluating coaches tend to pose. His face was impassive, but I noticed that each time the big fellow next to me burned one home the coach would stare for a moment or two at its point of arrival, as though in mental notation. Then he watched our windups again, waiting as he and others of his ilk did for whatever it was they wanted or hoped to see, knowing that it might come from anywhere and at anytime, and that when it did it was not to be missed. In this game they were descendants of the old prospectors who had had to break their backs panning for gold in running streams; but unlike those stubborn optimists of old, these men had merely to stand still and watch for the golden arm that in time could be molded to fit the mound at Fenway Park.

The memory of throwing next to those terrific fastballers came back to me years later in a conversation with the former ace Yankees right-hander Vic Raschi, at that point some twenty years retired. In 1936, just a youngster in Springfield, Massachusetts, Raschi's lively fastball had caught the attention of a Cleveland Indians scout, who invited the boy up to Fenway Park to work out with the team on its next visit.

Raschi arrived at Fenway, went to the Cleveland clubhouse and was given a uniform, then went out onto the field. The Indians manager, Steve O'Neill, told him to loosen up easily.

"In a little while," Raschi said, "he brought a catcher over and I pitched to him. I cut loose and threw as hard as I could, and felt pretty good about myself.

"Then this kid walked out and started to warm up. You couldn't help but notice him because he had this big, flashy windup. He started throwing harder and harder. Each pitch seemed so much faster than the previous. I'd never seen anybody throw a ball like that. Pretty soon it sounded like it was exploding when it hit the catcher's mitt. He was throwing bullets, just plain bullets. 'Good God!' I said to myself. No way was I going to compete with this guy.

"It was Bob Feller, of course. I hadn't heard of him yet at that time. But it was marvelous to watch him throw the ball, and demoralizing too. Heck, we were about the same age."

Marvelous, yes. Sublime talent elevated the game and set standards. If you were a baseball player, sharing a field, it was indeed exhilarating to feel you were part of it. Demoralizing? Yes, it could be that too.

One day, after running my brainless marathons from one foul line to the other, I sat down on the bench to watch infield practice. A coach named Jack Burns, who had been the St. Louis Browns' first baseman in the 1930s, was slashing hard, no-nonsense ground balls around the infield, yelling to the boys to "Gobble 'em up!" "Turn two!" "Fire it!" Then he would hang another ball in the air and whip his fungo bat into it, sending it tearing and bounding across the grass to challenge someone's ability.

One boy on the infield soon caught everyone's eye. He was quick, agile, strong-armed, with the "soft hands" so widely admired. These gifts belonged to my seatmate on the East Coast Champion, Frank Malzone. The Bronx boy had been a fine companion during the long ride, amiable, soft-spoken, all of the many facets of his athletic prowess quietly packaged.

Watching Frank move to his right or left or race in for a topper (the wily Burns would do that now and then) and take possession of the ball and with what seemed a mere wrist flick fire a chest-high peg to first base was pure baseball artistry. A pitcher sitting next to me watching this superb glovework said, "I don't care if he never gets a hit; I want him on my team." (But Frank did hit. In later years he was selected as third baseman on the all-time Red Sox team, a distinction he held until finally nudged aside by Wade Boggs.)

When he wasn't testing infielders with bouncing rifle shots, Jack Burns was often surrounded by first basemen seeking tips on playing the bag—feeding tosses to a covering pitcher, for instance, or positioning for relays, or footwork around the bag (you don't know how complex this can be until it's explained to you).

One day, at the completion of workouts, I joined him as he was walking back to the clubhouse, holding the fungo bat over his shoulder.

"Jack," I asked, "did you ever face Feller?"

"Sure," he said.

"How was it?"

"Uncomfortable."

"What about DiMaggio?"

"What about him?" he asked.

"Did you know him?"

"Slightly."

"What's he like?" I asked.

"He doesn't say much," he said. Then he added something that was to come back to me years later. "He doesn't have to." I was to find that as succinct a summation of Joe DiMaggio as I was ever to hear.

Baseball is the game of summers and stories. The pacing is deliberate and time must be filled. The players, most of them, sit idle much of the time, leaving too much scope to the as yet uncurbed imagination. Here we were, most of us away from home for the first time, freshly anointed professionals, not always entirely aware of the threshold we had crossed. The Red Sox obviously knew they weren't going to be convening a gathering of young seminarians, and within the welcoming speech on our first day together in camp was this: "Boys, don't ever forget—baseball is a very serious game." This is quite so, but occasionally some of its practitioners will stray from the doctrine.

There was a pitcher we called "Johnny Chicago." You can virtually see him, right?—striding through the Loop, wearing his Cubs cap, howling at Wrigley Field. But no, because baseball nicknames are not trustworthy: beanpoles are called "Shorty" and baldies answer to "Curly." The fact is, Johnny Chicago was from rural central Illinois and for some reason made it a point to inform his newly made friends that he had never been to that city, as though this somehow distinguished him. The perverse nickname was almost immediate.

Johnny was a quipster and an easy laugher, the type of kid who has set out to fill life's many moments with joy, even if it was sometimes advisable not to. Humorous mischief was one of the persistent tides of his nature, and once it took motion it would run its course, no matter whose shoes got wet. Almost any idea had a free pass to enter this fellow's head, nor did he ever seem to question the wisdom of the intrusion.

He told me that he once had introduced a small frog into his brother's bed, thrown the cover over it, then slipped into his own bed across the room to await the merriment. His brother came in a little later, got into his pajamas, turned out the light, pulled back the covers, and got into bed without giving the frog the chance to pop up and astonish him. To Johnny's disappointment there were no sudden yelps of surprise. Reckoning it best not to ask his brother if there wasn't a frog in his bed, he said nothing. In the morning the brother awoke to find his bed smeared and stained with bits and shreds of organic matter that no one could explain.

"I think he must have pancaked it when he sat down on the bed to take off his shoes," Johnny said. "Then every time he turned over during the night he must have been grinding it. The whole thing was a fiasco."

One warm morning, as we walked from the clubhouse to the field, Johnny opened his glove for my benefit; in the pocket lay what at first glance I thought was a batting-practice baseball but at second glance proved to be a rotten orange with a sun-scorched rind. Where he had gotten it from I didn't ask, and why it should be nestled in his glove also went without query.

This transportation of an incongruous object reminded me of the time my good old Maspeth friend Christopher and I were heading along Lexington Avenue for the subway on a snowy winter's day. Just before we descended into New York's netherworld, Christopher, another specimen of antic inspiration, swept his hands across the roof of a parked car and packed a snowball, which he carried with him below ground, through the turnstile and onto the subway. I didn't want to know why.

When our train roared into the station and stopped and the doors parted, we stepped in, and as we did Christopher deftly placed the snowball on top of the fedora of a man sitting next to the door reading the *Wall Street Journal*. Then we sat down opposite him. The doors closed and the train started on again. Its motion kept the snowball jiggling around on top of the man's head as a dozen or so of New York's most jaded stared impassively at it. When the coronated gentleman folded his *Wall Street Journal* and rose to leave at Forty-second Street, the snowball dropped at his feet. Baffled beyond expression, he looked down, looked up, around, and then barely made it through the doors with a final, perplexed backward look.

I soon found out what plan my teammate had for his burned-up orange. When we reached the field he casually dropped the object into the thick canvas ball bag containing the roughed-up and discolored batting-practice balls, which a coach soon carried out and placed behind the mound as we geared up for BP, for which Johnny was penciled in as first pitcher. Then he became very solemn of expression, as mischief makers are apt to do before unlocking the cage doors.

Instead of going into the outfield to shag balls, as I was supposed to, I remained on the bench, wondering if he would really do it. A frog in his brother's bed was one thing, but we were supposed to be professionals.

I watched him as he loosened up on the side. He looked to be concentrating on what he was doing. It occurred to me that all he had planned for that orange was for some other pitcher to reach into the bag and pull it out and hold it up for all to see before throwing it away. No one, not even Johnny Chicago, would throw that thing in batting practice. It would be unprofessional.

When he finished his warmups, Johnny strode to the mound, still solemn, which should have been the tip-off. The most ominous of looks can be the one of misplaced solemnity.

Clayton Sheedy, the Milford manager, took up his usual position behind the cage, studying the hitters as they came and went. Johnny kept mechanically winding up, striding, and firing. He had excellent control, and the sharp crack of batted balls was metronomic. The boys swinging away in the cage, particularly with the skipper standing a few feet behind them with an evaluating eye, were deadly serious. The fellow up there now, a fire hydrant known as Harry the Catcher, certainly was. He crouched, narrow-eyed, lips compressed, set to lean in and whale away.

Johnny glanced over at me, then reached into the bag, filled his hand, and went into his motion. His bit of extracurricular entertainment called for a perfect strike, a meatball designed to excite the hitter to murderous intent. And he delivered one, belt high and just a tad inside, the spot where Ted Williams once said, "You make history." Today, however, we were closer to folklore.

Harry the Catcher lashed out, but instead of the resounding knock of a well-struck ball there was a soggy squish as the orange exploded. Harry, who had been looking for a soul-satisfying bullet into left-center, jumped back as if stung. Sprayed with juice and pips, he cried out, "Jesus!" Then, rubbing his face and eyes, he glared out at Johnny Chicago and yelled, "You stupid fuck!" Johnny shrugged and held his hands wide apart in that universal declaration of innocence.

Clayton Sheedy began moving from his post behind the cage and, hands in hip pockets, began a slow walk to the mound. One thing I had learned: the slower the manager walks, the worse it is. The conversation on the mound went like this:

Sheedy: "Tell me about it."

Johnny: "I just reached in the bag and took it out."

Sheedy: "You thought it was a baseball."

Johnny: "I swear, Skip."

Sheedy: "You're a pitcher, and you don't know the difference between a baseball and an orange."

The skipper was not happy. I said to Johnny later, "He's going to send you back to Shitsville, Illinois, if you don't watch out."

"It was all in fun," he said morosely, as if Sheedy had shown a sad lack of humor.

The innocuous business of batting practice would have hazards other than rotten oranges. One day the BP pitcher took a line drive zinger right where all joy comes from. He scissored forward, then crumpled backward and lay stretched across the mound with barely a breath to draw on. In a storm of sympathy and concern we rushed out to him. In the shadows of his succoring teammates he lay while Sheedy crouched over him.

"I know it hurts like hell, son," the skipper said, "but you'll be okay in a little while."

Eyes shut, wanting to believe but not entirely convinced, the suffering youngster nodded. We helped him to his feet and walked him back to the bench, where he sat like a sack of jelly, bent double. I was then introduced to what I soon learned was an incomprehensible, inexplicable, but not uncommon masculine peculiarity. When they saw that their unhappy teammate was recovering and would be all right, there began a round of furtive, hand-covered smiles, moving from face to face. Heaven forgive us, but this particular misfortune, with its gagging rush of pain, is—after the fact—regarded as amusing and joke-worthy. One asks why. Is it psychological, an attempt to ward off some abyssal nightmare? How far back does this gritty humor go? Later, as we headed back to the clubhouse, our aching comrade was advised from now on to pitch with his legs crossed.

Things you laugh at and things you don't. Getting hit in the head with a pitched ball is not funny—not then, not later. *Almost* getting hit in the head with a pitched ball is risible. Once, in an intersquad game, a smoking fastball came close to rearranging the brains of one of our stalwarts (these of course were prehelmet days). He dropped to the ground and rolled over, eyes squeezed shut as though still expecting the impact. From his teammates came cries of support. "Good eye, Joe." "That's lookin' 'em over."

Trying to keep pace with my dream, I worked hard. Did my running, warmed up carefully, threw strikes in batting practice, learned how to cover first, how to field bunts, when to back up a base, how to improve my pickoff move. I learned the subtle strategy of what to do when the opposition put on a squeeze play: "Aim the fuckin' thing right between the batter's eyes." If you hit him the ball is dead (and maybe the batter too). If he goes down, the catcher's got it and the runner is dead. Properly executed—note the word—the strategy has mortal consequences somewhere.

Like the ghosts of Caesar's Legions, the memories tramp on, as fresh as every morning of those ethereal days. And even the forming memories were evocative of other things. For instance, that singular liturgy—call it what you will—of Righty Jack's.

Ballplayers are hives of superstition. The manias about not stepping on a foul line or not changing a sweatshirt during a hot streak are fairly common, but there are other quirks that call attention to themselves only after repetition, like the quick ritual performed by my roommate Righty Jack. This tough right-handed pitcher from a tiny Texas town on the Louisiana border would lace up his spikes and then snap his fingers first at one foot and then the other. It took me about a week to catch on to it.

"Why do you do that?" I asked.

"For luck," he said.

That's the exact place to end such a conversation, but I was intrigued.

"Does it work?" I asked.

My roomie looked directly at me; I think the question must have been new to him.

"Sometimes," he said.

"I don't have any superstitions."

"It's not superstition," he said. "It's for luck."

The conversation came to a halt right there, but it did evoke a memory and suggest a possible explanation for the "Five Egg Man," as my father called a peculiar customer who used to come into our grocery store. Elderly and morbidly expressionless, this guy used to stop in every few days. As taciturn as an owl, he spoke only to give his order. Milk, bread, some cold cuts, and five eggs.

My father, twenty-five years in the trade, was confounded. One day, after the oddball had left, he said, "You buy a dozen eggs or a half-dozen," as if this had been legislated.

"What do you care?" my mother said.

"I never heard of such a thing."

"Mind your business," she said.

Good advice, but I could see that was not going to happen. My father had at times a conflagrant curiosity which demanded its logs and twigs. When the Five Egg Man next appeared before the counter, my father asked him about the unorthodox purchase. The man, who wore a porkpie hat (which should have been a sign), said, "Why? Do you need the extra sale?"

"No."

"If you need the extra sale, then give me another egg."

"I don't need the extra sale," my father said.

"Because if you do . . ."

"I don't need the extra sale," my father said again, this time with an edge to his voice. He turned around, took an egg from the bin and added it to the modest order. "Here," he said. "No charge. It's on me." The man now had a half-dozen eggs, and the world was back on its axis. He accepted the largesse without comment, paid up, and left. We never saw him again.

"I told you to mind your business," my mother said. "Now you lost a customer."

And an egg.

So perhaps buying five eggs had been a device, contrived to ward off evil or to coax a few concessions from destiny, like Righty Jack's finger-snapping for luck. I was beginning to learn that the wider I explored the world, the more profoundly I was arriving at understanding.

Righty Jack and I really had nothing in common except our uniforms and the fact that we were roommates. He called me "City Slicker," which kind of tells you where he came from. (I was as "slick" as sandpaper.) He would speak of "back home," where he liked to fish and hunt, things as alien to me as subways were to him. The country boys always referred to "back home," whereas the city boys always named their place of origin: New York, Philadelphia, Cincinnati, Detroit. When I told him about Times Square and Broadway and millions of people filling the streets—which I think horrified him—I began to see the differences between fellow countrymen. Righty Jack knew grass and trees the way I knew concrete and traffic lights. He shot deer and I shot dice. He heard train whistles in the night while the big birds from La Guardia Airport thundered in the sky right over my roof. He camped out in the woods with his friends and drank whiskey; I sat in the schoolyard until midnight with my friends smoking Robt. Burns cigarillos.

The raison d'être for his nickname had an egalitarian foundation. If southpaws were always endowed with the handle "Lefty," why should their opposite numbers suffer discrimination? So he came to camp with the declaration, "My name is Jack but they call me 'Righty.'" He was obliged and became the camp's only "Righty."

I felt utterly detached from what just so recently had been my real world. Letters from home were like offstage whispers, answered with postcards giving my most recent pitching line and assurances of good health. My mind was too beclouded with my new excitements and self-discoveries. At night we sat in our rooms or in the lobby of the Bahama Beach Club (we were the only guests) and talked endless baseball and what was the latest bit of information from Sarasota, where the Boston club was training, and most especially about Ted Williams. We were frankly besotted with him. Most of the boys from the provinces had never seen him in action, and for them I became a source of Williams insights, most of them limited to the information that Ted could really hit.

Our meals, breakfast and dinner (lunch was at the ball field), were taken at the restaurant in the Oleander's Hotel in

Eau Gallie, a small coastal town just to the north, to which we were transported in the team bus. A section of the restaurant was reserved for us, and in we walked en masse, the ballplayers, trying to swagger without swaggering. Even among the people of tiny Eau Gallie the baseball dream was palpable, and here we were, in modest embodiment: being paid to play baseball. How much more special in the United States of America could you be?

We sat four or five at a table, ordered what we wanted, and signed for it. For breakfast it was all the eggs and bacon and pancakes you wanted, for dinner steaks and lamb chops and whatever had been freshly hauled out of the nearby Atlantic. It was a veritable Garden of Eatin'. The older fellows bantered with the waitresses with an easy glibness that I envied and yearned to emulate. The City Slicker was still a bit shy at this particular game.

We were young, vigorously alive, eminently pleased with ourselves. The only speck in the pudding was the dreaded cut-down day, and we knew that somewhere—and not far off either—that cloud was forming. It was the day when the rosters of the lower minor league clubs were drawn and quartered. Nor did you just go home; you were "unconditionally released," which sounds like quite a large kick in the ass.

But we didn't talk about it, and our gossamer-woven dreams remained secure. You couldn't have picked up the merest scent of self-doubt as we took our postprandial strolls through the few streets of Eau Gallie. We received constant psychic support from the townspeople, who greeted us politely, no doubt impressed by who we were and even more, perhaps, by who we might one day become, for, unlike much of humanity, we had in us the potential of rising from the teeming sea of anonymity and achieving notable success, of becoming heroes of the great game, and they could say, "I knew him in Eau Gallie. He was just a kid then."

Yes, being paid to play baseball on well-maintained diamonds, wearing a real uniform. Being lodged in a fine seaside hotel. Being fed and transported. Being cynosures of envy. Even signing a few autographs for deferent little boys who didn't realize that "Red Sox" on a uniform blouse didn't necessarily mean *Red Sox*. And, as will happen in the realms of the wondrous, there was something more, something not mentioned in the contract or shown on the menu.

Once upon a time they were called "camp followers" and at a later time "groupies." Not only did I not know what to call them, I hadn't known that such enticing baseball fans existed; they certainly hadn't around the New York sandlots.

They came by in groups of three and four, teenagers in flat shoes, bobby sox, skirts, snugly fitted sweaters. They cheered us, applauded daintily, leaned against one another, and giggled enchantingly. Their coquettish, Southern-hued voices stroked the sun-filled air. "Y'all." "Honey." "Sweetbread." "Tall stuff." (A few weeks before entraining south I had gone with several friends to a dance in Elmhurst in a place called Lost Battalion Hall. We straightened our ties and approached a gaggle of overcooked gum chewers, and when our advance man made his pitch he was told, "Get lost, fucko." The contrast in sunny Florida spoke well for the old Confederacy.)

I was in the outfield shagging batting-practice fly balls while some of our adoring auditors were sitting along the foul line, their honeyed drawls flowing forth. "Hey, Blondie. Blondie boy." Was that me? Nobody had ever called me that before. Then the same voice spoke out my number and I looked over. A morning-fresh brunette, sitting cross-legged on the grass, skirt pulled forward, cupped her hands around her mouth and said conspiratorially, "Get us a baseball." Staunch professional that I was, I was going to tell her we weren't allowed to do that when Righty Jack, standing nearby, told her, "You come by the restaurant in the Oleander's after dinner and pick it up. And," he added, "bring a friend." Then he winked at me. I winked back. Way to go, Jack.

That evening, during dinner, the brunette, accompanied by a trim little blonde, appeared at the restaurant, waved to us from the door, and disappeared. After dinner Jack, with a bit of contraband bulging in his jacket pocket, said, "Come on, 'Blondie,' let's see what a baseball can buy us."

They were waiting outside for us under the entrance canopy, Sally, the brunette, and Mayrene, the blonde. They were nicely proportioned, attractive, with the equivocal smiles of girls on the edge of mischief.

Jack gave the promised baseball—scuffed and grass-stained—to Sally, who dropped it into her purse. Then we wandered off as a quartet, eyed by our speculative teammates, who had time to kill before the bus left. We walked on the main street; some of the stores had slanted wooden awnings of the sort you saw in Western movies, with a few old boys in Panama hats and leathered single-climate faces sitting out front, mechanically nodding to whoever went by, as though activated by some sidewalk button you stepped on. Sally pointed out a white ramshackle bungalow where some relative or other maintained a dental practice. With its high lawn grass and weathered timbers it looked like a place where whiskey might still be the anesthetic.

The girls asked where we were from, then about baseball. About the latter we painted gaudy word portraits of prospects without end. We were in Melbourne, we told them, being sharpened up about the game's finer points; the organization didn't want to "rush us." It felt strange to hear myself saying aloud things I wanted fervently to be true, things I had been nurturing in one form or other for more than half of my sixteen years. Jack took a quantum leap and said we expected to be in Boston by midsummer. The girls were impressed.

We coupled off, Sally and I, Jack and Mayrene walking some twenty or thirty feet ahead. Sally asked if I had a girl back home. I took a moment to ponder this. If I said yes, I ran the risk of appearing unfaithful; if I said no, what kind of Rising Star was I? So I answered—deftly, I thought. I told her I had ended a romance just before leaving New York. She asked what had happened. I told her I'd rather not talk about it, which was good thinking since there was nothing to talk about. It must have sounded tragic since she merely nodded and let it pass.

I noticed that Righty Jack had, with what looked like practiced ease, slid his arm around Mayrene's waist, leaving me to wonder what was expected of me. So I, suavely I hoped, hoisted my arm unpossessively around my lady's shoulders, half expecting her to shrug it away. But there it remained. I thought she had very nice shoulders.

We wandered out to a little pier and stood there looking at a few power boats bobbing in the water. The Atlantic was on its best behavior, and standing there listening to it gulp around the pier was peaceful. Daylight had by now ceded to a filtering dusk, and something occurred to me.

"We've missed the bus," I said.

"Is that bad?" Sally asked.

I didn't know if it was bad, only that it wasn't good. We had no curfew as such because after dinner we always took the bus back to the hotel, and once there we had no place to go. Our overseer at the hotel was the team's general manager, an elderly gent who made it his business to bother no one. So it wasn't bad, wasn't good, but it was decidedly inconvenient— about a four-mile walk.

"We'll take you," Sally said.

She would go home, she said, borrow her brother's car, and drive us back. They told us to wait on the main street while they went off to get the car, looking back at us once and giggling.

"They're nice," I said.

Jack, who had been watching them go, turned to me.

"You got a rubber?" he asked.

"What?"

"You got a rubber?"

"No," I said.

"You better get one," he said, pointing to the general store across the street, where a few of the Panama-hatted old boys were sitting in front of the window lights on wooden folding chairs.

"Right," I said. I stepped off the sidewalk and began walking across, toward those staring old-boy faces. Halfway across I made a U-turn and came back.

"Chrissake," I told Jack, "everybody in town saw us walking with them and now you want me to go in there and buy rubbers?"

He shrugged.

"You think I'll need one?" I asked warily. I had never used one. Frankly, there had never been the occasion.

"Some of 'em won't roll without one," he said. The way he talked it sounded like we had a sure thing here. I began to get edgy. For want of a rubber it could all be lost; I could be wak-

ing up in the morning with one of Maspeth's most familiar re-
frains running through my mind: *I almost got laid last night.*

In my glamorous new world I had nothing to call upon
but a paucity of past experience, none of which was my own,
and a lot of that cautionary. One of my brother's good friends
was Fat Neil, a chesty lad of some boldness (he winked at
strange girls). When this luminary turned eighteen he bought
himself a used car. Upon the strength of this acquisition he
obtained a date with one of the neighborhood's better lookers,
Audrey, who had a "reputation."

"I'm taking her to the movies in Forest Hills," he told
Stanley, "then later I'm going to try and hump her in the back
of the car."

When I heard about this laudable plan I could imagine
only half of it actually occurring. But much to my surprise Neil
made it a clean sweep. Maybe it was the car, or the movie, or
his own hitherto hidden charms, but Fat Neil scored. The next
day, however, he was distraught.

"The bag broke," he told Stanley.

Later in life, as my horizons expanded and humanity
in all its many varieties began crossing my path, I came to
realize that there were certain people to whom certain things
happen. They have their pockets picked. They run out of gas.
They invest in zinc mines. Their bags break.

"What do I do?" he asked my brother.

Stanley always dispensed good advice, no matter if it was
manifestly the only advice.

"Wait," he said.

"If she's knocked up," the gallant Neil said, "I'm enlist-
ing. They can't touch you in the army."

Well, she wasn't knocked up, or down or sideways either,
and the U.S. military was spared the expense of having to house

and feed Fat Neil. But the idea of a defective prophylactic was
another thing to haunt a young man's mind. I prayed that the
article Righty Jack had generously, and furtively, slipped to
me would not rive under pressure.

The girls picked us up in an old sedan corroded around
the edges by the salt air. We rode from Eau Gallie along a
lonely palm-tree-lined road, crossed the small wooden bridge
over the Indian River, and soon saw the lights of the Bahama
Beach Club looming ahead, the last bit of illumination between here and the coast of Morocco. Jack pointed out that
it was a beautiful night and why didn't we take a walk on the
beach? When I questioned the advisability of this, he said
something to the effect that once you were late it didn't matter any longer how late. I wasn't sure how much sense this
made, but it sounded like having a license to legitimize and
compound all transgressions after the first.

We parked at a strategic distance from the hotel and
headed for the dunes, then crossed over them to the beach. It
was a warm night, the light sea wind fluttering like invisible
flags, coming and going like breathing, the moonless sky alive
with a pure heaven of stars, the black Atlantic tossing out
small waves with slow, somnolent splashes.

Righty Jack and Mayrene soon disappeared into the
darkness. Sally and I walked for a while along the sodden
sands at water's edge, then drew back and sat down. She
asked me if I would remember her when I was a big star. I
assured her I had a splendid memory and she would always
have a place in it. She said my life was going to be so enviably
exciting, with all the traveling, the big cities, thousands of
people cheering for me. Sitting there listening to her reciting
my dreams, with nothing between us and the sprawling stars
above, it all seemed plausible.

Then she got up and unbuttoned the sides of her skirt and let it descend to the sands and stood in the sensuous tropical night, shapely young legs boldly downward from a pair of silky white panties. To this day I cannot believe what I said.

"You're not going swimming, are you?"

She took it as cool humor, laughing. *Oh, what smart alecks these Rising Stars were.* She asked if I had "protection," and the message came through. I blithely assured her. (What Rising Star would walk around without protection?)

I wonder—is watching yourself in the long ago voyeuristic? I can see myself, though in many ways that is impossible, since I believe my eyes were closed the whole time. But yet some observing spirit must have levitated from me because there I am, though most of the details are lost to memory, if memory had ever been able to grasp them to begin with. All I am certain of is that the innate call of old Adam in all its primal exigencies was answered. The pyrotechnics, the detonations, the yips and yelps, all blurred away in mindless revelation.

It was as if she and I were merely nameless unthinking creatures in a storm that had burst from those yielding sands and then subsided, attended by the ceaseless nods and hymns of the Atlantic Ocean. Who my guiding Eve was that night and to where she vanished is lost to personal history. If she is still with us she is one of our sere leaves, grey and grandmotherly, with her own shelves of memories, among which I doubt that I count for very much. And that sanctum on the beach, that little patch of sand, is it still there, or has it been washed over by eroding Atlantic tides? But there it had been, and she, and I. And the protection, *pace* Fat Neil, had remained intact.

I imagine it's only fitting that one climax should follow another, for with the next sunrise came cut-down day.

After the workout the camp director, Roy Dissenger, came by, clipboard in hand. He called us all together and asked that those whose names he read out step to one side. There was an air of uneasiness. This wasn't good. He began reading from his clipboard, and one by one the players stepped away, I among them. When I looked around at my new companions I realized I was in dubious company. There was the wild left-hander from Cincinnati, who hadn't thrown a strike in weeks; the weak-hitting first baseman from Texas; the heavy-legged outfielder from Philadelphia who always looked like he was running uphill; and other questionable customers, among them Johnny Chicago, who what now seemed eons ago had thrown a rotten orange in batting practice. We were a foredoomed group and we knew it, and we didn't like it; we stood there as though each of us was contaminating the others.

When the final name had been read out, the other players, the survivors, began filing away, Righty Jack among them, leaving us to await the tumbril. We watched them go on to the clubhouse, observing them as we would passengers taking the last train out of a burning city. As if in commiseration they were moving quietly, without the usual hijinks. Compassion for their hapless comrades, or just an exhaustive sense of relief?

At sixteen you simply are not equipped to handle failure (or success either, supposedly, though I wouldn't have minded taking my chances with it). It was stark, sudden, brutally definitive. You no longer are what just a few minutes ago you thought you were. Truly man-sized emotions are crowding into your ill-equipped frame. You wonder: Is this all? Wasn't that contract supposed to be a prophetic document proclaiming that we were exactly what we thought we were? The contract gave not the slightest hint of failure.

"Boys," Dissenger said, "this is the saddest part of spring training." They were forced to judgment by finite numbers, he explained. Applying a bit of liniment, he said that evaluations were not infallible (I don't think he believed that) and perhaps they were making some mistakes. But decisions had to be made. Some very tough decisions, he said.

There were protests. The kid from Philadelphia said he had gotten seven hits in four games.

"You're too slow," the camp director said after glancing at the sheet on the clipboard. It sounded as if God and not the Red Sox had decided this.

A pitcher offered his line: so many innings, so few runs.

"You're not fast enough," the camp director said.

Too slow, not fast enough. The blunt, harsh truths had never been part of the dream. Who knew, as we excelled on our local ball fields, that we had been born with such physical deficiencies? Instead of covering them over, the uniform had without pity exposed them. The dream had been an illusion.

For myself, I didn't have to ask any questions. I knew what notation was next to my name on that clipboard. I had seen those other fastballs, express trains to my local.

His compassion spent, the camp director told us to see his assistant, who would be taking care of our "arrangements."

When I reached a silent clubhouse, Righty Jack had a consoling slap on the back for me, telling me the room wouldn't be the same. He asked what he should tell Sally, whose furnace of miracles I was supposed to be revisiting that night.

"Tell her I was injured," I said.

Twelve

⚜ THERE WAS a fellow in Maspeth who was known as "Peter Books" because of his penchant for "fancy" words. He once described the weather during a game at Ebbets Field as "raining intermittently on and off," and he spoke instructively of "endless infinity." I began to believe in this latter during the long, cheerless train ride home from Florida. The Old Confederacy didn't seem as lush with history on my way home as it had on my original journey a few weeks before. In my former world of promise and expectation, everything had been of interest; now I was bringing home with me something as radically different from what I had left home with as it was possible to be.

A lot of long journeys were being made out of Florida that day. A few of the boys were on the train with me heading north. Outside of contriving cover stories for the folks back home, we didn't talk much. The guy I think I felt sorriest for (other than myself) was Mike, a second baseman. He was from a small town in New Hampshire, where he had done exceptionally well and been a local celebrity. So celebrated had he been, he told us, that the night before he left the Chamber of Commerce had honored him at a dinner, and then the next day some members of the high school band had fifed and drummed him down to the depot. So that was going to be one lead balloon of a homecoming. I couldn't imagine it. In fact, I didn't think I was capable of imagining very much then, as if some source had broken down or maybe dried up. It could be posited that the state of being that is most alien to us as adults is our time of innocence. Life's ever-compounding experiences make it seem remote and incomprehensible and, saddest perhaps, quaint.

I must have been too ethereally detached to notice the train's rhythmic cadences on the way down; but coming home I did. They were melancholy and monotonous; they seemed to be calling for a longer and deeper look at the ever-vanishing world beyond the window. And on the train itself, in the dining car, the club car, the smiles and laughter of other people had distant qualities.

What comfort I did manage to muster for myself on that endless ride home came from my inner eye's view of that tableau on the beach, of the discoveries grand and amazing I had made with Sally (whose last name I don't think I ever knew). The whole thing had, in reexamination, a somewhat ordained aspect, what with the earth, the sea, and the stars in perfect, harmonious conspiracy with us. In living emotion it dwarfed and struck aside everything else. There had been nothing illusory about it. If baseball was a man playing a boy's game, then as a boy I had blundered wonderfully into the man's game, and if not quite yet the man, then at least a bit less the gauche teenager.

Mr. Ring offered me consolation. He said that signing a contract and going to spring training was to have experienced something that few other boys ever would. He suggested that excelling at the thing you most wanted to do was very difficult, in the larger sense implying that it was a very tough world (which I think I had begun to feel on the train ride home). Mr. Ring didn't sound very sentimental about baseball that evening. I think that in some ways he might have been drawing up memories of the 1928 season, the last of his career; for splendid big-league pitcher though he had been, he had labored through a summer of four wins and seventeen losses, and so had felt the pain of enforced farewell, as they all must at sunset, even Ruth and Feller and Mays, all of whom had stumbled at the end. Baseball could be as pitiless at the end of a long and gloried run as at an aborted beginning.

Does it make a difference if a dream is shattered or merely dissolves in the wind? It might. The shattered dream can leave behind permanent, damaging disillusionment, creating commonplace perimeters for what had been an unbounded future; the dissolved dream can leave the seeding ground as richly sown as ever. It was the idea of being something that was the thing. It helps, of course, if you are young, not given to deterrence, and look upon that wide pasture of unsprung time as a place of cultivation.

You can't play baseball in storms or blizzards, in hurricanes or tempests, or with a sprained ankle or bone chips in your elbow; but on my behalf the old clacking Underwood would persevere through all that and more. All it asked was to be fed sheets of paper and now and then freshly beribboned. It was my new battery mate.

This time it was not about a dream but a dream's more substantial cousins—ideas, concepts, perceptions, given reality by craft and language. I can never remember saying that I wanted to be a writer; it was something without source or origin, with no moment of decision or pronouncement. It seemed to have been woven and designed in the womb and thereafter, without prompting, set about working its will. There was never even the notion of ambition, for that would have connoted desire, with its implications of possible failure. In later years, when people commented on the incongruity of these career paths, I told them, glibly, that after being bounced out of one livelihood where you had to work just a few hours a day for six months of the year to sustain yourself, I needed to find another industry that afforded such workplace philanthropy.

What I think I always knew by instinct, that I would never be able to whisk my fastball by DiMaggio or Williams, I soon learned by experience—the publishing world does not lay down welcome mats for freelance writers. For several years my only writings that magazines accepted were checks for subscriptions. This "spring training," however, had no cutdown day despite a horrendous won-lost record. There was no contract to abrogate, no train ride home; you could stay as long as you wanted. A rejection slip merely fell out of an envelope; it didn't blast off and travel four hundred feet.

I went from the noisy, public world of baseball into the solitary sphere of the writer. The contrast couldn't have been more defining, for through all oscillations of the good and the bad, the writer, if he chooses, may remain invisible.

I can tell you about the invisible writer, for even into his life some ironies will fall. In those early days I would be up with the sun and commence work and continue, with a brief break or two, until around 5 P.M. An honest day's work, which in time produced my first three novels, a few dozen short stories, and a bit of local notoriety. At 5 P.M. ebb tide set in, and I walked over to the candy store to have a soda and talk baseball (oh yes, that) with the usual lurkers. Every day at around that time a work-weary, homeward-bound friend, stopping in to pick up his newspaper, found me sitting there. One day he said to me, "What are you doing these days? Still writing those books?" Yes. "Well," he said with a patronizing slap on the back, "if I had your spare time I'd write books too."

I took odd jobs for several months at a time, saved my money and then quit, returning full time to the typewriter, mailing my stories into their revolving doors. The family was remarkably tolerant. My brother aided the march of Western culture with gifts of reams of paper and typewriter ribbons; my mother, that inveterate book lover, was wholly supportive; my father, recovered from the disappointment of baseball's purblindness, took it all on faith, holding to a single doctrine: "If they don't like that story, write another one." His ultimately rewarded faith gave me an anecdote I grew to cherish.

He had sold the grocery store and was working as a salesman for Coca-Cola when a voice came down from Mount Sinai and I sold my first short story. When I brought home a copy of the magazine, he sat at the kitchen table and with a studious frown read the story, then pronounced it good. I caught him reading it again that night and then again the next day. A few days later, returning home from work, my mother asked him how things had gone. He'd had an hour or so to kill between stops, he said, so he went into a store and bought "the magazine" (there was no other in the world for him). Then he sat in the park and read "the story."

"You've read it five times already," my mother said.

He looked at her indignantly and slapped the table with the palm of his hand. "So now I read it six times," he said.

He lived just long enough to see the tide coming in—my first two novels and more short stories, two of which were adapted for Alfred Hitchcock's television series. And then he was gone. He went to work in the morning, and that afternoon my mother received one of "those" phone calls, the kind that make you think back later to that last goodbye, trying to remember exactly what it had been like. Had it been good enough? Who knew that his big, foolish, joyful heart would give out on that day?

The funeral home was packed. Representatives from his Masonic lodge performed a brief ceremony in his honor, an act of fraternal devotion since, typically of him, he hadn't shown up there for more than twenty years, despite to the end regarding himself as a loyal member.

So he was gone, leaving his history behind. The mischievous Polish farmboy, the Austrian soldier, the immigrant, the Dodgers fan, the grocer, the air-raid warden; Mason, Kiwanian, Pythian, Lion (how he missed the Elks and Shriners I'll never know). And tucked into this biography was the day he took my brother and me to Ebbets Field for our first game, the day Kemp Wicker won his only game in a Dodgers uniform. But above it all I will always see that loaf of bread flying away as a boy leaps for his life from a running train.

Thirteen

≪ "IS THERE any one book that made a significant difference in your life?" Writers hear that question. My answer is yes, there is one book, but before that there was another. Two dissimilar books conjoined to make the "significant difference." One of them I happened to be the author of, the other I was not, nor was it by any of the authors I had been steadily guiding myself by—Tolstoy, Dostoevsky, Balzac, Faulkner, Conrad, Stephen Crane.

I had been publishing regularly for more than fifteen years when I delivered to Doubleday a novel called *Illusions*. A prolific publisher, Doubleday could not reasonably be expected to put its corporate muscle behind every volume it set to sea. In my case, the publicity campaign was limited to a young woman holding up a copy of the book at a tenth-floor window during the lunch hour. In spite of this the book attracted little attention. The reviews were sparse, though one critic—and I blush to write this—declared it "a work of genius." But one must sift his sands carefully. We were living in a cultural environment where the likes of Andy Warhol had been anointed as "genius," and I had to accept the fact that some devaluation had set in. (One sage has written that when the word "genius" is used in a sentence, the name Mozart had better be nearby.)

When my champion at Doubleday, an editor named Bill Henderson, moved to the publisher Coward, McCann, & Geoghegan, I moved with him. He offered a contract for another novel. I told him that those things took time, and with *Illusions* having earned me nothing outside of some flattering commentary, there was the need to feed my bank account in a hurry (an urgency accelerated by the arrival of a bright-eyed little girl named Catherine). He suggested a book of nonfiction.

"What do you know about?" he asked.

"Nothing that would fill a book," I said.

"What about baseball? You're always talking about baseball."

I was then forty years old, and outside of a children's book about life in the minor leagues (talk about being haunted) and one short story, I had never written about baseball, for whatever unexamined reasons. It might have been a subconscious desire to separate myself from an ego-wounding experience (though my love for the game had never slackened). Or maybe it hadn't accorded with what I deemed my high-toned literary interests. In any event, I told Henderson I would give it some thought.

I drove back to Connecticut that night wondering if the Old Ball Game could possibly reenter my life, this time with blessings. I remember that drive home vividly, not because of coming to any decisive conclusions but because of an incident (I think a writer's always-exploring imagination draws these things into his orbit).

Because I had gone into New York for a princely expense-account dinner with my editor, I had (by my standards) dressed up for the occasion, my tie-and-all upholstery in-cluding a heavy tweed jacket. Halfway up the Connecticut Turnpike I began feeling uncomfortably warm. I pulled over onto the shoulder and stopped to remove the jacket, my mind barely registering the fact that I had just passed one of humanity's optimists—a hitchhiker. As I was getting my arms out of the sleeves, I noticed in the rearview mirror this gentleman, faith in mankind no doubt rekindled, making a dash out of the shadows toward the car. Not being in need of a hitchhiker and without time even for self-reproach, I quickly took off, leaving him standing there with his arms spread out. I hate to think what damnations he was throwing after me. (But if nothing else, I had at least moved his journey on by several hundred rapidly covered feet and provided him with a scurrilous tale to tell.)

It wasn't a matter of soul-searching; it was simply a matter of telling myself that if I didn't accomplish something soon, I too would be out thumbing for rides.

And so the second "significant" book of my life, the one that would lead me into many bright tomorrows.

Lawrence Ritter's *The Glory of Their Times* was ac-claimed an "instant classic" and has never lost that stardust encomium. If anything, the book's stature has grown steadily since its publication in 1966. It remains, along with Roger Kahn's *The Boys of Summer*, at the summit of baseball's vast body of literature.

The Glory of Their Times is a collection of interviews with former major leaguers, many of whose memories went all the way back to when the twentieth century was still fairly in-nocent—a long time indeed. I had marveled at Ritter's skill in coaxing forth and then recording these tales of the past from his galaxy of venerables, some of whom were ornaments of the game while others had passed through the old summers with less fanfare. But what Ritter had done so marvelously was to make them all vivid as human beings, to personalize them and evoke their times as a novelist and historian might. He cared about these men, and it showed; he struck up lasting friendships with them and indeed even shared equally with them the substantial profits the book was to earn. The genesis of *The Glory of Their Times* is a story in itself.

"I never had any intention of writing a book," Ritter said.

Divorced, this professor of economics at New York University (and co-author of two highly successful standard textbooks on this abstruse subject) had charge of his thirteen-year-old son during the summer. Uncertain as to how to keep a youngster occupied over this time, Ritter decided to unite this problem with a lifelong passion for baseball.

Contacting the retired players around the country and being assured of their willingness to talk with him ("They were more than willing," he said, "they were eager"), he and his son spent the next few summers driving about—as far as California—and talking with the elderly men, recording them on a rather cumbersome reel-to-reel tape machine, which was then the latest technology. The reason he contrived for his visits was that he was writing a book.

"The idea of being in a book impressed them," he said. "If I'd been, say, a journalist there to do a nostalgia piece, I don't think I would have gotten so much out of them. You have to remember, these men had been retired for decades; most of them were pretty much forgotten, and they knew it. They probably hadn't told or been asked about their stories for years. How many times can you tell them to friends and grandkids? So here I come, me and my son and that ungainly piece of equipment, wanting to hear it all."

Nor was this merely an economics professor and a tape recorder. A lifelong fan and devotee of the record books, Ritter knew the careers of these men, whom they had played with and against, what momentous games they might have participated in. He knew what to ask, how to delve, and—crucially—when to remain silent.

"Once they saw how much I knew," he said, "it put them at their ease, and they were able to relax, as though they were talking to an old teammate. You show them you're familiar with the details—I had researched each guy carefully—and they'll start telling you things they'd probably forgotten they ever knew. You can't ever forget how seriously they took baseball and how proud they were of their careers. So when they meet someone who knows the same things and cares the same way, you're in business."

After several summers Ritter ceased his travels and put his reels away in the closet. But then he started getting letters from the players.

"They all kept asking the same thing," he said. "'Where's the book?' I guess I had an attack of conscience. After all, I had gained entree into their homes based on the promise of a book."

So he had the tapes transcribed, and from these many hundreds of pages came the raw material from which Ritter, with loving and infinite care, distilled *The Glory of Their Times*.

Larry Ritter (who died in 2004 at the age of eighty-one) was a soft-spoken man, reticent in a large group, less so in more intimate gatherings. He was capable of some mischievous humor, once saying that a player frequently described as "underrated" by sportswriters was "the most overrated underrated player in baseball."

We met through the auspices of a shapeless fraternity known as the Bobo Newsom Memorial Fan Club. This was a group of ten or fifteen (it varied) wholly unconstrained and un-inhibited baseball junkies who convened three or four times a year in one or another's Manhattan apartment to "discuss" baseball. These discussions, which had all the decorum of a Socialist party convention, featured esoteric statistics, out-landish anecdotes, personal experiences, unforgivable puns, childhood reversions, senile excursions—all brought to the highest scholarly levels, with much of the scholarship enabled by sips of bourbon.

We were an aptly named band. Louis Norman (Bobo) Newsom, who pitched from the early 1930s into the early 1950s, was baseball's poster boy for itinerancy. Not even in this age of free-agent trampolining has any player come re-motely close to Bobo's travels in and out of baseball's ports of call. The only way convincingly to describe this Rand McNally career is with detail. Beginning with a brief stint in 1929, Bobo lent his services to, in order, the Brooklyn Dodg-ers, Chicago Cubs, St. Louis Browns, Washington Senators, Boston Red Sox, Browns, Detroit Tigers, Senators, Dodgers, Browns, Senators, Philadelphia Athletics, Senators, New York Yankees, New York Giants, Senators, Athletics.

No baseball player has ever heard "Goodbye" follow so closely upon "Hello" so many times. Lack of talent was sel-dom if ever the reason. Our patron saint was an individualist, with a snappy gift of repartee that was not always appreciated. Bobo could pitch himself into a job and just as quickly talk himself out of it. One day, soon after joining the Red Sox, the hefty South Carolinian found himself on the mound with a bases-loaded situation. Over from shortstop came the seri-ous-minded player-manager Joe Cronin with a word of advice.

Bobo stared at the skipper, listened for a moment, then said, "Who's telling Bobo how to pitch?" Well, it soon ceased to be Cronin.

Frequently unwanted, he was just as frequently wanted. Bobo could pitch. Three times a 20-game winner, equally he was a three-time 20-game loser. His career record stands at 211-222, meaning the bighearted right-hander gave as generously as he took. "Never a sore arm in over twenty years," he boasted. "Yes," a contemporary agreed. "He had a rubber arm and a head to match."

Teammate George Case recalled how Newsom would help break the tedium of long train rides. "He'd suddenly get up and begin preaching a sermon. He would stand on a suitcase in the club car, holding one of those Gideon Bibles in his hand, with a pair of glasses pushed all the way down the end of his nose, and preach a hellfire sermon in the style of a Southern Baptist minister. He'd have us rolling in the aisle . . . he was a natural."

So to honor Bobo we met several times a year. ("Don't let that get out," one member said. "My wife thinks it's every week.") Among the haze of cigarette and cigar smoke, and amid the aromas of potent beverages, you might find journalists Vic Ziegel of the *Daily News*; Joe Flaherty of the *Village Voice*; that prince of sportswriters Red Smith; Roger Kahn; pitcher-cum-author Jim Bouton; the accomplished biographer of Gehrig and Mathewson, Ray Robinson; author Wilfred Sheed; poet Joel Oppenheimer; novelist and essayist Edward Hoagland; *Village Voice* editor Ross Wetzsteon; columnist John Leo; and other distinguished members of society.

Because we were the only members to cross the border to attend, I was charged with picking up Red Smith, bringing him to the meeting, and delivering him back to his Connecticut home. This was a pleasure both ways, particularly the homeward bound side of it. Red was one of the most enjoyable raconteurs I have ever known, to the extent that our homeward drives were always much longer than necessary. I would drive well under the speed limit, and when we cut away from the turnpike into the shadowy lanes of Fairfield County I always contrived to lose my way, simply to keep Red going, to listen to more of those witty, always elegantly phrased stories that were unrepetitive and seemingly of endless supply. The only negative was that I had to watch my intake at the meeting; I needed a steady hand at the wheel, not only for the security of my venerated companion but to avoid a headline reading "Red Smith and Another Man in Road Accident." If you must go, at least you want to be the story.

Unshackled by any pretense of decorum, the gatherings of the Newsom Fan Club often turned into crosswinds of raucous and uninhibited repartee, leading Joe Flaherty once to regret that we weren't being tape-recorded. "For history?" someone said. "No," Joe said, "for blackmail."

We considered ourselves serious students of the game, and to demonstrate how, we sometimes deployed our scholarship creatively. Some prime time was used in constructing "Theme Teams," a not uncommon diversion among baseball fans. The "Fiduciary Team" would include players with names like Banks, Bonds, Pounds, Stock, Cash, Money, Price, Nichols, (spelling was optional); the team was owned by Cash & Carey and its games broadcast by, of course, Jack Buck. The "Anatomy Team" included gentlemen named Hands, Fingers, Head, Legg, Foote, Dickey, and everyone's favorite, Heinie Manush.

There were also some rather esoteric challenges. Someone would say, "vertiginous academic," to which the answer finally was "Dizzy Dean." Former Pittsburgh shortshop Gene Alley was the answer to "fallopian tube." And the answer to "subway tragedy" was the 1920s pitcher Urban Shocker. And so on into the gentle Manhattan night.

Under these ramshackle circumstances I became acquainted with Larry Ritter. We met for lunch several times, during which I badgered him to do another book, another *Glory of Their Times*. He had in fact embarked briefly on another volume, interviewing several players before losing interest. For one thing, his son had by now grown up and no longer found the summer-long excursions as interesting as before. A more telling reason was that Ritter had, to a large extent, become a victim of his own success. Old-time players everywhere had been given as birthday or Christmas gifts copies of *The Glory of Their Times*. (One player I later spoke with showed me three copies on his shelf, Christmas gifts from his three sons, who apparently hadn't synchronized their holiday shopping.)

"So now I was the celebrity," Ritter said. "I wasn't walking into the room anonymously as I had previously." He was walking in now as a celebrated author, and he found the men somewhat self-conscious, their replies more formal. "They weren't relaxed, and all the informal nuances that go into good storytelling were gone. I wasn't getting what I had gotten before, and so I gave up."

I kept at him, however, telling him that there were jewels of baseball history, large and small, scattered across the land, stories that were going unrecorded and soon into permanent silence if not preserved. He agreed completely. But if I felt so strongly about it, he said, then why didn't I go out and collect them?

"Because nobody can do it as well as you," I said.

"How do you know?"

"Anyway, it would be poaching."

"It's a free market," the professor of economics said, "and believe me, if you don't do it others will. The book has had too much success not to start spawning."

Admittedly it didn't take much persuading as Larry, a man of innate generosity, offered to help get me started. He told me how to contact the players, how to phrase the letter I'd be sending to them, how soon to follow up with a phone call, how to cajole someone who might sound a bit reluctant. He gave me tips on how to conduct the interview. "Never be afraid of silence," he said. "Remember, you're taking them a long ways back. Let them think about it." (This was why, he said, telephone interviews were inadequate, and in fact, to my own astonishment, a few years later I turned down a telephone interview with Ted Williams, who had said this was the only convenient way for him.) I was advised to let the players find out on their own how much baseball I knew; things would become easier after that. They'll make mistakes on dates and statistics, Larry said; never correct them in conversation—you don't want to look *too* damned smart. The corrections could be made later, in the writing.

When I discussed the art of interviewing with Red Smith during one of our rides of contrived longevity on the way home from a Bobo meeting (I don't think he ever caught on to what I was doing), he, as ever, had a story to tell. It dealt with an interview he had once conducted with New York Yankees outfielder Tommy Henrich in the clubhouse before a game.

"We talked for thirty minutes or so," Red said. "I wasn't taking notes, trusting to memory. If I had been taking notes there would have been a thick sheaf of them because Tommy was a good talker. When my column appeared in the paper the next day, Tommy caught up to me before the game and congratulated me. 'You never took a note,' he said, 'and yet you caught everything I said exactly right.' Well, of course I didn't use everything he said; I only used the wittiest and most perceptive things. He had forgotten the banalities, and so had I."

I met with Bill Henderson and told him what I wanted to do and that we had Larry's imprimatur for the book. A contract was drawn for a work to be called *Baseball When the Grass Was Real*. When I called my brother to tell him about the new adventure I was setting out on, he asked me whom I was planning to see.

"Among others," I said, "Bob Feller and Pete Reiser."

He paused, then said, "You mean somebody is paying you to do this?"

Well, they had been willing to pay me to *play* baseball, so why not pay me to write about it, which I thought I might be better at. I would write about baseball, earn some money, then return to home port and resume my life as a novelist. Which indeed I did—some fifteen years and forty books later.

Fourteen

⨠ HERE I MUST make a quiet request for a bit of indulgence. You see, it isn't always the occasion of the memory or the circumstances that is vital, but the "when." Memories formed in innocence, before even the merest scratch of cynicism or the knowledge that life isn't always going to be what it is right now, become like talismans to be cherished far into the unknown. To some this might seem like mere sentimentality, quaint at its best, at its worst maudlin naiveté. Nevertheless baseball is capable of these evocations and their amber-lit permanence, and the theme here is, after all, that game. The phrase "I remember . . ." is our verbal Fountain of Youth.

And so I remember. The year was probably 1937. Summer, of course, that magical soul-time of innocence for a little boy. The place was a wide and lovely tract of grass and trees and picnic tables in Forest Park, in Richmond Hill. You got there from Maspeth by riding the Flushing-Ridgewood trolley to its terminus in Ridgewood, under the clattery Myrtle Avenue El. There my mother, brother, and I stepped up onto another trolley, again the fare for the three of us eleven cents—a nickel for her, three cents apiece for us. We rode along Myrtle

Avenue through Ridgewood and Glendale to Richmond Hill, to Forest Park.

Indulge a child's memory further and see us, Stanley and me, on the swings and seesaws and then later, best of all, in the wading pool, for she took us there only on the hottest days (the only pool in Maspeth was followed by the word "room"). After the splashing came another treat—a Dixie Cup of ice cream, half chocolate, half vanilla (ice cream was integrated well before baseball was). You lifted the lid by a small flap, with double anticipation—for the cold flavors within and to see who you "got." You peeled away the round sheet of waxed paper and unveiled the baseball face under it.

The enduring memory of that day was the eye-widening sight of a fresh young face on the Dixie Cup lid, with the broad, confident smile of a teenaged overachiever. Look, I said to my brother with proper awe, Bob Feller!

It was as if that Dixie Cup lid had sanctioned something for me, established a tangible connection with that wondrous youngster whose name was already reverberating through my embryonic six-year-old baseball fantasies. "Rapid Robert," the "Cleveland Marvel," had startled the game like summer lightning. In August 1936, making his first big-league start (first start anywhere, in fact; he had never played in the minor leagues), the seventeen-year-old Iowa farmboy struck out fifteen St. Louis Browns (one short of the then league record; he eclipsed the major league record with eighteen two years later). This was in an era when hitters struck out far fewer times than they do today.

Bob Feller on the mound was an engine of pure, brute force. There was no guile in this boy. He simply swung into his energetic windup and, with a high-kicking delivery ending with an airborne right leg, fired off a fastball that some people said—heretically—was the equal of Walter Johnson's. Feller also threw a curve of such lethal hard-breaking proportions that hitters said it should have been outlawed.

Ruth had retired. Dizzy Dean, just a moment before the reigning King of the Hill, had through injury seen his arm turn virtually overnight from flashing saber to asparagus. Williams had not yet appeared, and DiMaggio was just beginning to stretch himself out. So the game's celestial overseers, always magnanimous when needed, had lifted Bobby Feller from the Iowa cornstalks and this time conceived something different—baseball's first, and thus far only, genuine prodigy. (When Dwight Gooden electrified New York and the world beyond in 1984 at the age of nineteen, he was considered a wonder-working "man-child.")

Two ingredients flavor the baseball feast—power and speed. The well-placed line drive and the corner-nicking curveball are part of the game's artistry; but the smoke-snorting dragons that accelerate the grandstand pulses are the long-ballers and the speed-ballers. "Instant legend" sounds like an oxymoron, but how else to describe a seventeen-year-old boy who parachutes in from nowhere and begins setting big-league strikeout records?

So he entered my six-year-old imagination—just as that fertile faculty was beginning to rise and grasp—like something from mythology. *They say he's as fast as Walter Johnson.* The older men scoffed. But I believed it. Walter was someone else's myth and not to be equaled. But I had my own incense to burn, and I had that Dixie Cup lid.

The secretary opened the office door halfway and said, "Mr. Honig is here."

"Tell him to wait a minute," a voice said from within.

So all those years later, when they have long ago been sealed away in the record books, you begin to meet them. You're meeting them for the first time, yet you feel a lifetime's acquaintance. With diligence you followed their long careers over those many summers, watching them from afar, talking about them endlessly and with awe, accepting with a philosopher's regret as they slowed into age and their wonders became fewer. For years you had read about them and were confident about all you had gathered. Previous interviews had gone well because at all times you had kept in mind Larry Ritter's caution: they might not be the best-educated people or the most articulate, but when it comes to baseball, they know it the way Einstein knew theoretical physics.

So I had done my research. I had my talking notes. I was ready. Except that this time it was Bob Feller.

When I heard the voice say, "Tell him to wait a minute," I suddenly felt my self-assurance draining. It was a debilitating miracle of reversion; I was six years old again, gazing wide-eyed at a Dixie Cup lid on a hot day in Forest Park. It is stunning what can come back to you as originally stored, and from so far away. In time I would meet all the field marshals of my youth—Williams, DiMaggio, Reiser—but only this time was there that reversion to near helplessness.

Indulge me once more. I have seen it happen to others. Old men gazing open-mouthed at the unapproachable DiMaggio (well, you could approach him, but as far as he was concerned you never really arrived). Starstruck Bostonians staring with frozen smiles at the restlessly garrulous Williams. And perhaps most memorable of all, a restaurant filled with allegedly sophisticated New Yorkers staring with mouthfuls of half-chewed food at Joe Louis sitting in his own misty world, eating his dinner, wearing a baseball cap. (Later they began moving upon him like ghosts, laying tentative hands on his shoulder and bending to whisper something to which the old champion would nod politely.)

Feller's office was in the Northern Ohio Bank Building in Cleveland. He was then employed by the Hilton Hotels Corporation—"Director of Sales—Sports" his stationery read. He was fifty-six years old, still robust in appearance (he would travel around the country for the next twenty-five years or so giving exhibitions at minor league parks, the always resonant name selling tickets to yet another generation).

I had thought during the flight out to Cleveland that I might mention my experience with the Red Sox. One old pitcher to another. Would Bob Feller be impressed? The question answered itself. In an attempt to soften him up for an interview, I had a few weeks before mentioned the fact to Lefty Grove, Feller's immediate predecessor as sovereign of American League mounds. Grove, like Feller a Hall of Fame–plus pitcher, laughed good-naturedly. "D ball?" he said. "That's way down there, huh? Way down there." So much for professional affinities. All men are not born equal, pitchers especially.

And then of all things, I thought about telling him the story of the Dixie Cup lid, as though to impress him with the epic longevity of the relationship, that my appearance before him was a moment of arrival, long destined. But then you remind yourself you're supposed to be there on business; the tape recorder is turning and you haven't asked him anything yet. You're looking down at your legal-size yellow pad with your scribbled notes, pretending to study them. You've run a half-dozen interviews before this and no problems. You just had to get started, that was all. As if I were writing an introduction to a literary classic, I thought about telling him how great a pitcher he had been (in case this fact had been kept from him). Not only was this notion gauche, but I was soon to find out that he would have been left unstirred by this sort of embroidery. He had achieved enough to have been able to retire his ego long ago, and in place of vanity one sensed pride and satisfaction.

I began by taking him back to when he had been the timeless boy, as I had been once, back to the one lone point where we had stood even, before he started throwing fastballs that still blister those unburied summer days that run across the sere calendars, fastballs that have never been worn down by the friction of running time, before he had propelled himself into what Williams and DiMaggio called "by far the greatest pitcher" they ever faced.

His boyhood memories were clear, vivid. Born on a farm in Van Meter, Iowa, he was raised by his father to be a ballplayer. A common enough story, but there are always degrees and differences. Mickey Mantle's father, for instance, sounds obsessed (even naming the boy after his favorite player, catcher Mickey Cochrane). Robert William Andrew Feller's father sounds like a man who had seen a vision. He prepared and tutored his boy as though a rightful inheritance lay in the coming years. When his only child (a daughter came along later) was six years old, William Feller bought a Delco plant to electrify the property (this was in 1924, years before the installation of power lines).

"We had a windcharger," Bob said, "and on a windy day it would charge the batteries and we would use the lights in the barn to play night baseball—if you want to call it that—two or three nights a week to keep my arm in condition in the wintertime." To keep his arm in "condition." At age six. Looking back, however, it doesn't seem so fanciful at all, not for an arm that was to become America's most famous.

I asked him if he'd always had that big, vigorous, high-kicking windup.

"Right from the beginning," he said.

"A kid who winds up like that," I said, "has to be very serious."

"Baseball was always serious. It's a game, but if you're not serious about it you're not going to be much of a player."

"I used to imitate that windup when I was a kid," I said, finally venturing forth.

"You would have been better off being yourself," he said.

I was going to say that at that age you have no "self," except that I was talking to someone who'd had one from the beginning.

"Kids have heroes," I said.

"I suppose they all do, but I don't think people should overglamorize ballplayers, or anyone else for that matter. You run the danger of overlooking something in yourself."

"Didn't you have a hero when you were a kid?"

"My father," he said.

"I don't mean that."

"You mean a ballplayer? Well, Rogers Hornsby was my favorite, but I wouldn't say hero."

I wondered if there was something in them, these future titans, that even at that age would intuitively not abide dreamy worship.

Pitching in the barn at night during the winter to keep his arm in condition. And there was more. This was an heir to the Johnson throne, and as befitted a fledgling crown prince he soon had his own duchy. When Bob was twelve his father fenced some pasture land, put up chicken wire, benches, a small grandstand, and even a soda-pop stand behind first base. A Field of Reality, to keep pace with a dream acquiring more and more substance.

When he was eight years old he could throw a baseball harder than any of the other boys. So could I, at that age. He often played ball in the house, with his father. So did I, at that age, with my brother. But he soon outpaced me. While I was playing on the corrugated fields of Maspeth with boys in overalls, he, at age twelve, had his own field overlooking the Raccoon River, and his own team (the Oaks), with matching uniforms. The same primitive instincts, the same grandiose dream, equal and coalescent, until the ruthless intervention and sorting out of fortuitous selection. It was all a matter of where the thunderbolt struck and who was standing next to it: St. Paul, Nebraska, for Grover Cleveland Alexander; Humboldt, Kansas, for Walter Johnson; Factoryville, Pennsylvania, for Christy Mathewson; Lonaconing, Maryland, for Lefty Grove; Refugio, Texas, for Nolan Ryan. For Bob Feller, Van Meter, Iowa.

I asked him when he had developed that lethal curve.

"I always had it," he said. "I brought it to the big leagues with me."

"I never knew that."

"You would have known it," he said, "if you'd ever batted against me."

That offhand sentence probably means nothing to anyone else, nor should it. But think how it sounded to me. Bob Feller saying, *"If you'd ever batted against me."* How far I'd come from the boy with the Dixie Cup lid. Never mind the context, Bob Feller had made a comment about pitching against me.

Early days, he said, he was a third baseman. But then somebody "liked my arm" and sent him to the mound. Somebody liked his arm. In 1935 a Cleveland Indians scout named

Cy Slapnicka began receiving reports from Iowa about a kid pitcher in American Legion ball. Scouts frequently receive these flashes which often, by their very nature, sound like hyperbole. The reports about the Iowa kid exceeded even that.

But a scout is a scout. Like a country doctor, he must attend. Slapnicka was planning a trip to Des Moines, some twenty-five miles from Van Meter, to evaluate Western League right-hander Claude Passeau (later to become a substantial winner for the Chicago Cubs). To appease his communicants in Van Meter, Slapnicka decided to park his car there for an afternoon.

"He came out there figuring he'd have a look at the farm boy," Feller said, "and then go on and attend to some serious business. Well, he never did see Passeau. He didn't buy Passeau. He bought me."

Slapnicka was astonished by what he saw. That wild, wonderful dream that motivates every scout tirelessly and optimistically to follow any trail anywhere had suddenly become unbelievably true. In baseball analogy, Cy Slapnicka at Van Meter had become James Marshall at Sutter's Mill.

The scout would not leave Van Meter until he had the jewel in his possession. And to possess, what did it cost?

"He gave me a big bonus," Feller said "—an autographed ball and one dollar to sign a contract for seventy-five dollars a month. I'm glad I didn't get a bonus. I think you're supposed to get paid after you do your job."

(No, the last, which today reads like heresy or science fiction, does not necessarily reflect the mores of 1935 but rather those of a young man raised by strong ethical and moral standards.)

Besotted with what he had discovered, Slapnicka returned to Cleveland to announce to his colleagues that he had found "the greatest pitcher in history." This from a man who had seen Mathewson, Alexander, Grove, Johnson. That was a remarkable proclamation, Feller said, for "Cy Slapnicka was a pretty conservative gentleman."

I thought myself by then too jaded for epiphanies, but as we sat talking across the desk I could feel the old enthrallment reanimating, verifying what I had felt as a boy. Here was the prologue from which had sprung the storybook baseball tale: the sky-high dream, the youngster embellishing the dream pitch by pitch under blue summer skies and in the winter in lighted barn, the skeptical scout coming to an Iowa map dot to humor the bumpkins and to his astonishment finding that another of those prodigious thunderbolts had struck, that his own dream had meshed with that of Feller and Son. As Bob sat and remembered—speaking matter-of-factly, without sentimentality, as was his way—I achieved in my mind a miracle romantic inversion of time that shed his years and mine and drew me back into the world of a six-year-old, when a smiling teenage face on the lid of a Dixie Cup had the power to excite and lift the imagination. Can you remember when it happened to you?

He had lost those four years to World War II service, coming back still a potent force; but in my mind he remained always a figure of the 1930s, his time of sudden, dynamic arrival. Those were the years of the American leviathans: Franklin Roosevelt in the White House, Ernest Hemingway shooting lions in Africa, Joe DiMaggio in center field, Joe Louis in the ring. And the youngest of them, the boy with the blurring fastball, on the way to his own pinnacle.

I had a yearning, unreasonable question to ask. I wanted to know how it "felt." To at least learn that much—how it felt to be able to throw a baseball so fast that it seemed he was practicing black magic on the mound, for as one batter described it, "The ball looks smaller when he throws it. I swear, it gets smaller." This goes against all logic of speed and mass: something that traveled *away* from you at great speed was what turned smaller to the eye, not an object that came *toward* you. The hand of Bob Feller, it seemed, delivered a baseball under different physical laws. I wanted to know how it felt to be able to do that. But I didn't ask him. I had learned by then not to put questions with amorphous answers to the pragmatic Mr. Feller.

I did ask him this: "Did you ever feel special?"

"Heavens no," he said impatiently. "All I was doing was throwing a baseball. Kids all over America throw baseballs."

Three weeks after his fifteen-strikeout game he set a new American League record by fanning seventeen Philadelphia Athletics.

"I was pretty excited over that," he said. "I knew I was approaching the record. I was counting those whiffs. And the closer I got to that record, the more I wanted to break it. I just kept pouring them in."

There may be no greater ferocity in sports than a mighty fastballer bearing down on a personal goal: Seaver burning away his record ten consecutive strikeouts; Koufax and Ryan throwing near-invisible pitches at the end of their no-hitters; Clemens wanting, and getting, his twenty-strikeout games. The climactic pitches must have been pure fury. So try to imagine how hard an adrenaline-pumping seventeen-year-old, already possessor of the fastest pitch on the planet, must have been "pouring them in" that day.

"That hit the newspapers like thunder and lightning," he said, "and I guess that's when people began to realize I was for real."

I told him that in 1936 he was America's most famous kid. He scoffed.

"You're forgetting about Shirley Temple, aren't you? And what about those kids in the *Our Gang* comedies? Anyway, I was seventeen years old. You want to call that a kid? Okay, maybe by baseball standards."

He had spent his long career, 1936–1956, entirely with Cleveland. It had almost been otherwise. In the winter of 1936 baseball's frosty and autocratic commissioner, Judge Kenesaw Mountain Landis, was prepared to declare the youngster a free agent. The Indians, contrary to baseball's then-existing rules, had been manipulating Feller's contract.

"You see," he said, "in those days major league clubs couldn't sign free agents. Minor league clubs would sign all the players and then sell them to the major league clubs to make ends meet financially. This was by agreement. Well, the major league clubs were all cheating. They were signing players off the sandlots, and Judge Landis knew it. I was one of them. So it became within his authority to make me a free agent. If he had done that, I could've picked up a hundred thousand dollars or more in bonus money. There were scouts sitting in the Chamberlain Hotel in Des Moines with blank checks in their hands, just waiting."

But Feller and his parents felt a loyalty to the Cleveland club. And they told Landis so. The judge remained adamant—the old gentleman had by this time become accustomed to speaking from mountaintops. But he had yet to deal with an Iowa corn-and-hog farmer.

"My father told him it was our intention to play for Cleveland," Feller said, "and that if he tried to stop us we were going to sue him in civil court, because we had a civil law contract and we wanted to test it to see if baseball law superseded civil law."

The judge, who knew his law, wanted no part of that, and Feller stayed with Cleveland.

I couldn't help feeling slightly incredulous.

"This was when?" I asked.

"Nineteen thirty-six," he said.

"The heart of the depression."

"That's right."

"Do you realize how much a hundred thousand dollars was then?"

"I damn well knew then," he said tartly, "and I damn well know now."

"It was then about fifty times the average national income."

"Probably."

"And you turned it down."

"You find that foolish?" he asked.

"I find it hard to grasp."

"Then I'll explain it to you. I figured if I was worth that kind of money, I'd make it later, after I'd proved I was worth it. And if I wasn't worth it, then I had no business having it."

He said this quite plainly, as though there was nothing remarkable about it.

"I made plenty of money later on," he said, "when I'd proved what I could do. And I wasn't shy about asking for it."

He soon became the game's biggest drawing card, nor were those sold-out stadiums lost on him—he was the first to have attendance clauses written into his contracts.

I told him about the friends of mine who still grieved over his "four lost years" and tried to average them out to see what his record might have looked like. The consensus was another hundred or more wins to go with his 266, and other speculative but hardly fanciful numbers. He was not interested.

"It didn't happen," he said, "so I see no point in talking about it."

He could have avoided military service, he said. By late 1941 his father was dying of cancer and Bob could have received what was called a 2-C deferment as a farmer (though he would not have been able to play baseball). But "the right thing to do," he said, was to enlist.

"I went to war college in Newport, took a gunnery course in Norfolk, went to PT-boat school. I was pretty good at anti-aircraft gunnery. I ended up in the South Pacific, on the *Alabama*. Battleship."

"Did you request combat duty?" I asked.

He had.

"You could have sat it out in Honolulu drinking beer and pitching for a service team."

"The hell with that," he said. "I figured if I was in, I might as well be in all the way."

I asked how much combat he had seen.

"The *Alabama*," he said, "was with the Third Fleet, and we got into quite a few of those scrapes. Tarawa, Kwajalein, the Marshalls and Gilberts, Iwo Jima, the Philippines."

I had been twelve, thirteen years old then. Sometimes I would think about them, Feller and all the others, wondering what they were doing. It never occurred to me that they would ever be in any danger.

"Our job," he said, "was to protect the carriers. We'd have those air battles, and the Japanese planes would try to get at the carriers. And sometimes they'd come after us. Torpedo bombers. They'd come in low, to get underneath our shells, sometimes so low they would fly right into a wave or a big swell. I'd be up there on the main deck with a bunch of kids, banging away with a Bofors. The one that gets you you never see, that's the scary thing. You can never be sure about anything one minute to the next. That's for keeps, that racket."

I flew home from Cleveland that night thinking about fastballs and strikeouts, about the refusal to accept unearned money, about volunteering for combat duty, about Japanese warplanes trying to kill Bob Feller.

You're a writer, I told myself. Writers have instincts about people. You've always had good instincts about people. Even when you were six years old.

Fifteen

❧ I WOULD IMAGINE that some forty or fifty years from now elderly men named Derek Jeter and Albert Pujols will be sitting down to talk with some young, baseball-buzzed interrogator wanting to know what it was like "back then," when the century was young. What was it like to bat against such long-ago bronzed and enshrined duffers as Roger Clemens, Randy Johnson, Greg Maddux? How well did you get to know them? What do you remember about them? What stories? There have to be stories; otherwise, no matter how eminent, men become little more than pages in the record book.

What will today's stories sound like to a distant generation? Tales of actual games will differ little from those of any era. Runs, hits, splendid glovework, all endemic no matter when, and those ninety feet between bases—"The most perfect geometric configuration ever conceived," Red Smith said—will still be there (unless, in the name of "a more fan-pleasing game," they are reduced by a foot or two, which is all it would take to complete the subversive process begun by inspirations like the designated hitter and the mysteriously shrinking strike zone. It would be the baseball equivalent of global warming and rising sea levels. But with the World Series now degraded by barely .500 teams emerging as world champs, nothing is beyond the range of the siren dollar-call).

It changes, and yet not. The game has a fixed and stubborn soul. Those runners will always have to fly around the bases to score runs, and pitchers will still have to throw strikes, even if through keyholes. The world around, however, still evolves, with Old-Timers Day ornaments Jeter and Pujols telling us about it, probably regaling us with tales of how much more fun the players had back in those days, in the early part of the century. There was more team cohesion then; the players were able to spend more time together during those six-hour transcontinental plane rides, unlike "today's" forty-five-minute coast-to-coast hops. Back then, Jeter and Pujols would recall, the whole team stayed in one hotel, unlike "today," when players own their own condominium in every league city.

Larry Ritter recorded the tales of men who played in a time when professional baseball players were regarded by genteel society as little more than hard-drinking rowdies and their teams were debarred from the better hotels. Nor was this discrimination entirely without warrant. Players were known to reel drunkenly through corridors, rebel violently against overcooked steaks, lead women of unconventional virtue up fire escapes, and dive into hotel fountains. One scholar of the game was known to go sliding across lobby floors to demonstrate to his colleagues the art of stealing home.

Changes? Never mind what and how many. Today's players—and we can understand this—luxuriate in the only one that matters to them: the Niagara of money in which they bathe themselves. This largesse, which is hurled at them by scatter-arm clubowners, contrasts with what Pittsburgh's old Hall of Fame outfielder Lloyd Waner once said. Growing up poor on a farm in rural Harrah, Oklahoma, in the years before World War I, he and older brother (and fellow Hall of Famer) Paul were ravenous for baseball; often sans bat and ball, the boys swatted at corncobs with sawed-down broomsticks. Imagine these youngsters making it to the major leagues and excelling. How did he feel about it, I asked Lloyd. "I would have played for nothing," he said. And if he were playing in today's money-padded times? Mr. Waner gave it a moment's serious thought, then said, "Well, today, I might have asked for expenses."

After appearing in the 1927 World Series against the Yankees, the two young, likable Waner brothers signed up for a tour of vaudeville theaters. They stood on the stage tossing a baseball back and forth while engaging in amusing patter. "That money came in handy," Lloyd said.

There was other handy money to be made, some of it unthinkable today. Postseason all-star teams were knocked together and took off on barnstorming trips, displaying their talents in nondescript ballparks in what one player described as "one-mule towns," competing against local teams. These barnstormers included some of the best big-league talent. Detroit Tigers second baseman Charlie Gehringer, the finest all-around second baseman of his day (as well as of most days), remembered touring through North Dakota after the season, when "it was so cold Lefty Grove was pitching with woolen mittens on." That's right: thirty-game winner Lefty Grove, possessor of baseball's most hallowed left arm, was risking it in freezing Dakota weather to earn a few extra. Sometimes saying the obvious is so unavoidable it is necessary: So—can you imagine a thirty-game winner doing that today?

Changes come. They are inevitable, sailing under the name of progress. We have always been a progressive people.

But if you've been soaked to the core with this game, you have concerns for its essence, the things that keep its devotees on their season-to-season treadmill and the youngsters playing on their fields rough and smooth, hustling upon that heraldic diamond design.

Preservation and remembering are part of baseball's enduring fascination. The game was born with a sense of its own history; every at bat (today, every pitch), every out, hit, run, every everything has been studiously recorded, as if with a sense that people a hundred years later would want to know about it. Today these numerical multitudes are harvested and analyzed and anatomized to the point where the experts can see exactly where their forecasts went wrong the year before. Its statistics continue to give the game the imprimatur of instant history, the procreation going on and on, accumulating, growing, expanding, becoming more and more precisely detailed, a feast for the omnivorous computer maw, until the latest editions of *The Baseball Encyclopedia* finally grew to the dimensions of second base.

But without the men and tales of their dreams and dramas, their fun and foibles, the numbers are cold. Like a connect-the-dots exercise, lines of narrative need to be drawn to give us the flesh-and-blood picture. The joys of baseball are quadripartite: playing it, watching it, studying it, talking about it, with a subdivision for the latter: listening to the talk, especially when the talk is coming from those who know it best.

"Did you know," the fifty-year baseball man (player and manager) Jimmy Dykes said, "that Walter Johnson had no follow-through in his delivery?"

I didn't know, nor did I entirely believe it, except that I was listening to a man who had played against Walter for ten years.

We were sitting in the living room of his Norristown, Pennsylvania, home. Dykes was half shouting, probably because he was hard of hearing, or maybe because he was talking about Walter Johnson. Or maybe it was simply because he was talking about the game that had absorbed a half-century of his life. Having lost my way somewhat in my search for Norristown, I was a half-hour late in arriving. "He's been wondering," Mrs. Dykes said at the front door, and when I walked into the living room the old baseball soldier wanted to know where the hell I'd been.

His first big-league at bat, he said, had been against Walter, and he seemed almost proud of the fact that he had struck out.

"Bang, bang, bang," he said, describing the three pitches he'd seen. "Back to the bench. Didn't disturb anybody. I didn't even disturb the air because I never swung. I could have telephoned in that at bat. I went home that night and told my dad, 'If they're all like him, you'll be seeing a lot of me around here.'"

The syndrome was not unfamiliar. Certain pitchers would describe with awe and admiration a home run ball they had served up to Ruth. Its height, its distance—as though describing a work of art for which they had provided the frame. ("I once gave up one to Jimmie Foxx," Burleigh Grimes said, "that the guys in the bullpen said they were watching for two innings.") They had a grip on the coattails of a legend, sanctioning them as big leaguers. Good enough to compete with Ruth, Johnson; later it was Williams and Feller; still later, Koufax, Mantle, Ryan. Never did they ever mention getting the better of an icon, as though it would have in some way diminished the prestige of having been there. If you struck out Ruth—and many did—it was less Babe, and that wouldn't do.

"That right foot stayed planted," Dykes said of Walter. "He stepped forward with his left foot, gave this little underhand flip, and the ball shot up there like a bullet. The right foot never moved. No follow-through. He threw with his arm only."

"That must have been rough on his arm," I said ingenuously.

"Very rough. He only won over four hundred games, pitching for teams that hit like the Bloomer Girls."

With my clinical mind, I asked: If Johnson had followed through, thrown his entire body into the delivery (the mantra of pitching coaches), might he have been even faster?

"Faster?" Dykes shouted. "Don't give me nightmares."

"Was he faster than Feller?"

"How can you tell something like that? The difference is so slight there is no difference. It's what the ball does that matters. Does it have any action on it? The ball that Walter threw was alive. So was Feller's. Who was faster?" The old skipper pointed his finger heavenward. "He's the only one who knows that."

They endure because the marinated tales fit snugly into the imagination, tales told right up to the rim of fantasy but never quite across. Babe Herman, Brooklyn's colorful and mighty slugger of the late 1920s and early 1930s, had his own Walter reminiscence to share.

"I batted against Walter Johnson when his playing days were over," Herman said as we sat in the den of his Glendale, California, home, some fifty years after the fact. "He was managing the Washington Senators then. I was with Brooklyn, and we were playing them an exhibition game. Walter was pitching batting practice for them. I was watching him, and I must have had a look in my eye because Heinie Manush, who was an old friend, said to me, 'Hey, Babe, did you ever bat against the great Walter?' I said no, so he gave me his turn at the plate.

"Walter sent one in there and I put it up in the seats. Well, I don't think he liked that, because he pulled forward on the peak of his cap and fired in about eight in a row that I couldn't get around on. I barely fouled off each one. And I was right in my prime then." (Herman batted .393 that year, 1930.) "Best fastball I ever saw. But, according to Manush, Walter could only throw like that for a few minutes, then needed a few days before he could crank it up again. Now, I hit against Feller and Dean, but Walter Johnson—in his forties—was the quickest thing I ever saw."

Billy Goodman, Boston's fine contact hitter and future batting titlist: "One game Cronin sent me up to pinch-hit against Feller. 'Make him throw you a strike,' he said. Well, I did even better. I made him throw three of them, all in a row. I went back and sat down and said to myself, 'Man, you're in the wrong league.' I'd never seen anything like that."

Johnson, Feller, Grove, Koufax: emperors of the fastball. (We are talking here about the nine-inning fastball, as uncooled at the end as at the beginning.) Ryan? Clemens? They belong surely. Smoke and statistics alone, however, do not necessarily a legend make. The memories of an era must first be gathered and collated and allowed the mellowness of dreamy recollection. In baseball, as in every field of endeavor, posterity runs the elevator and creates the aureole; but it is the echoes and the graphic tellings that etch the lasting image.

Away from the field, baseball is a game of opinions, many of them neighborly to prejudices. Take that fortissimo question: Who is the greatest player of all? The easy answer is Babe Ruth (with his hitting *and* his pitching), but that won't do; it's like asking who was the first president. Answering with Babe Ruth takes away the question's entertainment value. So, leaving Ruth aside, the question is asked again. Each generation, of course, presents its credentialed candidates, leaping from Cobb to Ruth to DiMaggio to Mays, on up to Alex Rodriguez and Barry Bonds (with footnotes for the latter).

The best way to defuse the troublesome question is to give a brief litany of baseball's permutations: dead ball, lively ball, differences in home-field configurations, crumbling color barriers and the infusion of all that new talent, expansion and more expansion, artificial surfaces, the lowering of the mound and the contracting of the strike zone, the designated hitter, the split-finger fastball, relief specialists, and of course the joys of steroids. (You have to be careful today about saying you "needled" a teammate.) If the same men had played for a hundred years, someone would have emerged as an answer to the question. So the question is unanswerable. The mass of big leaguers played in different eras under widely varying conditions, facing different pitching in different leagues. Try picking your all-time outfield. Try picking three of the following: Cobb, Speaker, Ruth, Williams, DiMaggio, Mays, Mantle, Aaron, Musial, Clemente, Frank Robinson, Gwynn, Bonds. (It's easier to pick the three or four greatest pitchers, because you're going to be right and wrong at the same time.) And don't look to the record book for help, for that is an entirely misleading document that should be closed and reopened every twenty-five or so years.

Who is the greatest player of all? I suppose there is an answer: it's whoever you think it is.

One day in 1937 the Monarch of all Fastballers was at Comiskey Park in Chicago to watch young Mr. Feller at work. When asked later about what he had seen, Walter Johnson

155

pronounced thusly: "I don't know if he is as fast as I was, but he's the fastest thing I've seen in twenty years. That boy can pour the ball in there." But sportswriter Shirley Povich wanted more. "Tell me, Walter," he said, "does Feller throw that ball as fast as you did?" Walter hesitated, for there was no more compelling question in the Universe of Baseball at that moment. Then he answered, no doubt as honestly as this honest, modest man could. "No."

What did Feller think of Walter's appraisal?

"Well," he said, "of course he's going to say that, but I'm sure he was absolutely honest and sincere about it and probably 99 percent right. In my opinion Walter Johnson has to be the fastest pitcher of all time, for the simple reason that he didn't have a curveball and he struck out so many batters. I would say he had to be a harder thrower than I was."

"I still don't see how he could tell," I said.

"It's what he believed."

But it's still a game of opinions. Who is the fastest pitcher of all time? It's whoever you think it is.

Sixteen

❰ "YOU TAKE Interstate 94 out of St. Paul into Wisconsin, then you pick up Route 29 just north of Elk Mound. At Cadott you pick up 27 and follow it north to Holcombe, where I'm right on the lake. You can't go wrong." That last always strikes a note of what I think is unwarranted faith. You can go wrong. You often do. I did.

The speaker was Burleigh Grimes, Hall of Fame right-hander, Brooklyn Dodgers ace of the 1920s, winner of 270 big-league games. The person he was speaking to over the telephone was me, and I think I must have stopped listening before he was finished speaking, because I did go wrong, though not too far—I was still in the State of Wisconsin. I didn't mind terribly being lost; I always started out with time to spare, and it was, as the poets say, "a picture postcard day," the early October air filled with a cool, radiant sunshine, the sky keenly blue and afloat with big, slow-traveling white clouds. I was motoring along in my rented car through what I took to be the Wisconsin dairy belt, for there were cows standing like sculpture in golden pastures and along the slopes of green hillsides. It was all so plainly peaceful and harmonious it gave the feeling that only nice people lived here, that the homes were immaculate, the children obedient, and crime against the law.

I was driving up from Edina, Minnesota, where I had spent the preceding day talking with Ossie Bluege, who had served in the big leagues for eighteen years (1922–1939), playing third base for the Washington Senators. Bluege had spent a lot of time talking about Tyrus Raymond Cobb, who seemed to have left an indelible impression on him, as Cobb did with just about everyone he shared a playing field with (a twenty-four-year lifetime *average* of .367 does connote something maniacal). Almost to a man they detested Cobb, and almost to a man they proclaimed him the most illustrious player of all.

Along with descriptions of the Georgian's vivid talents, Bluege kept returning to tales of Cobb's ferocity on the base paths, his snarls and oaths and high-flashing spikes. Throughout the early stages of our conversation Bluege's large German shepherd several times entered the room and started barking. Exasperated finally, the old third baseman jumped to his feet, confronted the noisy intruder, and shouted, "That's enough, Tyrus Raymond!" Then, with a somewhat sheepish expression, he turned to me and, sounding almost helpless about it, said, "I call him Tyrus Raymond."

This recent interview was running through my mind as I went astray between pasture and hillside, over crossroads and through small towns. Maybe it was thinking of the defiant Cobb that did it, but when I saw the state trooper starting to pull out of a side road I kept right on going, figuring the hell with him; I had the right of way, and Tyrus Raymond would have done the same thing. Then I looked in the mirror and saw that state-owned vehicle coming after me with its dome light in a state of agitation. When that happens you know your day is about to be divided into Before and After.

I pulled over and waited, believing myself innocent of any wrongdoing, though in the long run that can be of little consolation. He drew up behind me, his door slowly opened, and he eased himself out. When he appeared at my rolled-down window, tall, uniformed, dauntingly hatted, he said, "Didn't you see that Full Stop sign back there?"

Well, obviously I hadn't; I had been watching him. You don't zip cavalierly through a Full Stop sign with a state trooper as your witness as if you're expecting him to wave his hat and cheer you on. I produced my license, pointing out that I was driving a rented car, as though the infraction was the car's fault. After examining the license, he said, "You're from Connecticut, your car's rented in Minnesota, and you're running stop signs in Wisconsin." That sounded like a lot for a little.

I told him that I was lost, that I was heading for Cadott and had missed my turn. As evidence I produced the paper with Grimes's directions on it. For Cadott I had written "Kodut" (which might explain why I had driven past it). The way he looked at the misspelling I think began to give him the feeling he had less than he bargained for here. I told him I was heading for Holcombe, where I had an appointment with Burleigh Grimes. Hailing originally from New York City, Wisconsin looked underpopulated to me and I supposed they all knew one another.

It's the language of America, this baseball, as music is of the universe. No matter how remote the place you find yourself, no matter how seedy the film noir of a motel you land in, mention the national game and nameless strangers become fraternity brothers.

"The old pitcher?" the trooper asked, handing me back my license.

I don't know how many Wisconsin state troopers had heard of Burleigh or were even baseball fans, but this one qualified on both counts. (If he had heard of me it would have been a clean sweep, but you can't have everything.) I explained my mission—I was traveling around the country interviewing former ballplayers for a book I was writing. He pushed his hat up from his forehead, rested one brawny forearm on my door, and asked whom else I had seen. And there at the roadside in what might or might not have been the dairy belt we talked baseball for a good twenty minutes while the drivers of passing cars probably empathized with me (or not). The conversation ended only when his car radio began to cackle something in what sounded like a UFO transmission. He wished me luck, said he would look for the book, got back into his cruiser, made a screeching U-turn, and shot away into the Wisconsin sunshine, leaving behind his learned writer who didn't know how to spell Cadott. Our conversation had been engrossing, so much so that I had forgotten to ask for directions to that elusive place.

My father was right. He had said, on the night I signed my Red Sox contract, that if I worked hard, used all my talent, and believed in myself, I could make it to Cooperstown. Well, I had tried my best in all respects and there I was, in Cooperstown, where Abner Doubleday had become famous for not inventing baseball. I was not there, however, to make an acceptance speech with a plaque in my hands. I had come as a prospector, to mine the ore in the memory of Burleigh Grimes, one of the enshrined veterans who return to that village of wholesome Americana to attend the annual midsummer gala known as Hall of Fame Weekend, when the newest inductees are honored.

I had written to Grimes at his Wisconsin home asking for the interview. He had sent back a curt note reading, in its entirety, "See you in Cooperstown." I was delighted with the note's brevity—age hadn't mellowed Burleigh: throughout his long career he had been known for being frank and always direct. A tough-minded, no-nonsense character with, when provoked, an explosive temper. While his heyday had been with the Dodgers, Burleigh had traveled the big-league trails with several other teams, being at one time or another teammate or opponent of such empyrean figures as Grover Cleveland Alexander, Honus Wagner, Rogers Hornsby, Babe Ruth, and Lou Gehrig while pitching for managers like Wilbert Robinson, John McGraw, and Joe McCarthy. Here was another full serving of memories to be recorded and preserved.

When I introduced myself to him in the lobby of the Otesaga Hotel, the sturdy, nearly bald, eighty-three-year-old Grimes sized me up and said, "Oh, it's you. Well, all right."

"Are you ready to turn back the clock?" I asked, giving him my good old opening line.

"Well," he said guardedly, "maybe rewind it a little."

We sat down on a sofa commanding a view of the crowded lobby, where knots of men stood in hearty baseball conversations, Hall of Famers and their families came and went, and young people and old were hawkeyeing about with ballpoint pens and baseballs and autograph albums.

"What the hell do people do with those autographs anyway?" Grimes asked moodily.

"They collect them," I said. "It preserves the moment."

"What moment?"

"The moment of meeting somebody like you. The emotion."

"Emotion?" he asked skeptically.

"For a lot of people, meeting a great star is an emotional experience."

Burleigh grunted. I don't think being the generator of other people's emotions moved him very much.

"Do you know," he said, "that sitting here in this lobby are three men who pitched in the 1920 World Series? Jesus, that's over fifty years ago."

It was the Series with a memorable Game Five, in which Cleveland second baseman Bill Wambsganss turned the only World Series unassisted triple play, Cleveland outfielder Elmer Smith hit the first World Series grand slam, and Cleveland's Jim Bagby hit the first World Series home run by a pitcher. And sitting next to me at the moment was the man who had started that game for Brooklyn.

"You remember that game?" I asked him.

"Would you?" he asked sullenly.

In Game Two of that Series he had pitched a shutout, but he lost the final game to right-hander Stanley Coveleski, the Series pitching star with three complete-game victories, during which he had given up just two earned runs. Coveleski was sitting across the lobby with his wife. Grimes stared at him.

"Stanley's a nice fellow," he said.

Coveleski was one of Ritter's "boys." When *The Glory of Their Times* was published to its wholly unexpected fanfare, the publisher brought to New York as many of the players as could come (sixteen of the twenty-two) to publicize the book. They were interviewed by newspapers, magazines, and on television. It was in a TV studio that Ritter gave a glimpse of his mischievous side.

Mrs. Coveleski had not been present when Ritter went out to Pennsylvania to interview her husband. When he saw the pitcher's wife sitting in a studio anteroom, he went over, sat down next to her, and asked who she was.

"I'm Mrs. Stanley Coveleski," the woman said proudly.

"Coveleski?" Ritter said. "What's he doing here with all these great players?"

Mrs. Coveleski frowned and said indignantly, "My husband was a great player."

"But he doesn't compare with these men."

The poor woman compressed her lips and, Ritter said later, glared at him like an irate schoolmarm, so offended she was at a loss for words. Then Coveleski came over.

"Ah," he said to his wife, "you've met my friend."

"He's no friend of yours," she said sternly.

Stanley, Ritter said, was baffled.

"But this is Mr. Ritter," Stanley said. "He wrote the book."

Whereupon Mrs. Coveleski compressed her lips again, turned to Larry and, shaking her finger at him, said, "Shame on you. You shouldn't tease an old lady."

Burleigh's eyes found the venerable left-hander Rube Marquard, his Dodgers teammate and the third of the 1920 World Series pitchers present.

"You see that big galoot?" Grimes said of the six-foot-three pitcher. "He got caught scalping tickets before one of the games. He somehow got hold of a fistful of tickets and went outside to sell them." Grimes chortled. "Of all the people out there, he picked on a plainclothes cop. He's lucky he wasn't arrested. Though for all the good he did in that Series, it would have been better if he had."

Have you ever seen a bird dive to the ground for a morsel of something? If you have, then you've seen other birds soon attracted begin to follow, and others to follow them. The pattern of autograph seekers differs little. Burleigh began by signing one, which told others milling around the lobby that here was a morsel worth picking up. Some of them, older men in particular, wanted reminiscences along with an autograph. Did Burleigh remember this, or that? What did he think of . . . ? Did he ever . . . ?

Burleigh answered most of the queries with an uninterested grunt or nod of the head. He was becoming a barometer of rapidly diminishing patience. He signed his name, he grunted, he nodded, he shook hands, from time to time glancing at me with eyes that had storm signals at their centers.

And then he was confronted by a tall, elderly, fungo-bat-thin gentleman with a broad smile that would not relent, as if his lips were unable to meet. He had followed Burleigh's career assiduously, he said. Burleigh had been his favorite. And on and on. And then the gentleman leaned forward and asked, "Tell me, Burleigh—did you ever pitch for the Dodgers?"

I thought that was very funny, but when I turned to Grimes I saw the blood flooding his bald head and his lips tightening. It looked like Mount St. Burleigh was about to erupt. But he merely looked up at the man and muttered tersely, "Go away."

Then he said to me, "Look, this is no damned good. This is no place to talk. If you want to do this right you'll just have to come out to Wisconsin."

I found Cadott—it had been there all the time—and made my way north. The roads began turning narrower and less traveled, going from pavement to solid Wisconsin ground, until the last turn led me along what looked like a leftover wagon road. Lake Holcombe came into view, blue soul mate of the sky, smooth and sunlit, with a scattering of tidy, unpretentious houses along the shoreline. I wondered about a man who had known the madding crowds of the great cities settling in what was almost a precreation stillness. Was it to clear the way for memories? I soon learned that Burleigh had been born not far away in a town "so small that only the people who lived there knew where it was." It was the old siren call of native ground that had brought him back.

The riled-up autograph signer of the Otesaga lobby proved a most pleasant, considerate, and quite forthcoming host. We sat in the large living room, in front of a handsome fire that my host continually kept in full, rosy health. There was whiskey, cigars, lunch, and then dinner as the reminiscences flowed. The meals were prepared and served by Burleigh's attractive, much younger, and adoring wife (who with a sly wink described her octogenarian husband as "a Hall of Famer all the way"). There was another eyewink later, when Mrs. Grimes said she had to drive down to "the city." The wink came from Burleigh. "Chippewa Falls," he said dryly.

With a thought to his water bills, Burleigh took his lesser emergencies to the lakeside, to a reasonably secluded spot. So at one point in the early evening we strode out the back door and, standing shoulder to shoulder, urinated into Lake Holcombe while Burleigh discussed the wide variety of breaking pitches thrown by Grover Cleveland Alexander, though for the moment unable to demonstrate their many trajectories.

Burleigh's memories were vivid, amusing, filled with fond nostalgia and firm opinions. I asked a basic question and he answered: the greatest pitcher he ever saw was Alexander, allowing for the fact that he had seen little of Grove or Feller, and Koufax only on television, which wasn't "the same as being there." But he couldn't imagine anybody being better than Alex, the only pitcher he'd come close to "hero-worshiping." And he insisted his greatest player was Wagner.

"He was forty years old when you saw him," I said.

"You asked me," he said, "and I answered you."

"He must have been really impressive ten years earlier."

"He was still impressive ten years later."

I asked him to name an all-star team from his era.

"What's the matter," he asked, "have you run out of intelligent questions already?"

But he indulged me. The "smartest" catcher he'd ever pitched to was Jimmie Wilson. His infield was filled out with the standard brand-names: Bill Terry at first, Rogers Hornsby at second, Wagner at short, Pie Traynor at third. Then he began rattling off outfielders: Zack Wheat, Edd Roush, the Waners, Chick Hafey, Chuck Klein, Ross Youngs, Mel Ott, Lefty O'Doul.

"That's nine outfielders, Burleigh," I said. "You can't have nine outfielders."

"There were times when I could have used them all," he said, ruefully.

"Pick three."

"I can't. You're the expert—you pick 'em."

So we ended up with an all-star team with nine outfielders. I allotted him three pitchers and that proved easy: Alexander, Carl Hubbell, and his Dodgers teammate of the 1920s, Dazzy Vance, whom Burleigh insisted nobody ever threw harder than. He mentioned that in 1924 he and Vance together had won fifty games for the Dodgers (Vance with twenty-eight). Then he asked what was the best Koufax and Don Drysdale had done as a Dodgers tandem. Forty-nine, I told him, in 1965. He puffed his cigar with evident satisfaction. Even far into retirement they remain competitive, these old-timers.

I reminded him that he had been on the scene at two of baseball's most storied moments, one a hard and sudden fact, the other baseball mythology at its loftiest.

"Sure I saw it," he said of Bill Wambsganss's unassisted triple play. "I'd been knocked out of that game in the fourth inning, but I was still there, sitting on the bench. You don't let your team play a World Series game all by itself, do you?"

"It must have shocked the hell out of you," I said.

"Well, I would say it did. It took us all a few seconds to believe what we'd just seen. Two men on, none out, line drive—wham! Maybe three seconds, and three outs. I think the most surprised guy was Wambsganss himself. He looked around like he couldn't believe what he'd just done. Then it must've come to him, because he ran off with a big smile on his face. You never saw a happier young guy. Three seconds and three outs. When people tell me they love baseball, I think yeah, it's those unexpected things like that. But then I think, Kee-rist, how can you like a game where a guy hits a line drive and it makes three outs? Whoever said life isn't fair must've seen a ball game."

"What about that other business?" I asked. "In the '32 Series."

"Ruth calling his shot? Yeah, I was there. Ringside seat in the dugout. Every time you were near Ruth it was a ringside seat because you never knew what he was going to get up to. I was with the Cubs then, near the end of the tether. Did he call his shot? You want to waste time on this?"

"It's probably baseball's greatest moment," I said.

"That's because Ruth touched it up later with a little bullshit," Burleigh said. "Look, I was sitting right there watching him, and no, he didn't. Charlie Root was pitching, and he whipped over two strikes. We were yelling at Ruth—that whole Series was pretty nasty, with a lot of bench jockeying—and he looked over at us and held up one finger, the bat in his hand, to show us he still had one strike left. Do you think Charlie Root would have just stood there and let him call a home run? Charlie was as mean as a straight razor on the mound and would've turned Ruth upside down with the next pitch. And anyway, if he'd been calling a home run he wouldn't have been pointing to center field, which the story has him doing. He would've pointed to right because that's where most of his shots went."

"You're killing a good story, Burleigh," I said.

"Maybe I'm giving you a better one. He didn't do it and that's that."

By that time I had spoken to five men who had been at that game, Burleigh being the fifth. Cubs second baseman Billy Herman said that Ruth had not "called" his shot, but Herman loved the story anyway and hoped it would go on. Two Yankees, third baseman Joe Sewell and pitcher George Pipgras, followed a party line and insisted that Ruth had indeed called it. Yankees manager Joe McCarthy, however, hadn't seen Ruth point anywhere, "but I might have turned my head for a moment." Then he winked at me, a wink that said a lot but remained mute to a tape recorder.

As pitcher Waite Hoyt, Ruth's teammate on the 1920s Yankees and one of the most urbane of players, said, "Whatever you hear about Babe Ruth, no matter how fantastic—believe it." And so the story too good not to be true, becomes true, a case of legend outdistancing fact.

The best talk always came from men who sounded as though they were sitting alone, reminiscing aloud to themselves, a mood Grimes fell into as the evening wore on and the chill October night darkened the windows.

"I know men," he said, staring into the fire, "who are lawyers or doctors or carpenters or what have you. Most of them can't remember what drew them into their trade or profession. A ballplayer always knows. He's a kid who's out in the sunshine doing what he enjoys most and thinks he's pretty good at. I played baseball because I loved it. We had our own team. The Redjackets. We were pretty damned serious about it all. I was about twelve years old then. So this was around 1905."

"Who were your heroes back then?" I asked.

Burleigh laughed. "Heroes?" he asked. "We didn't have any heroes. I knew there was such a thing as big-league baseball, but I'd never heard of Honus Wagner or John McGraw or Christy Mathewson or any of those fellows. The news hadn't got through the timber yet."

I tried to see that, a boy playing baseball without a lodestar to guide and motivate him. I couldn't imagine my friends and myself without a Feller or a Williams or a DiMaggio to style ourselves by and show us where the summit was. It leads one to suspect that Burleigh and his young friends were purer and more spontaneous players. I could remember energetic Feller windups on the rugged fields of Maspeth, stolidly poised DiMaggio stances, and, later, young center fielders dropping fly balls as they tried to emulate the Willie Mays basket catch. For the young Burleigh and his mates in their insular world, aptitudes and mistakes were natural, their own entirely.

"And then one day," Burleigh said, "while you're doing what you love to do, somebody comes along and tells you they'll pay you to do it for their side. You're never going to forget *that* day, are you? You realize that what you were doing just for the hell of it can be a serious business after all."

"Does getting paid for it take some of the fun out of it?" I asked.

"Well, it should, shouldn't it? But I don't know. Serious fun, maybe. Does that make sense? Probably not."

"How old were you when you signed that first contract?"

"Around eighteen. That's when you know it all, right? I put in five years in the minors and then pitched in the big leagues for nineteen years. That's a haul, isn't it? I was known as a spitball pitcher, but I didn't throw it as much as people think, and I didn't throw it as much as they expected, which is the key thing. If you want to confuse people, dodge around your reputation a bit. It was the fastball that got me to the major leagues and the fastball that kept me there. The reputation kept them looking for the spitter. That pitch was banned after 1919, you know, but they grandfathered the rule and let the established spitballers keep throwing it. I was just about the last one throwing it. Legally, anyway."

"Nineteen years in the major leagues," I said. "That's a hell of a lot of train rides."

"It sure is," he said. "And you just keep getting on those trains as long as they're paying you to do it. Until one day somebody walks up to you and tells you that uniform belongs to somebody else now. How does that feel? Not good. But you can see it coming. Guys who were never able to get around on you are suddenly drilling them down the line. You see that and you say to yourself, 'Oh-oh.' Well, hell, you're forty years old. Listen, I saw them whaling the tar out of old Alexander at the end. I told you how good he was. Well, you see it happen to Alex and you don't feel so sorry for yourself. You say, Well, hell, I'm in Alex's class now. Finally caught up to him.

"How'd it feel playing in the big time for almost twenty years? You feel you belong, that's all. The big thrill wears off. You keep on doing the job, that's all. You watch the ones who can't cut it come and go, but you don't feel so special yourself."

I confessed that I had been one of those who hadn't been able to "cut it." He asked me how old I'd been.

"Sixteen," I said.

"And you felt like hell. Well, it doesn't feel so good at 41 either. Listen, you probably saved yourself a lot of grief. Look at it this way, bud. I won 270 games, but I also lost 212. And every one of those killed me. The way I look at it, in 19 years I had 58 better days than the other kind."

"You're being philosophical," I said.

"No. It's arithmetic."

"But you filled out your dream."

"About what? Playing in the major leagues? No, that just came along in its own way. The dream came later. You want to know about it? Sometimes I dream I'm warming up before a game, and I've got terrific stuff. But the game never starts. I'll bet I've had that dream a hundred times. You dream at the end of the line too, buddy."

Burleigh sat quietly for a time, smoking his cigar and gazing through the weave of grey smoke into the fire. I had learned not to intrude upon silence; you never knew through what long unvisited corridors a player might be wandering.

As Burleigh Grimes sat puffing his cigar and contemplating the autumnal fire, I awaited his return, to hear what memory he had conjured. Was it some farcical glimpse of his "Daffy Dodgers" of the 1920s, the snap of an Alexander curve, the crackling aria of a Hornsby line drive, the whip of a Wagner peg, a McGraw fulmination, a Ruthian rainmaker?

I let him be, and the minutes passed to the languid sound of the fire. Finally he removed the cigar from his mouth and looked at me. I wondered what nugget he had lifted from his golden treasury.

"What," he said, "did you think of that son of a bitch who asked me if I'd ever pitched for the Dodgers?"

I drove away that night filled with the warmth of hospitality, sated, gratified, enlightened. And in the dark Wisconsin night I even found the turnoff for Cadott.

Seventeen

⫸ RECOUNTING the careers of former big-league players becomes a synergistic exercise, the writer requiring the stories for his book and the player needing the book for his legacy. The players realize that with passing time they grow steadily dimmer in baseball memory, something they accept with varying degrees of equanimity. But there can be a buoyancy in these careers. Old-time outfielders Harry Hooper and Goose Goslin, both featured in *The Glory of Their Times*, attributed their elevations to the Hall of Fame directly to that book and didn't mind saying so. And while he certainly didn't need *Baseball When the Grass Was Real* to certify his Cooperstown credentials, Johnny Mize said to me when I congratulated him, "I suppose the book didn't hurt," which for the laconic Mr. Mize was an oration.

With only the elite players remaining fast in the general memory, the rest become the province of the truly hard-core fan, the one who believes that yesterday in baseball is just as important as today and will thus relinquish nothing. Being one of the latter, I often found myself, after mentioning some bygone name, blankly stared at by someone who (I thought) should have known better, experiences that leave you wondering whether your ballyard knowledge is esoteric or bizarre, or if you simply have made the wrong friends.

No pitcher, before or since, has done what Cleveland Indians right-hander Wes Ferrell did in each of his first four full big-league seasons (1929–1932)—win twenty or more games; and when he had two more twenty-game summers with the Red Sox in 1936–1937 it gave him six ace years in his first nine. In addition, Ferrell was one of the best hitting pitchers in baseball history, with a lifetime average of .280, while his thirty-six career home runs are tops for a pitcher (he had two more as a pinch-hitter).

This handsome fellow (a Hollywood studio offered him a screen test in the early thirties: he turned them down, saying he already had a job) was also known as "tempestuous." His reactions to baseball's sometimes fickle caprices were legendary. He was said to have chewed apart his glove in the dugout, stamped on his own wristwatch, smashed locker doors, and hurled a clubhouse stool or two. It was always self-directed, though a manager was now and then known to come into his swirling orbit.

By the time I saw him in the summer of 1973, Wes had been gone from the major leagues for more than thirty years, his name but vaguely remembered; he had the fidelity of the record books but little else. When I called him at his Greensboro, North Carolina, home to ask if we could get together, his mildly incredulous response was, "You want to come all the way down here to see *me*?" I don't know which was greater, his surprise at my interest or mine at his response. This was, after all, a record-holding, six-time twenty-game winner. He said he would be pleased to see me.

A day or two later I got into my car and headed south, in my ear a caution from Red Smith. Red, who had known Ferrell well, said, "He's a bright, likable guy, but you be careful you don't set him off." So on I drove, whether to talk baseball or practice diplomacy, I wasn't sure.

It had been a long, hot drive into the Southern summer. I'd stopped at a roadside convenience store along the way and bought a bottle of 7-Up and poured it into my small thermos, in case of thirst along the way. I placed the thermos on the floor, and there it had been rolling back and forth, unopened, keeping beat with the car's ongoing motion.

When at last I arrived in Greensboro and pulled into his driveway, I found Wes outside waiting for me. He rose from his lawn chair with a friendly wave.

"Hot as hell, huh?" he asked, coming at me.

Not wanting to begin a long conversation with a dry throat, I took up the thermos and unscrewed the top, then pulled out the cork, and promptly unleashed a hissing geyser of liberated 7-Up which plumed up and flew out like a carbonated genie, the expulsion catching some of Wes's sport shirt, trousers, and oxblood loafers.

Jesus, I thought, Red Smith's injunction leaping to mind. Wes jumped back, looked himself over, then laughed.

"What do you do before you interview a man?" he asked. "Baptize him?"

Evidently, time had defused his charges.

I spent two days in Greensboro, and Wes Ferrell never stopped talking. Pent up for years, the stories followed one upon the other, funny, poignant, self-deprecating. From North Carolina farm boy to the big leagues, going to war against an array of baseball's golden names: Babe Ruth, Lou Gehrig,

Jimmie Foxx, Al Simmons, Hank Greenberg, Charlie Gehringer, Joe DiMaggio.

I asked the "tempestuous" Wesley if he had thrown at
batters. Only to a purpose, he said, and went on to explain.
The Philadelphia Athletics had backed up in their lineup two
of history's most ferocious right-hand hitters, Foxx and Simmons.

"I always knocked Jimmie down but never Simmons,"
Wes said. "Al asked me about that years later, when we were
at some dinner. 'Look,' I told him, 'you were kneeling there
in the on-deck circle and you saw Jimmie going down. When
I knocked Jimmie down I was knocking you down, because
when you came up you were looking for it, and before you
knew it you were behind two strikes.' He thought about it
and laughed and told me that, doggone it, I was right. So you
might say I started pitching to Simmons while he was still in
the on-deck circle."

What about chewing up his glove?

"Never did that," he said. "But I did tear apart a few
with my hands."

And stamping on his wristwatch?

"A few times," he allowed. "It made me feel better—until I looked down at it and realized I had to buy myself a new
one. Then I really got mad."

On the second afternoon he took me out on a tour of a
nearby Revolutionary War battlefield. As we walked among
the scattered monuments he mentioned with pride that Fer-
rells had fought there. We were walking on a carpet of pine
needles, through a grove of old, whispery Southern trees. It
was quiet, there were few other people about, and he seemed
affected by some enclosing mood. Ferrell blood had run into
this ground, he said. Almost two hundred years ago now. He

had grown up hearing the old family stories, he said, but they had "thinned" out with time.

I asked him if he came out there often.

"Once in a while," he said. "Sometimes I try to imagine all the mayhem that went on right here, all the shooting and yelling." He said it was hard to believe those things had gone on here, where it was so intimately quiet now. I told him it was probably part of the battle's afterlife, that I had walked on fields large (Gettysburg) and small (Concord) and felt that same close, almost touchable quiet.

During most of the hours we'd spent together he had been chatty, amusing, a first-rate storyteller. When we sat down on a bench under some shade trees, however, he was wistful.

"You know," he said, "I was an idol in Cleveland in those early years. Go to a crowded restaurant and they'd move me right up to the front of the line and give me the best table. They used to stop the traffic when I crossed the street. Now?" He laughed ruefully. "I could get thrown down by a cab there and nobody would care."

Wes's chapter was one of the best in *Baseball When the Grass Was Real*, good enough to catch the attention of the editors of the *Atlantic Monthly*, which featured it in their pages just before the book was published. When the magazine came out I called Wes to alert him. He must have gone right out to pick up a copy, for he soon called me back.

"The drug store guy says it's one of the most important magazines in the country," he said, the pride evident in his voice.

"That's right," I said. "It is."

"He says it's read by the most hifalutin' people."

"That's right," I said, "and now they all know who you are."

And sometimes the book you write turns into a hot plate right under you. In 1981 Ritter and I, apparently with nothing better to do, compiled and published a book called *The 100 Greatest Baseball Players of All Time.* Courageous? Foolhardy? We didn't think so at the time, though it seems we should have known better, that these were the kinds of concepts that merely in conversation can lead to internecine warfare within even the most loving of families, create Red Sea divisions between lifelong friends, bring foam to the lips of otherwise well-adjusted people, and prompt imputations about one's sanity. But, as baseball fans, aren't we all, by definition, "experts," with total entitlement? The wise men who spend lifetimes in monkish cells trying to decide between Mays and Mantle should at least be respected for their dedication if for nothing else.

"I like the idea," our editor said to us when we presented it to her. "But you're going to be making 100 friends, many of them dead, and God knows how many enemies, all of them alive."

For some reason I was reminded of the fellow who refuses to say whether he is a Democrat or a Republican. "As soon as I announce," he said, "I will automatically be considered ignorant by half the people, and that's too many. Of course, I will be considered intelligent by half the people, and that's not enough."

If you utter debatable opinions you can always rely on the wind eventually to carry them away; but if you state them in a book they look oracular, and people can stare at them while their ire rises to unbearable levels. The most heated comments concerned our including in the book three players whose careers had ended after barely beginning: Smoky Joe Wood, Herb Score, and Pete Reiser. Each had demonstrated a breathtaking gift for baseball before being cut short by injury. By enrolling them among the greatest we felt we were professing a "romantic" view of baseball supposedly inherent to all fans: the great *What if?* We were saying, in effect, that what had not been would have been, if it had been. How different were we from the abstracters who reconstruct "the lost years" of Williams and Feller on computers, or those who try to forecast the future careers of active players? But no sale. Too many gifted players had been omitted from the book to permit such dreamy indulgences to go unscalded.

We knew that baseball fans did indeed thrive on differences of opinion; what we hadn't realized was that among them were zealots who sharpened their knives on it. We went on call-in shows to publicize the book, and the phone calls came fusillading in from people who sounded as though we had molested their daughters, besmirched their patriotism, questioned their piety. Usually we could justify why a particular player was included; it was the exclusions that sent our critics into hailstorms of opprobrium.

"From now on," Ritter said one night as we walked out of a New York City studio, "we'll do the shows separately. This way, when I'm on I can blame you, and when you're on you can blame me."

Soon after that, I was in Washington, D.C., at the Smithsonian Institution. I had been invited to participate in a three-day "Celebration of Baseball." The event was extremely well organized and attended, with an estimated 175,000 people passing through at one time or another (this in the midst of the 1981 players' strike, which had shut the game down). There were exhibits, clinics, symposiums, panels of notables telling stories and answering questions. The impressive roster of participants included Bob Feller, Waite Hoyt, Monte Irvin,

Johnny Mize, Negro Leagues star Buck Leonard, Brooks Robinson, Lou Brock, Bobby Bragan, Enos Slaughter, and many others, including journalists like Bob Broeg, Peter Gammons, and Jerome Holtzman. The *100 Players* book had just been published (and, by the way, was selling remarkably well). One of the nicer moments for me was when Brooks Robinson came over to thank me for his inclusion in the book. All I could say in response was that it wouldn't have been much of a book without him.

I was scheduled one afternoon to sit on a panel with Feller, Hoyt, and Slaughter. We were seated on a small stage, faced by an audience of several hundred baseball fans.

About six years earlier, for a book called *Baseball Between the Lines*, I had met and interviewed Slaughter on the campus of Duke University, where the old nonstop St. Louis Cardinals hustler had been employed in the Athletics Department. When I greeted him in Washington he remembered neither me nor the book; evidently both had slipped between those lines. But that was all right—Bob Feller had greeted me warmly.

Sitting up front was a robust-looking middle-aged gentleman wearing a baseball cap and sunglasses. As soon as we had settled in he raised his hand and said he required an answer to a question.

"Mr. Honig," he said, "you recently published a book naming baseball's one hundred greatest players. May I ask why Enos Slaughter's name was not included in that book?"

With Enos sitting right there, I found the question imprudent as well as perhaps embarrassing for him. Unprepared for this sort of target practice, I tried to frame an explanation that would have embraced an extravagant tribute to Enos's many skills, the excruciating rigors of selection, and the fact that one hundred was a finite number. But before I could say a word, Slaughter popped in.

"It's books like that and writers like that," he said, "that's keeping me out of the Hall of Fame."

"Good luck," Bob Feller whispered to me.

"To my mind," the agitator with the sunglasses said, "Enos Slaughter was one of the greatest players ever."

Enos (who in later years did make it to Cooperstown) went on.

"I played this game for over twenty years," he said sulkily. "I always hustled. People know that. But you see that doesn't count for anything when they make up these lists."

The guy with the sunglasses gave several slow, loud claps of applause. He was the only one.

Enos wasn't finished. He supplied us with some of his stats, said that he had played on some great teams and had appeared in five World Series. (I had never heard a major league player extol himself in this manner in front of an audience.)

So I was in the dock. I thought about mentioning some of the outstanding players who hadn't made the cut, to show Enos he was in some very distinguished company, but I was concerned about boiling more water. There was no telling whose partisans might be sitting out there.

They were all looking at me. I could have ameliorated the situation, I suppose, by singing paeans to my ill-humored panel mate, saying that he had been No. 101, and that if we had it to do all over again, etc. But I didn't think that would appease him one bit, and anyway, there was no need for appeasement, nor for any *mea culpa*, which under the circumstances would have been as sincere as a coerced apology.

I acknowledged that Enos had been a marvelous player. "But," I went on, "there are thirty pitchers included in that book. That reduces the number of position players to seventy. And neither I nor my co-author considered Mr. Slaughter to be one of the seventy greatest players ever. Not then and not now."

If that sounded definitive, it was meant to. Apparently Enos had run out of tunes to play on his horn, for he remained silent. The audience was quiet, unused, I would imagine, to hearing a highly regarded player so bluntly defined. (And anyway, I was an "authority," right? Who else in their right mind remembered the details of Kemp Wicker's only win as a Dodger, at Ebbets Field in May 1941—and that Enos Slaughter, by the way, was in right field for the Cardinals that day?)

And then Waite Hoyt, the '27 Yankees ace, in his eighties then, known throughout baseball as one of its premier raconteurs and sharper wits, cleared his throat and said, "Would anyone like to hear some funny stories?"

The players and other participants in the Smithsonian Celebration took their meals in a small dining room within the Institution. During one of these breaks I found myself sitting next to Buck Leonard, who had been known as "the Lou Gehrig of the Negro Leagues," a clubbing first baseman who had spent some prime years with the Homestead Grays, for a time the most feared team in the Negro circuit. With the Grays, Leonard had teamed with catcher Josh Gibson, whose long-distance hitting had earned him no less a sobriquet than "the black Babe Ruth" (though Josh was a right-handed rocket launcher). Both men had been just a few years too late when Jackie Robinson leaped across the moat, though each later found Hall of Fame distinction (Gibson posthumously).

During the summers of 1944–1945 I worked as batboy for the Bushwicks, for many years the country's premier semi-pro team, equivalent, it was felt, to a Triple-A team. The

Bushwicks employed at their Dexter Park home in Queens many former minor leaguers and a few cup-of-coffee former major leaguers. They played two night games a week and a Sunday doubleheader, the latter frequently outdrawing many big-league clubs, the crowd often exceeding ten thousand, more when the Grays and their two renowned sluggers were the attraction.

Being the baseball-intoxicated boy that I was, I asked my boss if I could move over to the visitors side when the Grays came in. I wanted to handle the bats for, and sit in the dugout with, Gibson and Leonard. And so I did. One Sunday afternoon I saw Gibson hit one out to Dexter Park's endless center field that easily carried five hundred feet (and that with one of the soggy wartime baseballs). Standing at home plate with his bat in hand, I offered my handshake congratulations.

"Nice shot, Josh," I said.

"Did you think so?" he asked amiably, engulfing my hand in his for a moment.

Things you remember.

So, sitting at lunch with Buck Leonard at the Smithsonian more than thirty-five years later, I gave him a surprising bit of information.

"Buck," I said, "you know I used to be your batboy."

He looked me over for a few moments with a quizzical smile that implied I sure didn't look like a Homestead Grays batboy. When I explained the circumstances, he laughed. Thereafter, whenever we met, which was most often at Cooperstown, the whimsical Mr. Leonard always went out of his way to introduce me to people as his "old batboy," leaving them to puzzle it out. So to some I was the author of this or that book while to others I was, quixotically, the former batboy of the Homestead Grays.

The Bushwicks had played Negro Leagues teams on a regular basis, and it was at Dexter Park that I saw Satchel Paige and the Kansas City Monarchs (the team Jackie Robinson had played with before signing with Brooklyn). I also saw outfielder James (Cool Papa) Bell, reputed to have been the quickest man of his day, who routinely scored from second base on fly balls. (This is the same Mr. Bell who, with his baseball colleagues, visited San Pedro de Macoris in 1937.)

One of the first of the Negro Leagues players to be elected to the Hall of Fame, Bell was a charming and ingenuous man who greatly enjoyed his Hall of Fame Weekend visits to Cooperstown, delighting in signing autographs and answering questions. You could find him sitting on a sofa in the Otesaga lobby, watching the baseball people and the "civilians" come and go, a warm, interested smile on his face. One afternoon I joined him.

"How are you, Mr. Bell?" I asked, sitting down next to him.

"Well," he said, reaching back and touching the nape of his neck, "I bought this new suit and the material is rubbing and giving me a rash."

I sympathized, and we talked. He told of all the wonderful things that had befallen him since his election to the Hall. There had been dinners honoring him, invitations to speak, newspaper interviews. (The St. Louis resident was probably being feted in places that no doubt would have wanted no part of him years ago.)

We were approached by Monte Irvin, the former New York Giants star and veteran of the Negro Leagues.

"Bell," Irvin said, extending a hand. "How are you?"

"Well, Irvin," Bell said, once again reaching illustratively to the back of his neck, "I bought this new suit and the material is rubbing and giving me a rash."

Irvin sympathized. Then they exchanged some small talk and Irvin moved on.

Bell mentioned what a marvelous player Irvin had been, a superb all-around athlete. (There had, in fact, been some people in the Negro Leagues who felt that Irvin and not Robinson should have been the pioneering figure, the concern being that Jackie "wasn't that good" and that a failure to succeed could set the "cause" back for a long time.)

A few minutes later a familiar, highly extroverted voice came booming across the hotel lobby: "Cool Papa!" To the ears of baseball fans there was only one voice like it—distinctive, evocative, filled with the joy of being alive.

Mel Allen closed in and shook Bell's hand.

"How are you?" Mel asked.

"Well," Bell said, once more reaching back to his sore neck, "I bought this new suit and the material is giving me a rash here."

Mel paused, then said, "Sorry to hear that."

After Mel had gone, I asked Bell if he didn't have another suit.

"No," he said shaking his head. "You see, I just bought this one and it . . ."

You can learn many things in the lobby of the Otesaga Hotel on Hall of Fame Weekend, from the hazards of a new suit to the most demoralizing experience that many of us can have—that we're not as smart as we think we are.

One afternoon in 1974 I sat down next to John Bertrand (Jocko) Conlan, bit player with the White Sox in the 1930s and later a National League umpire of distinction, enough distinction to be voted into baseball's Valhalla. As an umpire, Conlan had been a feisty, no-nonsense figure, qualities I had caught a glimpse of some months before.

The Baseball Writers Association of America holds an annual midwinter dinner in a New York hotel. It is a gala, star-studded event, held in a large banquet room, the many tables filled with writers, former players, club executives, and those in need of a wintry taste of their favorite game—a dose of summer amid the frost. The dais is lined with a dozen or so luminaries being honored, mostly for being themselves, but prominent among them the most recent Hall of Fame selectees. That year they included Jocko Conlan.

It is an unwritten law of these events that those on the dais are introduced, come forward, say a very few words, and sit down. Jocko, however, came with a speech in hand. Not a very interesting speech, as we soon learned. After what seemed like some rather long minutes, an irreverent voice called out, "Sit down, Jocko."

The old umpire would have none of it. He looked out into the audience and peevishly said, "I came here all the way from Arizona, and I'm going to finish." At which another voice rose up to say, "Thank God he didn't come from Japan." Jocko finished his speech to polite applause.

When I approached him in the Otesaga lobby that July day Jocko appeared to be in somber contemplation, as though he may have had that episode in mind.

I introduced myself, congratulated him, and took a seat next to him. You always want to start off by letting them know you've been around the block, though with something obviously correct rather than anything especially esoteric (you slip that in later). So, putting my expertise on the table, I casually said, "Warren Spahn must have been a pleasure to umpire," the illustrious Milwaukee-Atlanta Braves left-hander having been known for his pinpoint control.

Jocko turned to me as though I had just forecast a blizzard.

"Warren Spahn," he said sourly, "was a nightmare to umpire."

Timidly, I said, "He was?"

Jocko held up his hand with his thumb and forefinger an inch or two apart. "Spahn was always this much on or off the corner. It was nerve-racking. You could get a headache umpiring him. When Warren Spahn was wild he threw the ball right over the heart of the plate."

"And he was seldom wild," I said, trying to redeem myself.

"That's right," Jocko said. "He was a nightmare."

"A nightmare," I said. "Yes, I can see that."

It's a lovely game, our baseball, designed as entertainment, which it is, supremely so. Some people, however, can get a tad serious about it. In a book I wrote, *Baseball America*, I referred to all-time St. Louis Cardinals favorite Stan Musial as "numbingly amiable." This may not be the gaudiest of compliments, but it certainly is no ragged insult. But according to the barrage of letters I received (all postmarked St. Louis, a city perhaps better called "St. Stanley"), the remark was seen as a calumny upon that, well, that amiable star. I was informed what a gentleman Musial was, how beloved, how luminous a credit to the game, and a few were even transgressive enough to remind me that he had been a great hitter.

I think the biggest rumpus I ever set off was when, as a guest on a call-in show, I offhandedly stated that I thought big-league players were "the finest athletes in the world." (I should have learned by that time not to make these grand pronouncements, but there is something about sitting in front of a live microphone and sending your voice off into the vast and airy night that gives a sense of omniscience.) Well, who would have thought so many basketball fans were listening to a guy talking baseball? The show's engineer said later that he thought the switchboard was about to explode.

A person's sensibilities and partisanship can cohere into quite a sticky mess. You would have thought I'd been belittling the basketballers, who unquestionably possess scintillating athletic skills. But no athlete in any sport, I maintained, had to have the variety of high-caliber talents required to play big-league baseball. I leaned first on Ted Williams's oft-quoted declaration that "the hardest thing in sports is hitting a pitched ball." And what Ted meant was a ball out of the hand of a big-league pitcher, when a batter has approximately two-fifths of second to determine whether it is a ball or a strike, fastball or breaking pitch, what kind of sink or break, and then try to hit it solidly. The ability to do that calls for a truly remarkable fusion of eyesight, judgment, and reflexes.

In addition to this rare packet of coordinates, a player needs a strong (and of course accurate) throwing arm, reasonable speed afoot, and all of the quickness, agility, and, again, judgment required to handle bunts and sharply hit ground balls and line drives and long outfield flies (that some of this is made to look easy is further tribute to a man's talents). The precision timing needed in executing the middle-infield double play—the most balletic of baseball's maneuvers—is sheer artistry.

I fully acknowledged the superb skills of NBA players; nevertheless I was slandered and vilified without mercy, though I did think "baseball chauvinist" was not entirely off the mark. By program's end I was pockmarked with insults. Later, when I asked the show's screener if no one had called to agree with me, he allowed that some had but he had thought it more "fun" to turn loose the others. "Controversy is always better," he said. For him, maybe.

There was one big-league attribute I failed to mention, though it had been very much on my mind: the plain audacity it took to stand at home plate when a millimeter's miscalculation in the pitcher's release point ran the danger of having a thoroughfare driven through your head, especially with the uncertain control shown by speedballers like Bob Feller and Nolan Ryan at varying times in their careers. (You do see some hitters cross themselves when stepping into the box. A petition for success or survival?)

I think it is a miracle of sorts that throughout all of baseball's many seasons and millions of pitches only one on-the-field fatality has been recorded. That, of course, was Cleveland shortstop Ray Chapman, who in 1920 was struck in the head by a ball thrown by Yankees right-hander Carl Mays and died the following day. (Perhaps fortunately for him, Mays was a man of ice-cold sensibilities. According to Yankees teammate Bob Shawkey, "It never seemed to bother him afterward." During spring training the following year, Shawkey said, "Mays corralled some of the younger pitchers and told them, 'If you got to knock somebody down to win a ball game, do it. It's your bread and butter.' He says this after killing a man! That's the type he was." Apparently Mays's less than saintly character did not go unnoticed; despite a high-caliber Cooperstown-worthy career, he never got close to that finishing line.)

There have been many serious collisions of ball and nog-gin, some career-ending, but again one marvels at the survival rate at home plate, particularly when one considers that for many years batters did not wear helmets and pitchers had carte blanche to engage in target practice without threat of fine and suspension, which is now the case.

"Stick it in his ear!" was a managerial injunction often howled from the safety of the dugout, either to intimidate the batter or to give him a friendly tip that he was soon to be in the path of a lethal missile. Rising from the dust—if they did rise—some batters chose the reprisal tactic of pushing a bunt down the first-base line, hoping to find the pitcher covering and then run him over in a smashing collision.

One manager, however, devised his own anti-beanball strategy. Giants star Willie Mays was a frequent target of pitched balls. In one series against the Cincinnati Reds in 1956, when the Giants were still playing in New York, Willie was being leveled during every at bat, infuriating his man-ager, Bill Rigney. Whether the assaults were at the direction of Reds manager Birdie Tebbetts or not was irrelevant to Rigney.

"They were throwing at Willie's head, body, legs," Giants catcher Wes Westrum said. "It was really nasty. Our guys re-taliated, but it made no difference. They were after Willie."

After watching this for a game or two, Rigney became concerned about seeing his mighty center fielder leaving the Polo Grounds with a toe tag. Approaching Tebbetts during batting practice the next day, Rigney said, "Willie's getting fed up with this crap."

"Those balls are just getting away, that's all," Tebbetts said, offering the standard line of defense.

"Well," Rigney said, "I'll tell you what I'm going to do if it happens again. When your pitcher comes to bat, I'm bringing my center fielder in to pitch to him."

"You can't do that," Tebbetts said.

"Show me the rule that says so," Rigney said, walking away.

Tebbetts must have reported the conversation to his pitchers, who no doubt then considered the prospect of standing sixty feet away from a man—a retaliative man—whose cannon arm could fire line drives from deep center field.

"It was amazing," Westrum said, "how those Cincy pitchers got their control back overnight."

"Would Rigney have done it?" I asked.

"That was for them to find out," Westrum said. "I can tell you this—Willie wouldn't have said no. He was fed up."

While on the subject of fastballs errant and otherwise: I was in Fort Worth interviewing former major league catcher, three-time big-league manager, and at the time president of the Texas League Bobby Bragan. Bragan was a marvelous interview; he would ask you as many questions as you asked him. One of those questions was this: "Who's the hardest thrower in baseball?"

This was in the early 1970s, and the answer seemed to me obvious. Nolan Ryan was then striking out batters in record-setting droves.

"Ryan," I said.

"No," Bragan said. "The hardest thrower in baseball is Johnny Bench. He can fire it harder than Ryan or anybody else. If he was a pitcher, Johnny Bench would be on his way to the Hall of Fame from that direction."

Only baseball gives you something like this to ponder.

Eighteen

⧖ I OWE A DEBT to Jim Bouton and his merrily irreverent book *Ball Four*, a risible, bawdy, cutting-edge revelation that big-league ballplayers can be people just like you and me, an insight that the baseball establishment had for decades been trying to keep secret. Bouton's boys were drinkers, sexists, peeping Toms, amphetamine gulpers, childish practical jokers. The game had never been put under such a grinning klieg light. Certain teammates and opponents were portrayed as petty buffoons, others as buoyantly free-spirited, some coaches and managers as something less than citadels of wisdom. From the untouchable Mickey Mantle (about whom Bouton seemed at times ambivalent) on down, the book was candid and refreshing. (Bouton's collaborator on the book was New York sportswriter Leonard Schechter, a man whose acid wit no doubt contributed much to a book that Commissioner Bowie Kuhn described as being "detrimental to baseball.")

Readers devoured the book while official baseball tried to devour Bouton. The former Yankees twenty-game winner-cum-author soon became a baseball pariah, in some quarters as nefarious as Hal Chase. Among those I found most offended by the book were some of the former players I was trying to arrange interviews with. From these I heard the question, "You're not writing a book like Bouton, are you?" Once they received my assurances they became exceedingly receptive, as though I were on assignment from *Good Housekeeping*. I arrived on their doorsteps as the anti-Bouton and was made welcome.

Ironically, in the course of my conversations I was told stories that might have made Bouton blush. Baseball players, it seemed, had become frolicsome the moment Abner Doubleday turned his back. One of the most uninhibited of the naughty narrators was right-handed fireballer Kirby Higbe, who had won twenty-two games for my 1941 Dodgers pennant winners.

I was in Columbia, South Carolina, having just finished a long sit-down with Ewell Blackwell, the sidearming "Whip," who had won sixteen straight for Cincinnati in 1947. Although I had not previously contacted Higbe, I knew he resided in Columbia and decided to call him, to make the trip more cost effective and have the pleasure of talking with a former hero. I got him on the phone, made my pitch, and in a rough man's heavy voice, Higbe said no. Normally when receiving a turndown (I did have a few) I said a polite thank you and hung up. But with Kirby it was different: I felt like I was talking to an old friend. After all, hadn't I, at that impressionable, sensation-absorbing age of ten, been a fervent fan of his, celebrating his wins and mourning his losses? We had gone through a lot together, Kirby and I. This man was no stranger.

"For Christ's sake, Hig," I heard myself saying, "I'm right here in town. Let's get together." And then I nailed him. "Don't let me drink alone." That last must have struck home.

He paused, then grunted. He said he wasn't feeling well, that the doctor had prescribed Canadian Club for him and that he was all out.

"I'll bring a bottle with me," I said.

My old hero had doubled in size. He was a tough, intelligent, hard-drinking rogue, resembling in girth and speech Hollywood's idea of the backwoods Southern sheriff. He was comfortable with himself, his ego in place (the fastball pitchers seem never to lose that). He soon spun off a few tales that for manly peccadilloes exceeded anything in *Ball Four.*

"You want that in the book?" I asked him each time.

"Use your judgment, boy," he said.

My judgment was not to. Even though the subjects of his tales were dead, the families were probably still breathing, and I didn't want anyone embarrassed and turning pictures to the wall. In the course of my adventures I heard many a ripe tale but chose to omit them. Besides not wishing to singe sensibilities, there was another reason for this discretion: I wanted to continue doing these books, and if I began writing about players at their most playful I would be running the risk of being labeled a crypto-Bouton and having welcome mats snatched from under my feet.

To give an idea of Higbe's tales beyond the white lines, perhaps the one about a formidable St. Louis Cardinals pitcher will suffice. In 1941 and 1942 the Brooklyn Dodgers wrapped themselves in a pair of epic pennant races with the Cardinals. The competition between the two clubs was intense, and with teams playing each other twenty-two times a season at that time, a strong, mutual dislike for each other soon emerged. Their games were tense and hard fought; tempers grew edgy; there were beanballs, spikings, sulfurous shouts from the bench, and a few wrestling matches in the middle of the diamond.

The Cardinals pitcher that Higbe spoke of was known as a man among men, with a reputation of prodigious proportions in the more notorious manly virtues. One day, with the Cardinals in Philadelphia on the eve of a series (crucial, of course) at Ebbets Field, an idea entered the fertile mind of Dodgers manager Leo Durocher.

"I'll tell you what he did," Higbe said. "He got hold of a chorus girl he knew, gave her some money, and sent her down to Philly. He told her what the hotel was. She was to go in there, pick up this guy at the bar, and spend the night with him. Get him drunk, keep him at it all night, wear him out. He was pitching the opening game against us, you see."

When the Cardinals arrived the next day, the target of Leo's machinations took the mound and turned in a low-hit shutout performance.

"I went into Leo's office after the game," Higbe said. "He'd just got off the phone with the broad. He wanted to know what had gone wrong with his investment. 'Hig,' he says, 'she says she picked him up at the bar, she went upstairs with him, he screwed her four or five times, drank a fifth of whiskey, and hardly got any sleep at all.' 'Leo,' I said to him, 'maybe you should give me some of that medicine.'"

I told Kirby of a recent meeting I'd had with a contemporary of his, former Pittsburgh right-hander Rip Sewell. Sewell, whom I'd met in Plant City, Florida, was the inventor and primary exponent of the "blooper ball," a pitch he could parachute over home plate from an arc of some twenty-five feet. In his later years Rip had suffered severe physical problems, culminating in the amputation of both legs. The doughty old pitcher fought back, was fitted with artificial legs, and boasted of his golf game.

"I saw Rip Sewell," I told Higbe.

"Good ol' Rip," he said without interest.

"He has artificial legs now."

"I heard."

"He say's he's out playing golf."

"That so?"

"He's got a lot of guts," I said.

"Ol' Rip always had a lot of guts," Higbe said. "He had to, to go out to the mound with the shit he threw."

"You don't want that in the book, do you?" I asked.

"Use your judgment, boy."

Only once did he explicitly forbid me to include one of his tales. It concerned some Dizzy Dean gambolings. Of all the players past and present that he mentioned, only Dean received his unreserved esteem. (They had for a short time been teammates on the late-1930s Cubs.)

"For all of us Southern boys," Higbe said, "Dean was the Southern pitcher. More than Wes Ferrell or Bobo Newsom or any of them. He was up there representing us. That's how we looked at it. We all wanted to be Dizzy. One of the greatest guys that ever lived."

I think Dean's attraction for Higbe and the other Southern boys went deeper than pride in mound exploits. One cannot discount a satisfying sociological element. The shrewd and witty Dean had come muddy-shoed to the big city and with calculating cornpone charm put a reverse spin on the accepted concept of sophistication. If the big-city folk were laughing congenially with him, Dizzy was laughing even harder back at them. Higbe would echo his hero's tactical credo: "I never tried to outsmart nobody. It was easier to out-dummy them."

In the beginning, when I was preparing to write what was to become a series of oral histories about baseball, I was like a man standing before a high-piled buffet table of many temptations. They were all mine to choose from—from Hall of Famers to the long-serving .270 hitters who provide the game's vital vertebral structure. They ranged from the foothills to the cloud-wreathed summits, and when it came to the art of the narrative you never knew which modest journeyman might have the gifts of a Mark Twain.

You can't escape history in Massachusetts; it spreads across the land like natural growth. The Boston suburb of Milton, where I was headed, lay between Dedham, with its Sacco-Vanzetti notoriety, and Braintree, site of the John Adams homestead. For me, there was a special attraction in Milton, both historical and personal.

Elbie Fletcher was as mandatory a choice for my pages as Bob Feller or Pete Reiser. When I told my brother whom I was off to see, he said, "Don't forget to tell him he was my favorite first baseman." A good reason to take the northeast roads to Milton, but not the only one. Elbie was one of those backbone players (.271 lifetime) who crowd the lower ranks with their steady if uncelebrated distinction. With the Boston Braves and Pittsburgh Pirates from 1934 to 1947 (with two years out for military service), Elbie had been known for his flashy glove and his .270 line drives. Higbe had told a Fletcher story.

"For some reason," Kirby said, "Durocher was scared to death of Elbie Fletcher in a clutch situation. One day I'm on the mound at Ebbets Field in the ninth inning against the Pirates, we're up a run, the tying run's on second, there's two out, and Fletcher is up. I see Leo wigwagging from the bench to put him on. I keep shaking my head at him—that's the lead run, you don't put him on. Leo finally comes stomping out to the mound. He wants Fletcher walked. I tell him that's crazy, I can get the guy out. So he agrees and goes back. Well, I give him my best curveball and Elbie rips it. He really rips it. Dixie Walker goes back to the right-field wall and jumps up and makes a great one-hand catch. Game over. I walk off and there's Leo, looking bug-eyed at me. 'I told you I could get him,' I said. But I'll tell you, that damned Fletcher could be tough."

I found Elbie in his office in the Milton Parks and Rec-reation Department, where he was employed. Behind his desk was a large cork bulletin board covered with official-looking papers and memos, among them an eight-by-ten glossy of a handsome young Elbie with his Pittsburgh manager, Pie Traynor, the only evidence that within these portals toiled a former National League first baseman.

"Elbie Fletcher," I said with a fondness based on an old nonexistent but nevertheless deeply felt fellowship, my memory tailing far back—with one spin covering more than thirty years—to that junkyard first baseman's glove handed to my brother by Uncle Fendel.

An exuberantly friendly man, Elbie rose and welcomed me with a strong handshake. Unlike most of my subjects, he had shown a keen interest in the book when I spoke with him on the phone, asking me how it was going and whom I had seen. When I mentioned Bob Feller, Billy Herman, Johnny Mize, Charlie Gehringer, Lefty Grove, etc., he laughed and said, "God, that's some lineup. What do you need *me* for?"

Elbie was in the midst of organizing a senior citizens' bus trip to Lancaster County's Pennsylvania Dutch country. While I waited for his lunch break, several of the old-timers came in to sign up for the trip. One old woman shook her finger at him and said, "Don't you forget to put my name in, Elbie."

He seemed to enjoy the admonishment, reassuring her. When she had gone, he said, "I'll get them down there; it's bringing them all back that's tricky. They wander around, and then when you're getting them back on the bus you miscount by one or two and then there's hell to pay. You've left somebody's grandmother in the boondocks."

"Has that happened?"

He laughed guiltily. "Once."

"What do you do?"

"What else can you do? You turn the damn bus around, go back and send out a scouting party and hope *they* don't get lost. You'd think if you left with fifty and came back with forty-nine you'd done pretty good. But that's not the way it works."

Elbie took me to lunch at a very fine local restaurant. Nearly all the diners waved to him when we walked in; he returned all greetings with smiles and quips.

Sitting at a white-clothed table in the crowded restaurant, I told him of the illustrious position he had occupied in my brother's life those years ago. He was delighted and somewhat incredulous.

"Why me, for heaven's sake?"

"He had the glove," I said.

"But there was Dolph Camilli, Johnny Mize, Frank McCormick. And that's just the National League."

"He liked your name."

"Elbie Fletcher?" he asked, pronouncing aloud his own name in a quizzical tone, as though searching it for hidden qualities.

"He used to scoop up low throws and yell out, 'Elbie does it again!'"

"That's great. But what did he say when he missed one? I hope he left me out of it."

"There used to be a guy in Ebbets Field whose favorite player was Cookie Lavagetto. He'd sit behind third base and yell 'Cookie' the whole game. Then he'd let off balloons."

"I remember that," Elbie said. "Ebbets Field," he added, fondly. "You knew you were in a ball game when you played there."

"Baseball fans. How do you figure them?"

"You begin by not trying."

"Were you a big fan as a kid?" I asked.

"As crazy as anybody else. Worse, probably."

"Who was your hero?"

"George Sisler," he said. "He finished up with the Braves in '29 and '30, and I used to go out to Braves Field to watch him. I always bought a ticket behind first base and watched him like a hawk. Boy, was he slick. He had all the moves. I tried to model myself on him."

By this time we had established a rapport; Elbie's easy-going way made him a quick and natural friend. This enabled me to say, "Maybe you should have watched him at the plate a little." (Leaving the game with a .340 lifetime average, Sisler had peaked with .420 in 1922.)

Elbie laughed good-naturedly. "It wouldn't have made any difference," he said. "I believe you're born to hit a certain average. They assign it to you in the cradle, like you get a name. And they give you a certain amount of doubles. In my case, anyway."

"Doubles?"

"Look at my record: from 1937 to 1946 I never had fewer than twenty-two or more than twenty-nine doubles in a season. No matter what I did, what I ate, who I saw, what I said, I was going to hit around twenty-five doubles in a season. It's like the Good Lord gives you a quota every spring. Same thing with batting averages. Three years in a row I was in the .280s. I know that's not bad, but . . ."

"That's what the long schedule does," I said. "It shows what kind of player a guy is. It enforces a statistical gravity."

"That sounds pretty fancy."

"Did you know that from 1917 through 1919 Ty Cobb batted .383, .382, and .384?"

"Cobb did that?"

"He was in the same rut you were."

He laughed. "Except for that little '3' in front."

In 1934 the eighteen-year-old Elbie won a newspaper contest held to see who was the Boston area's most promising young ballplayer. The prize was a trip to spring training in Bradenton, Florida, with the Braves.

"I'd never been away from home before," he said, "and I was awed by everything. You know what got me the most? They told me that when I went into the restaurant I could order anything I wanted and just sign the check. The first morning I went in I saw 'breakfast steak' on the menu. I couldn't believe it. Back home I'd be lucky to see steak once a month. So I ordered it, never believing they'd bring it."

They brought it. And they kept bringing it. Elbie ordered his breakfast steak every morning for a week.

"The waitress wrote it down the minute she saw me walk in," he said.

After a week of epicurean joy he began feeling sick.

"I was all bound up inside," he said, "and was getting sicker by the minute."

Word got around the training camp that the youngster was ailing. The word reached the ears of manager Bill Mc-Kechnie, a most fatherly and kindly gentleman. McKechnie also learned the cause of the problem. He called the boy into the clubhouse one morning.

"He was holding this big bag filled with liquid," Elbie said, "with sort of a nozzle on it. I looked at it and wondered what he was up to. He handed me the bag. I didn't know what in the world this thing was. He saw the puzzlement on my face and explained how I was to work the thing."

"Are you telling me," I asked, "that in your first big-league camp the manager gave you an enema?"

"Are you going to put that in the book?"

"How could I possibly leave that out?"

"All right," he said laughing lightly. "But give it some dignity."

When we returned to his office I reopened my tape recorder and Elbie talked on. I didn't need many questions; Elbie was a natural, one story flowing into another. Big brother Stanley had chosen a most ingratiating hero indeed.

Describing the professional demise of Babe Ruth, Elbie grew sober. The boy had returned to spring training with the Braves in 1935, the spring Ruth joined the team to melt away his final playing days.

"He was forty years old," Elbie said. "He couldn't run, he could hardly bend down for a ball, and of course he couldn't hit the way he used to. One of the saddest things of all is when an athlete begins to lose it. And to see it happening to Babe Ruth, to see Babe Ruth struggling on a ball field, well, then you realize we're all mortal and nothing lasts forever."

For Elbie this phase of his mortality came in 1947. Like all the rest of them, he felt the accompanying pangs.

"You know it's coming," he said, "but you never think it's going to quite get here. I remember when I was a kid, maybe five or six years old, I had this favorite toy. When I misbehaved my father would take it away from me for a few days. I always felt miserable when that happened, like my whole world had emptied out. That's how I felt at the end, when they told me I was being let go, just the same as I'd felt when that toy was taken away."

As I was leaving he asked to have his regards sent to my brother.

"Does he still have the glove?" he asked.

I told him it was long gone.

Nineteen

⧉ "YOU COULD have been our Musial," I said.

It sounded accusatory, like I was making an arraignment. It was unfair and probably unkind. But the hour was late, and it was a hotel room; you know you're never going to be back there, so you tend to say things in hotel rooms, especially when the hour is late and the quart of Jack Daniel's all but spent. We were about a dozen floors up from the wide lanes of Chicago, from which the occasional spire of sound rose high enough to reach us. The bottle's slow depletion had rolled back memory and inhibition both, and I found myself, from out of a brooding nostalgia for what never was, reprimanding Pete Reiser for having been the relentless ground-burning baseball player I had watched at Ebbets Field in 1941 and 1942 and could still see today in those mirages of remembering.

Look at the box score of that—for me—very first game, when Kemp Wicker scored his only victory as a Dodger, and you'll see that Brooklyn center fielder Pete Reiser (as yet an unproved quantity) left the game early. Running down a fly ball, he had struck a gate in center field, severely cutting his back. He left the game soon after. It wasn't one of his major injuries, and I don't think he missed much time, but what he was saying to me that day was, *This is the way it's going to be. Get used to it.*

Baseball lore pares you down—if you're going to be remembered at all—to that lasting image. It's a matter of taking what you can get, since even some of the mightiest left behind nothing of themselves, neither shadow nor footprint. Pete Reiser, youngest National League batting champion ever, a player of talent beyond measure, is remembered for running into walls and wrecking his career. The reputation earned him invitations to come and talk to the children at the Missouri School for the Blind. He was willing, but curious: Why me? Because, he was told, the children there always had problems with walls and had heard that Reiser was similarly bedeviled. He was one of them.

That was in 1947, by then too late to change anything. The injuries had opened vents throughout his body, and out of each was running one facet or another of those many talents which, when consolidated, had made him a one-of-a-kind player. (As good as Mays, Durocher said. If not better.)

The walls were the most famous part of it, but there were other stoppages, like breaks and fractures, and strains and pulls, and beanings. In '42 he played for months with a serious concussion because, as Kirby Higbe said, "Twenty-five percent of Reiser was better than anybody else." In time he ran up a Mantle-like dossier of injuries, in further resemblance to the Yankees star: switch-hitters (though Pete settled in from the left), unbeatable speedsters, all-out hustlers, and even, as youngsters, beginning as shortstops (a position Reiser could play at the big-league level). Mickey persevered, gritting his way through a full-length career. Reiser had no such luck. The undertow was too strong. Injuries, three years in the army, more injuries, and for all that it mattered it was over in 1947 after one last, near-fatal crash into that Ebbets Field concrete. The padded wall that came later was like the red light installed at an accident-ridden intersection.

You could have been our Musial. Yes, unfair, a combination of the late hour and the near-empty bourbon bottle and my own juvenile reversion, an old, piqued resentment at having been deprived of his career. I was like someone left with the frame from which an Old Master had been torn.

When I had told him I was off to see Reiser, a friend from the Bobo Club, one with his head lost farther in the clouds than even mine, said, "A great opportunity. Like being in heaven and asking Keats about unwritten odes, or Schubert about the what-if symphonies." How did a man feel about being baseball's most intriguing "What if?" It's a wretched question to ask, as impertinent as telling him what he could have been . . . if only . . .

Along with Feller, Reiser was the irresistible name on my list. Of my two boyhood champions, I felt closer to Pistol Pete because there he had been, coming through the radio every summer's day to raucous Ebbets Field orchestration. And of course that short trip to watch him in center field where, unlike the classical DiMaggio, he was a short-fused missile ready to launch pell-mell in any direction, relentless to the point of recklessness, fixed on the single thing. And no different on the bases.

"You know," Elbie Fletcher said, "a lot of times a fellow would get a base hit, and we'd stand on first and shoot the breeze a little. I was a friendly sort of guy. But Reiser wouldn't talk. Never would say a word. He'd get on base, and he'd be all concentration. And you just *knew* what he was thinking about. How am I going to get to second? How am I going to get to third? How am I going to score?"

That concentration. On the next base, on scoring, and in the field on that ball coming his way. *A ball in the air has to be caught.* It was absolute, to the exclusion of anything else.

In the bottom of the ninth inning of the seventh game of the 1955 World Series, the Brooklyn Dodgers held a 2-0 lead over the Yankees and were one out away from winning their first championship. For the Dodgers and all their millions of long-suffering fans it was the brink of the moment of moments. Someone later asked their veteran rock-solid shortstop Pee Wee Reese what he was thinking about. Reese laughed, and said, "Don't hit it to me." (It *was* hit to him, and Reese did make the play.)

I asked Reiser what he thought about in center field.

"Hit it to me," he said. "Hit it to me."

"Why?"

"I wanted it," he said. "Every pitch. I wanted that ball."

"You could have been our Musial," I told him, my mind soggy with whiskey.

"Stan was some kind of player," he said.

Reiser was fifty-five years old then, balding, a bit thick around the middle, deep-voiced, with baseball's hot suns and trackless miles in his face.

He remained indelible in the minds of his contemporaries, and he was never without a job. "Pete's a boy you want to have around," one old-timer told me. He had been a minor league manager, coach, batting instructor, and now the newly appointed third-base coach of the Chicago Cubs, so recent an addition to the club, in fact, that we had missed our original appointment in Salt Lake City.

When I called him at his California home he sounded as surprised as Wes Ferrell and Elbie Fletcher had been that I wanted to see him.

"That's a long time ago, Ebbets Field," he said.

"We can make it sound like yesterday," I told him.

"I don't like to talk about the past."

"It wasn't all bad."

"That's not what I mean," he said. "I like to look ahead."

I assured him we could do both. We agreed to meet. He was then working for the Cubs as a roving instructor in their minor league system. At that point in the summer the farthest east he would be was Salt Lake City. He gave me the date, where he would be staying, and the arrangement was made. I then called my brother.

"Guess who I just spoke to?" I said excitedly. "Guess who I'm going to see?"

"Pete Reiser," he said.

Deflated, I asked, "How the hell did you know?"

"I could tell," he said.

I wasn't really all that excited; I got to Salt Lake City only one day early—sort of to clean the streets and arrange the furniture for Pete Reiser, prepare the city for this summit meeting.

I checked into a Ramada Inn, unpacked, made sure my tape recorder was in working order, then went out to explore the Mormon city. After marveling at what was purported to be the widest main street in America, I did what I always did when invading a new location—visited the library to see if I was represented on its shelves. The Mormons didn't disappoint me.

The following day I waited. The appointed time for his arrival came and went. By early evening, still no Reiser. I wondered whose luck it was this time, his or mine. Finally I put in a call to his home. I reached his daughter, who had a message for me: her father had had to go to Chicago and wanted me to meet him there the next day, at the Executive House hotel. What had happened was this: while I had been sailing with whetted excitement through the blue skies of America, the Cubs had fired their manager, Whitey Lockman, and replaced him with Jim Marshall, whose first request as skipper was for Pete Reiser to be his third-base coach. Since Pete had been unable to reach me, I had gone blissfully to Salt Lake City while he had set off for Chicago. Baseball people are often in a state of transience; get too close to the orbit and you can get snatched right up into it. (Whenever I spoke to Reiser over the telephone in later years, one or the other of us would end the conversation with the catch phrase, "See you in Salt Lake City.")

So the next morning I flew back over the Rockies and soon set down in what many years ago I took a writer's vow never to call the Windy City. I checked into the Executive House, asked about Mr. Reiser, and to my delight learned that he was quartered two doors along the corridor from me, on an upper floor.

The Cubs—at home during the days I spent in Chicago— were not yet playing night games at Wrigley Field, so Reiser and I had two long nights in which to sit and sip bourbon and return to a time precious to each of us, when I was ten years old and a zealot and he twenty-two and a batting champion. In all ways to sundown, he was the past to me, with power to draw waters from that deep well.

That talent. At fifteen he had fibbed about his age and attended a Cardinals tryout camp in his hometown St. Louis. The camp, as was customary, was attended by scouts from other major league clubs. The youngster was immediately weeded out and sent home. A Cardinals scout appeared at the Reiser residence the next day, with an explanation for the disappointed boy and his father.

"We didn't want anybody else to see him," the scout said. "That's why we sent him home. We know who he is."

They had been watching him since grade school, the scout said. Since *grade school.* So they secured him then and there, at fifteen, even though he wouldn't be eligible for another year. (Mr. Reiser had to sign the contract for the boy.) But the Cardinals lost him a few years later when Commissioner Landis, fed up with the club's manipulation of their many minor leaguers, declared one hundred of them free agents, Reiser among them. "We lost our jewel," Cardinals general manager Branch Rickey said later. The Brooklyn Dodgers signed the jewel for a bonus of one hundred dollars. (When Rickey joined the Dodgers as GM a few years later, he and his gem were reunited.)

It is said that in baseball, sentiment comes in through the turnstiles. That night I was the one turning the stile. Reiser did not seem a man awash with nostalgia; the memories had to be drawn from him, but once they were, they flowed easily. He wasn't bitter about his "bad luck" but rather wholly accepting of it, like a man with a determinist philosophy, or one who had taken pains to form one. I wasn't surprised by this, nor was I not surprised. I had no way of knowing. When we first began talking I was that reverted ten-year-old, knowing only what I had known those nearly thirty-five years before, that this was a man I couldn't take my eyes from and who had caused seizures in my imagination (and because of whom I had once tried to steal home). Sometimes Stanley and I had taken seats in the first row of the center-field bleachers to be as close as possible to him, to wait for him to burst from his stationary posture and explode across the grass because, as he said, "That ball has to be caught." Charley Gehringer said that for Cobb every at bat "was a crusade." I think Reiser in the field had some similar frenzies; he seemed to disdain the routine fly ball; difficult ones were more interesting. The crusader would wilt in the mundane.

"I'd see an easy pop fly going into short left," he said. "Reese would drift back for it. He had it all the way, but I had to stop myself from charging in and calling him off. I wanted everything."

Still unable to break away from ten years old (nor did I think I wanted to; this was too wondrous, too wish-fulfilling; if I was ten, he was twenty-two and the injuries hadn't happened yet, could still be blocked, avoided), I said, "We used to sit out in center field and yell at you." We wanted him to turn around and look at us; he never did, but sometimes while trotting out to his position he would glance up. The most exciting thing was when he had to come back to the wall and pull one in, when we could look straight down at him and watch him take in a descending ball, sometimes hearing the leathery *plop* in the glove.

I was reluctant to talk about the injuries, but it would have been like ignoring .400 with Williams and strikeouts with Feller. But more than anything else, this was his story, and I wondered how a man would talk about something that not only blighted his life but had become its caption.

I told him I had seen him steal home once, during a doubleheader with the Cubs in May 1942. My father had taken me.

"Your old man took you to a doubleheader?" he said. "He must've been a fan."

"What about yours?"

"He put a baseball in my hand the moment I could stand up."

"I guess he knew something," I said. Like Bob Feller's father.

I told him about my first game, the time he'd run into the center-field gate. He remembered it. He had cut open his back.

"I was bleeding like a pig," he said.

"You stayed in the game for a while."

"They said they'd sew it up after the game. Leo told me not to slide. I said to him, 'What the hell do you mean, don't slide?' So he took me out."

"You would have slid with a ripped-up back?"

"What the hell was I doing in there otherwise? You're in the game, you play the game."

"But then Leo played you in '42," I said. He'd run flush into the wall in St. Louis and suffered a deep concussion.

"I volunteered," he said.

He wouldn't hear a word against Durocher. He didn't blame Leo, he blamed himself. His average sank from .380 to .310. An umpire, Babe Pinelli, told Leo to get him out of there, that Pete wasn't seeing the ball.

"Another knock on the head could've killed you," I said.

"You don't think about that."

"You were all baseball, weren't you?"

"Listen," he said, "when you're twenty-three years old you don't want to sit on the bench and watch a game. You want to be in there. I couldn't have sat out in a pennant race any more than I could have swum the Atlantic Ocean."

I was eleven years old that summer, sitting at the radio for every tension-ridden game. Suppose I had known then that an errant pitch could have finished my hero forever? What in God's name did he think he was doing? It was, after all, only baseball. But yet, how appropriate was it for me to make so critical an appraisal of a man's intrinsic values, especially when those values had been laid out for all to applaud or mock? He was adamant in his refusal to rue or regret, nor did I get the idea that he ever felt he was entitled to any of that. "I never wanted to cheat anybody on a ball field," he said, "not my teammates, not the fans, not myself." Then by whom or what had I been cheated (and not me alone but all of those fans who distill the game through the dreamier avenues of the imagination)? Fate? Destiny? Bad luck? I was fixed on getting this out of him, but not yet.

Yes, the finest young player in the National League was playing with a deep concussion, when there were no helmets, when the abrasive Durocher would deliberately provoke opposing teams and beanballs would fly indiscriminately.

Reiser was plain and direct; he recited things as they had happened, the underlying motivations always the same: it was the only way to play baseball. He sounded like a man of the highest principle: he had played vigorously by the canons and precepts of the game, playing to his fullest obligation. But in the end it could have been described as fanaticism. I wanted him to share my regrets at his aborted career, to take a stab at outlining those "unwritten Keatsian odes." A .400 season? He said he could have done it in 1942. He was hitting around .380 at the time of the injury and was "just starting to get warm. I could've hit .400 that year. No doubt in my mind about that." He was stating a fact, very conversationally, without pretense.

(It was the only time he talked about what might have been, probably because it really wasn't about what might have been but about what had been happening.)

Unwittingly he made an ironic comment. In extolling Durocher's provocative style of managing, he said, "Leo kept you alive out there."

"And almost not," I said.

"I don't want to hear anything against Leo," he insisted. "He was the best baseball man I ever knew."

I tried to snare him. "He says you were as good as Mays. Maybe better."

"Willie had a great career."

There it was again. Did I have the temerity—and the unkindness—to tell a man what he might have accomplished, if only—? Did he need me to tell him about it? How much did he actually think about it himself? It would have been fascinating to hear. But as far as I knew, none of them had ever spoken about what might have been, not Joe Wood or Herb Score, not Dean or Koufax. If the pragmatic Feller had not seemed particularly interested in a reconstruct of his "lost years," how did a man conceive a lost career? That exercise, apparently, was the province of the most unreconciled of the unreconcilable.

In September 1946, in another tight race with the Cardinals, Reiser slid back to first base on a pickoff attempt.

"I could hear my ankle crack," he said.

Durocher came running out and told him to get up, that he was all right. Not this time, Reiser said. The bone was sticking out.

Then, in '47, he had "that bad accident" in Ebbets Field. To add more seats, the Dodgers had taken in the center-field wall by some forty feet.

"So there's this long fly ball to center," he said, "and I tell myself, 'Hell, this is an easy out.' I'm going full speed . . . and oh, my God, I'd completely forgotten about the forty feet that wasn't there anymore. When I woke up, I couldn't move."

He received last rites in the clubhouse and was taken to what was for him a familiar place, Peck Memorial Hospital. (Pete did have a wry perspective on things. One spring when a newspaperman asked individual Dodgers where they thought they'd finish that year, Pete's answer was, "Probably Peck Memorial.")

He was back five weeks later. In Pittsburgh, during batting practice, he was pursuing a fly ball and was knocked out when he bumped heads with another player. Soon after, he noticed a knot on his head. It was a blood clot. If it moved it could have killed him. He was flown to Johns Hopkins in Baltimore to be operated on. They told him he'd never play again.

"But I went back," he said. "Played the last two months and hit .309."

The Dodgers went to the World Series that year, against the inevitable Yankees. In the third game he fractured his ankle sliding into second.

"It's like you were hexed," I said. By this time it was after midnight and the bottle was far down.

"That's bullshit," he said heatedly. "That's like saying you're not responsible for your own life."

"If a case can be made for a man being hexed, you're that man."

"No way," he said shaking his head. "If that was true, then I'd really be pissed off."

"You're happier with it being all your own fault."

He didn't like that either, the idea of the word *fault*. I think it implied to him something wrongheaded and self-destructive.

"The night I broke my ankle in that Series," he said, "I was in the hospital to have a cast put on. The doctor was sympathetic. 'This has happened before,' he said. 'Last year,' I told him. So he tried to be helpful. He was a nice guy. 'Perhaps you slide too hard, harder than necessary,' he said. What was I supposed to tell him—that I was sliding that way since I was five years old and had done it thousands of times?"

He showed up at Ebbets Field the next day with the cast on his ankle. A cheerleader, supposedly. That was Game Four, the World Series game with the most spectacular ending of all World Series games, Mazeroski, Fisk, and Joe Carter notwithstanding. It was Brooklyn's own "Bobby Thomson game."

It was the game in which Yankees right-hander Bill Bevens was pitching a ragged nine-walk no-hitter until two out in the bottom of the ninth, holding a fingertip 2-1 lead. The Dodgers had the tying run on second. Burt Shotton, then managing the Dodgers (while Leo was sitting out a year's suspension for this, that, and the other), pointed to Reiser. Yankees manager Bucky Harris knew about the ankle cast. "I knew he couldn't run," Harris said later, "but he could still swing." So Harris went against "the book" and called for one of baseball's more unorthodox moves: he ordered Reiser walked, putting the potential winning run on base.

Think of it, two veteran managers guiding themselves by a man's now tarnished refulgence, the one sending up a batter with a cast on his foot, the other unwilling to pitch to him.

"It was a nice tribute to me," Reiser said of Harris's move, "but it cost him."

Bevens's tenth walk of the game put the winning run on, and it scored a moment later in the guise of pinch-runner Eddie Miksis when Cookie Lavagetto drove a pinch-hit, two-run double against the right-field wall. The Dodgers won it, 3-2, on Lavagetto's double and Reiser's reputation.

But by then what had gone was not coming back. The head injuries had left him with frequent pain and spells of dizziness.

"It had always been so easy for me," he said, "but now it became a struggle. I was only twenty-nine, but the fun and the pure joy of it were gone."

Maybe the joy had been too pure, maybe a few restraints on it . . .

There were a few lingering years with other clubs, but it was mostly illusion now.

"You were bullheaded," I said.

He acknowledged that he had been. Writing about the early-nineteenth-century English actor Edmund Kean, Hazlitt said, "In one who *dares* so much, there is little indeed to blame." But late on a night, high above sleeping Chicago, with that whiskey tracking through me, I was not in agreement.

"You tried to do too much," I said.

I think that stung him.

"How much is too much on a ball field?" he asked. "You know, people talk as if I was some kind of nut, banging into walls and all, like I was running after balls that were going way up in the stands. Well, when I hit the wall in St. Louis in '42 and the one in Ebbets Field in '47—those were the bad ones—each time I had the ball in my glove. In St. Louis I dropped it, in Brooklyn they carried me off with the ball in my glove. In other words, those were catchable balls. What was I supposed to do—stop and check the wall while the ball went over my head?"

Outfielders have been known to do just that on occasion, shy away from barriers and have fly balls drop behind them. I tried to imagine the scene, Reiser coming into the dugout and explaining it: *I was wary of the wall.* No. It simply was not in the Canons and Precepts of Baseball as studied and integrated by Pete Reiser.

"I played baseball the way I believed it should be played," he said, in a sense elevating the game into a higher sphere of discipline, and in a further sense sublimating it beyond what I knew about it. I wondered: Is this what a sumptuous overload of talent demands from a man, no matter his vocation? "There are times when you can slow up—right? No—you can't. You slow up a half-step and it's the beginning of your last ball game." That was highly personal; I didn't think he was lecturing on the ethos of baseball. "It might take you a few years, but you're on your way out. That's how I look at it. You can't turn it on and off anytime you want to. Not if you take pride in yourself. It's born in you, it's part of you. It *is* you."

How do you debate a man's credo with him, his sense of honor? His pride? You don't, not when pride trumps the calamities. Foolishly, I wanted to ask if he wished it could have been different. Of course he did, but in what terms could it have been? He had already declared his terms. Durocher said Reiser had everything but luck. As simple as that, or did a zestful *joie de vivre* somewhere enter into it, a young man defying the gods as if to say, *Catch me if you can?*

Now he was this fifty-five-year-old man sitting in front of me. And in the talk of all that I so well remembered, the veils had fallen and he had turned younger. That was me, of course, what I wanted to see—a young dynamo who had promised so much, so many years of so much. But all I had was what I had come there with, a phantom record-book page that ran all the way to 1959, when he was forty, retiring with all those batting titles that Musial instead had taken. But I had this too—an understanding, at least, of why.

"Well," I irresistibly had to say, "when you were on top of your game, there were none better."

"I don't have any regrets," he said. "Not about one damned thing. I've had lots of good experiences in my life, and they far outnumber the bad."

By then we had sipped the night away to the bottom of the bottle. He held his whiskey like a champion, and I had to wonder how many nights, how many hotel rooms, how many bottles through the decades for this traveling baseball man.

"I'll always remember the good ones," I said.

"Life is hell if you don't," he said with a smile. Then he said, "Listen, you never think of yourself as being somebody's hero. You're just a ballplayer, trying to do your damnedest."

If there was an apology in that, I was shameless enough to accept it.

We met a few times after that, when he came east for a banquet or an Old-Timers Day. We stayed in touch by telephone. He was pleased with the book, he said. His chapter was reprinted, excerpted, widely quoted. In the early autumn of 1981 I called him in California. Answering the phone he sounded angry.

"I can't talk long," he said. "I'm not feeling too well." After a pause, he muttered, "I got fucked again."

He died a few weeks later, "after a long illness," the newspapers said. He was sixty-two.

Twenty

≫ I CAN TELL YOU about the time the earth tilted, or seemed to anyway, but wait till we get there. First there are Old-Timers Days, those occasions of decidedly mixed emotions, or so I find them. It is nice to see back in the sunlight the men of yesteryear, especially those who have been gulped by time and long lost to sight, though we must be prepared for some sobering verifications that the years have accumulated.

On one of these occasions, in the early 1980s, the New York Mets displayed a fine sense of history by bringing to Shea Stadium, among others, Bill Wambsganss, the Cleveland Indians second baseman who had snapped from the air a hard-hit line drive and turned it into three seconds of imperishable personal glory and baseball history—his unassisted triple play in the 1920 World Series. He had been twenty-six when his great moment occurred—and it truly was but a moment. Now he was up to his shoulders in years, almost ninety of them, and the once-vigorous young athlete—the one Burleigh Grimes had watched run smiling off the field more than sixty years before—could hardly walk, tottering from side to side as he made his way.

"He has trouble remembering," said Joe Sewell, shortshop on the 1920 Cleveland team and also at Shea that day.

I had had the pleasure of interviewing Sewell for a book called *The October Heroes* in Cooperstown in 1977, when he was being inducted into the Hall of Fame. The diminutive Mr. Sewell was possessor of baseball's most uncanny eye. Across 14 years and a total of 7,132 official at bats he had struck out just 114 times, or approximately once in every 62 at bats. More remarkably, over his last nine years (1925–1933), the soft-spoken Alabaman came to the plate 4,785 times and had just 48 strikeouts, or almost exactly one in every 100 at bats. His steady contact earned him a .312 lifetime average and a place among the game's most eminent. When I asked him to account for this almost supernatural skill, the unpretentious old gentleman leaned toward me and confided, "You got to keep your eye on the ball."

He had been playing minor league ball in New Orleans in 1920 when Carl Mays delivered the pitch that fatally struck Cleveland shortstop Ray Chapman. In need of a replacement, the Indians reached down for Sewell. He arrived, got into twenty-two games, batted .329, and helped his team win the pennant. And there he had been, at shortstop, watching Bill Wamby's three stunning seconds of immortality.

Now, there we were, more than sixty years later, Mr. Sewell and I, sitting in dugout shade at Shea Stadium.

"I'm surprised he's here," I said, noting Wambsganss's frailties.

"Oh, he wanted to be here. He's very happy. But he has trouble remembering."

Bill Wamby was having trouble remembering. I watched him as he went slowly out on the field in his limply hanging old Cleveland uniform, being introduced as "The only man to ever . . . ," and I wondered how much of his radiant moment was still in memory, or was it by now merely an afterglow of "something."

"I'll bet he still remembers the triple play," I said half-jokingly to Sewell.

"Oh, yes," Bill Wamby's old double-play partner said assuredly. "They were asking him about it in the clubhouse. The newspapermen. He remembers all the details." Which were simple enough, I guess: he leaped, snared a line drive, stepped on second, and then tagged out a befuddled base runner who had run disbelievingly right up to him. Three seconds in a man's life, some sixty years before, and today a crowded Shea Stadium was applauding him for it.

Old-Timers Day is supposed to be about the past and the players, but one of those occasions called me back as well, as an unapplauded, somewhat retired fan.

By 1951 the New York Giants had returned from years of dormancy to begin haunting the Brooklyn Dodgers, whose grip upon my affections was still unreasonably strong. That season culminated, of course, in Bobby Thomson's stomach-turning home run, which a chronicler of history is supposed to be objective about. But to a certain one of those chroniclers that home run sails on as a yet unindicted crime. If at the end Thomson was the executioner, the arch villain throughout that summer was Giants right-hander Sal Maglie. Not only did this relentless curveballer trim the Dodgers with maddening consistency, but he did it with what looked like hubristic malice, knocking them down, spinning them around with "close shaves" (hence his nickname, "The Barber"), and in general throwing sand on our cornflakes. And there was even more:

he looked the part of the villain. He had the face of a man who lives through 90 percent of a gangster movie—swarthy of complexion, tight of mouth, cold of eye.

To perturb and distract a player by "getting inside his head" is a baseball axiom. One day Dodgers Carl Furillo thought Maglie was trying to do just that to him with a baseball and responded by throwing his bat at the pitcher. It was anger and it was frustration, for over the seasons 1950–1952 the Giants ace was 15-3 versus the Dodgers (who at that time were fielding one of the greatest teams in National League history). Given that record and that baleful face and trigger-man's dispassion as he dispatched our Dodgers gunners, you can see why we didn't just shout slander and invective at him. For emphasis we rose to our feet and, hands cupped around mouths, fired off our best salvos.

So if you were a Dodgers fan in those days, even if you were a somewhat self-regarding twenty years old and had already read Dostoevsky, you had every right to despise Sal Maglie. The ticket that got you through the Ebbets Field turnstile when he was pitching was a license to hate. It embarrasses me to this moment to think of some of the disasters I and my fellow partisans wished upon this man. Ours was a venom purer than any adder's. Our case was simple: this man was tunneling through our lives.

If you think this animosity juvenile or a manifestation of unsteady mind, well, you weren't there. What was happening in New York City in those years must be considered with sobriety of thought: it was at the time an incurable affliction, the sufferers remaining in its throes until, mercifully some might say, the Dodgers and Giants hove themselves westward. In later years I was to write histories of the New York Yankees and Brooklyn Dodgers. When I suggested to my publisher that we complete the trilogy with a volume on the New York Giants, the response was, "Nobody cares about the Giants." For me this was costly but smugly satisfying. And anyway, how do you write a book about the New York Giants without including the 1951 season?

Nevertheless it did happen, and no amount of burning incense will make it go away. Aided and abetted by the severity of the rivalry, it is the game's commanding moment. But try to imagine the moment without the rivalry, or the rivalry without the moment. Without that home run, time in its gallop would by now have put quietus to much of that history, with all its fables and foibles. Ebbets Field and the Polo Grounds are long down and underfoot. But the home run continues to breach oblivion, a case of baseball snatching breath from the flying gusts. What Thomson's ever-orbiting home run did was to sound the crescendo moment and raise a lasting monument to those teams and their times.

And so as I wandered about the crowded clubhouse on that Old-Timers Day, I noted a solitary figure sitting before a locker, bareheaded, wearing a heavy sweatshirt and baseball pants. He was older, yes, but unmistakable: the care lines etched deeper into his swarthy face, the formerly sinister eyes now merely watchful, as unrevealing as ever. With my old Dodgers psychic disorders now securely behind me, I stared at Sal Maglie with curiosity and a growing, clinical interest. *Good Lord, what had that been all about? How long ago?* The once-upon-a-time archetype of all that was evil on a ball field looked piled on not so much with age as weariness. He looked down at his stockinged feet, then raised his head and moved those expressionless eyes around the clubhouse, and down again.

Naturally I called my brother that night and told him that I'd met Sal Maglie.

"*Sal Maglie?*" Stanley said. "What was he like?"

Of course. More than Feller or Reiser or any of them, Sal Maglie had to be *like* something because he had always *been* something—not just ace pitcher but torment. Static in your sleep. The most demoralizing name among tomorrow's probable pitchers.

I had to laugh at myself: did I forgive him? If such nonsense had been actively in mind it would have been more appropriate the other way around, for I had been the one with the scabrous thoughts, the one who had wished for trucks to pinwheel him through the air, for boa constrictors to lie in wait for him, for his right arm to turn into a pencil. And the things I had screamed at him in the open air.

Maglie. The name itself had had a dark Dickensian toll, a synonym for malice, threat, danger. And yet we had for a brief time embraced him, as baseball, in its sometimes bizarre turns and courses, brought him to the Dodgers in 1956. This was via Cleveland, to where the Giants had waived him the previous July. In 1956 the thirty-nine-year-old pitcher, who many believed was just about wrung out, turned in his last productive season, going 13-5 (including a no-hitter), helping his onetime adversaries to a pennant they won by a single game. But even then the grumble was, "He owed us that."

Now, stirred by some vestige of atavistic emotion that should have long ago been put to rest, I was prepared to dislike him, as though there were some need to justify the old howls and curses. I shook the hand that had snapped out curveballs like a lion tamer with a whip and frozen nobles like Reese, Robinson, Campanella, Hodges, Furillo, and the rest. His eyes sat sadly in his time- and mile-worn face; what had once been baleful was now merely tired. His eyes made his faint, occasional smiles look wan. He was close to seventy then. He looked like a man who had been born with a history.

I asked him how he was and he mentioned some recent surgery. (It had been a brain aneurysm. The surgical procedure had been quite delicate, and successful.) I told him it was good to see him back, that he belonged in New York, though in truth, with that worldly face he looked like he belonged everywhere and nowhere.

There had always been more to Maglie than that unrevealing face and those chin-scraping pitches. In the spring of 1946, then a nobody with the Giants, he had committed "treason" (if you will excuse a teenager's fastidious credo) when, with a handful of other big leaguers, he had jumped to the newly formed, checkbook-waving (and foredoomed) Mexican League. As a consequence Maglie and his fellow renegades had been blacklisted, banned forever from organized ball. "Forever" had lasted three years, when they were reinstated. So this exotic character was indeed a man with a history. Upon his return to the Giants in 1950 he became an instant ace, going 59-18 during his three big years, capped by the black magic he wove over the Dodgers.

"I wasn't going to come down for this," Maglie, whose home was in Niagara Falls, said, "but I guess I was feeling sentimental."

A sentimental Maglie? Once, it would have seemed an anomaly.

"You miss it, do you?" I asked.

"I don't miss pitching," he said, "but I do miss baseball."

That may sound incongruous, but it isn't. It's baseball with its long reach. You can't play forever, but in departure you leave behind the game's inner soul—the rowdy clubhouse banter, the sound of spikes clacking on concrete, the camaraderie of a team. The other world of baseball, more privileged. It brought a tired man down from Niagara Falls, as it had a tottering almost-ninety Bill Wamby from Ohio, even though he was "having trouble remembering." One imagines that sometimes just "being there" is all the embrace that is needed.

I recalled that Maglie, pitching beautifully and well enough to win most days, had been the victim of Don Larsen's perfect game in the 1956 World Series.

"Not many people remember me in that game," he said.

"What was the feeling on the bench?"

"We were surprised how he kept it going, with the hitting we had. Each inning we kept figuring, all right, somebody's going to start it off."

To my own disbelief and discomfort, it still was slightly jarring—that "we." Sal Maglie and the Dodgers.

"But Larsen had good stuff," he said. "He was right on the money with every pitch."

"That must feel like hell," I said. "You pitch a great game yourself and you run into that."

"I did the same to a few guys," he said with a shade of smile.

"Did you like pitching in Ebbets Field?"

He shrugged. "If I had my stuff, I didn't care where I pitched."

He was soft-spoken, surprisingly so to my ear, at least. I still wasn't sure what I had been expecting. A grim old warrior, sullen with unexpended malice? Was he the more deadly for being soft-spoken and polite?

"It seemed you always did well there," I said. "Did you get up for those games?"

"We always got up for the Dodgers. The whole team did."

"Monte Irvin once told me that a Dodgers-Giants game was tougher to play than a World Series game."

"He's right. It was a whole different atmosphere."

"Those fans in Ebbets Field," I said, "they'd get pretty overheated."

"You don't pay attention to that," he said dismissively.

Of course not. Why should a man pay the slightest attention to a howling pack of partisans fire-hosing him with obscenities? But he could have glanced up at us, for a moment at least. Glared at us. Shown some contempt.

"They really gave it to you at Ebbets Field," I said.

He allowed his wan smile and passed me a veteran's glance of mild disdain.

"The feelings were pretty strong back then," I said.

"Giants-Dodgers," he said in explanation at once succinct and comprehensive, a blanket to cover the whole corral.

"Did you think you had a better team?"

He frowned, then gave a noncommittal shake of the head.

"You don't see it like that," he said, "that you're better. That doesn't get you anywhere. You think you can beat them, that's how it works."

"Confidence."

"You'd better have it."

"You used to get those fans riled up."

"Which fans?"

"Brooklyn."

"I think they riled themselves up," he said.

"There was a lot of animosity between the two clubs, wasn't there?"

"I wouldn't say that. Some guys you like, some you don't. It's the same way with every team."

"Who didn't you like on the Dodgers?"

"It's a long time ago."

"You worked them over pretty good," I said.

With a wry smile, he said, "They weren't too shy out there either."

"I saw Newcombe flatten Willie with a fastball."

The wry smile again. "Only once?"

"You used to come in pretty close," I said.

I have heard some old-time pitchers recount with glee or sardonic humor these sorts of escapades. Higbe said he never threw at a man's head, "only at his cap." There were others who looked with retrospective amusement at near-homicidal incidents at home plate. I heard none of this from Maglie.

"You have to let the hitters know you're not afraid of them," he said. "I never tried to hit anybody, just move them back. Not every pitcher is willing to do that."

"That you're tough."

"It isn't a matter of being tough. It's pitching."

"Give them something to think about."

"You could say that," he said.

"You had an advantage," I said, some unreconstructed iota inside me still begrudging him his success. "All those right-handed hitters: Robinson, Reese, Furillo, Campanella, Hodges . . ."

"They wrote out the lineup, not me."

I felt it was time for my confession. I didn't know what was so important about it; it was the sort of thing that never meant a damn to them, nor was there any reason why it should have. But as fans, it was really all we had to offer, our place in the pantheon of the indiscriminate many.

"I was a Dodgers fan back then, Sal."

The unbosoming was received with total indifference, though it made me feel as though I had been sitting there as some sort of *agent provocateur*. I asked him if he thought about those days very often.

"Well," he said, "people talk about them a lot."

And well they should, I thought, because those days were unique, and not because they were mine as we all tend to think that our days of early passage were unique, but because those were the days of Dodgers-Giants and the one city, of Sal Maglie, Willie Mays, Jackie Robinson, Branca-Thomson, and ghosts in old uniforms. Try reassembling that somewhere.

The hand that shook mine, the hand that had snapped off those fearsome and infuriating snakes, was of surprisingly gentle grip. I wished him well.

A nice guy, I told my brother that night. Pleasant, gentle-voiced. A really nice guy.

"You liked him," he said.

"Hard to believe, huh?"

"I'll need time to get used to it."

"How soon we forget, huh?"

"*Soon?*" he said archly.

Well, given the age of the planet Earth, thirty years really isn't that long.

Leaving my old tormenter, I went back out on the field, mingling amid the swirl of old-timers, journalists, photographers, and those familiar faces who seem to turn up at all of the game's celebratory occasions, from the winter banquets to Hall of Fame Weekend.

Standing on the top step of the third-base dugout was a familiar figure, to an old New York baseball fan a very familiar one. Leo Durocher looked to have aged into a waxen image, sportily tailored in blue blazer and white slacks with creases sharp enough to shave with. He was gazing out upon the field with a sea captain's eternal eye, as befitted a man who had once commanded many a similar vista and who gave the appearance of having relinquished it all with regret. He looked now like a man thoroughly and irrevocably California-ized, from his impeccable sportiness to the tan that lacquered a face that may or may not have received the skills of a Dr. Nip and a Mr. Tuck. One had the feeling that it would have taken a pair of forefingers to pull free a smile from him. The "Hey Leo" cries raining down at him from the grandstands appeared to be melting before reaching him; he'd had more than a half-century's practice in ignoring the sound of his own name.

People who had disliked him (a crowded fraternity) were nevertheless always united in the one thing: Leo was as good a baseball man as there was. Seasoned baseball men have told me this about managers: the one and only measure of a good skipper is, does he win with a contending club? Leo Durocher sometimes succeeded when he should have, sometimes not. But whatever his managerial virtues, he had run back on the field an illustrious young star who was suffering from a deep concussion. Whether this was from panic, callousness, or criminal indifference, I didn't know. But I had tried to find out.

When I was writing a book about managers in the mid-1970s I had written to Durocher at his Palm Springs, California, home asking for an interview. Having already spoken with such eminent captains as Walter Alston, Joe McCarthy, Dick Williams, Al Lopez, and others, I felt Durocher would be an excellent addition to my table of contents. Leo, however—as was his privilege—thought otherwise. He evidently sent my letter to his attorney to make the response. In sending me a polite letter of refusal on Mr. Durocher's behalf, the attorney (or more likely his secretary) inadvertently included in the envelope my original letter to Leo, on which the old skipper had scrawled, *Tell this guy to go fuck himself.*

"Hello, Leo," I said. I suppose there is a link, however nebulous, that you have with someone who has suggested you have carnal relations with yourself.

He looked me over, eyes narrowing at the corners, then gave a slight nod, as if to confirm my existence. I understood. A man who revels in his friendship with Frank Sinatra, Don Rickles, etc., tends to hoard his syllables when strangers come lurking. (Not only had Leo heard Sinatra pronounce his name, he had even been heckled on a TV talk show by Rickles: "Leo was the only guy who owed points on his batting average at the end of the season.")

Leo Durocher stories are legion, beginning with his days as a young, feisty, sharp-tongued shortstop on the 1928 Yankees and an alleged dispute with Babe Ruth over a missing watch (Ruth's). And then Leo as a combative, light-hitting but slick-fielding, sharp-tongued shortstop with the St. Louis Cardinals' "Gashouse Gang" of the 1930s. And then as Brooklyn's sharp-tongued skipper in the 1940s, his tenure including a loud and decidedly sharp-tongued defense of Jackie Robinson's right to play. And then his truly startling mid-season move from the Dodgers to the Giants in 1948 (for incredibility, only Svetlana Stalin's defection to the United States can equal it). And leading the Giants to their remarkable 1951 pennant and then a world championship in 1954. And on and on, including the assertion that he "blew" the 1969 pennant to the Miracle Mets by burning out his Cubs players. And much more, several biographies' worth.

I'm sure Leo would have given me a memorable, sharp-tongued interview, but it hadn't happened. Now I found myself with little to say, or at least being encouraged to say little. So I said what little I had to say.

"Do you remember Pete Reiser?" I asked. One of my more inane questions.

He glanced me over with frosty curiosity.

"He was a friend of mine," I said.

"Pete was a good boy," he said.

"Hell of a player."

"That's right."

"He always spoke highly of you."

"That's good," he said.

"He was injured a lot, wasn't he?"

"Pete played hard."

"He played with injuries."

The corners of his eyes appraised me curiously. I wondered if he knew what I was thinking. Probably not; I doubted whether he ever thought it himself, how callously he had handled his stellar young star. Leo's philosophy had always been that today's game was the only one that mattered. The flesh and blood was winning, not how you did it. Billy Herman said that Leo never cared what his players thought of him. Leo had always driven and demanded, and he had fought, with umpires, opponents, his own players, even the fans sometimes. His last managerial job was with Houston, in 1973. He had quit after that season, carping about "the modern player." They refused to do things "his way." The purists notwithstanding, in many of its aspects, the "new way" is better.

So I hurled no *J'Accuse* at Leo. Reiser was dead, Ebbets Field was gone, the Dodgers were in California, Leo was retired. And in the back of my mind I could hear Pete: *Let it go.*

Twenty-One

⏣ BUT YOU want to know about the day
the earth tilted. It happened on another Old-Timers Day, at
Shea Stadium. They were honoring New York's memorable
center fielders that sun-bright afternoon, and quite a galaxy
it was.

The baseball tides at all times flow from two opposite directions, one of the tides slow and languid, the other running
with the game's lifeblood. In his premature departure from the
scene, Reiser left behind an open door through which soon
passed the Dodgers' Duke Snider, the Giants' Willie Mays,
the Yankees' Mickey Mantle (the ensconced DiMaggio left
after 1951). The new men were arranging themselves for long
years of power-laden production. It puts in mind the lines
from *Troilus and Cressida*, where Shakespeare has Ulysses, in
his "alms for Oblivion" speech, say:

> For Time is like a fashionable host,
> That slightly shakes his parting guest by the hand,
> And with his arms outstretched, as he would fly,
> Grasps in the comer: the welcome ever smiles,
> And farewell goes out sighing.

A thick knot of people were crowded into and around one corner of the Mets dugout. The twin cynosures of this lively group of admirers were Mickey Mantle and Whitey Ford, bright ornaments of any occasion: two relaxed, bantering men, completely at their ease.

Along with Larry Ritter, I stood at the fringe of the group, listening, taking in the laughter that was equal for Yankees quips that were witty and for those that were not. And then it happened: the earth tilted. The auditors began falling away, in twos and threes, until Mickey and Whitey were all but alone in their corner. What had taken place? It was this: After putting on his uniform in the clubhouse and walking through the tunnel under the first-base grandstand and then along the passageway and up into the dugout, Joe DiMaggio had emerged into the sunlight, for the moment a solitary figure. He was one of the last out of the clubhouse, yet he would know he hadn't missed anything because it never really started until he appeared.

It had been in the papers: Joe DiMaggio, etc., at Shea on Old-Timers Day; so everyone knew he was there, the main attraction they were waiting for. The atmosphere changed when he came out, even though all he was doing was standing in front of the dugout. Old men were staring at him with clearly delighted, almost proprietary smiles while the fathers of young sons were leaning into the boys and pointing to the field as they informed the youngsters of what had just happened.

Part of the reason for the long and never wavering or diminishing fascination with the long-retired DiMaggio was that there was no evident reason for it—something that might be arbitrary or debatable—making him an unassailable phenomenon. The image had launched itself at the very beginning, in his 1936 rookie season, had found an orbit and never faltered, coming finally to exist like a piety. Most icons, particularly those raised from athletic arenas, enjoy a bonfire fame that blazes for a given term and then burns itself into an ordered place and becomes part of the nebula. Not this man. He had an uncanny way of stoking his fire, remaining a virtuoso among celebrities until his death in 1999 at the age of eighty-four. Apolitical, noncontroversial (one teammate, Lefty Gomez, had described the young DiMaggio as "mysterious"), he gave the public what it seemed to want of him: a persona reserved, dignified, unchanging. Symbol. Talisman. Embodiment of some ideal that was beyond definition. His only rival in adulation was Ruth, but Ruth, the ebullient extrovert, had reveled in it; he waded into it, embraced it, could never have or give enough, and it had nothing to do with ego. Joe seemed to shun it, seemed to prefer having it conferred. He controlled his adulators as if by fiat, by some natural regality.

My old Red Sox coach Jack Burns had said, "DiMaggio doesn't say much. He doesn't have to." That was a long time ago. It hadn't changed. Joe had found the formula—if that's what it was—and never tinkered with it. It was as if a vocal DiMaggio would have marred the image. He was explained away as "shy," "quiet," "aloof" as well as "wary" and "suspicious." Some writers were perturbed by these guarded stances, but for the fans, whose devotion and adoration never wavered, it worked. And whatever was included in the DiMaggio recipe, it worked with teammates as well. As were heard in those hoary paeans to Ruth and Walter Johnson, teammates were proud to have been in the same clubhouse with Joe, while he in turn was regarded as a caring, generous friend. "You needed tickets for some hot Broadway show," Yankees pitcher Spud Chandler said, "Joe got them for you. You needed him for some banquet or testimonial, he'd be there."

The foundation of the edifice was, of course, an athlete who was a glossary of baseball skills that were demonstrated with a smooth and athletically cultured efficiency, the likes of which seemed to denote a new species of player. The old Boston Red Sox players used to say they were never concerned about being a run or two behind in the late innings because they knew "Ted would do something." The DiMaggio Yankees felt the same about their man. Spud Chandler said, "Joe knew things." What did Joe know? Well, a few years before, the long-retired DiMaggio was visiting the Yankees spring training camp. During batting practice a long high fly ball was hoisted into left field. "That's out," someone said. "No, it isn't," DiMaggio said. The ball dropped at the base of the wall. When they all looked at him, the old center fielder said, "I can tell the second it's hit within five or six feet where it's coming down." (So that's how he'd done it in center field all those years, where he never seemed to break a sweat and was always there ahead of the ball, waiting for it.) Joe knew things like that, and in multiples.

"He was the perfect player," DiMaggio's longtime manager Joe McCarthy said, a note of pride in his voice.

Somewhat mischievously, I asked, "Tell me, Mr. McCarthy, this perfect player of yours—did he know how to bunt?"

The old gentleman smiled. "I don't know," he said, "and I never had any intention of finding out."

"He set a standard not just for playing," Spud Chandler said of DiMaggio, "but for the team." There was nothing worse in the Yankees clubhouse than a DiMaggio glare for some perceived baseball transgression (like not hustling) or affront to Yankees dignity. "You felt it," Chandler said. "You really did. You wanted to climb into a hole." Corporations are remote and impersonal; DiMaggio's Yankees were corporate in their systematic winning—six pennants and five world championships in his first seven years.

Mickey and Whitey, sitting in the corner of the dugout watching their admirers move away toward the man upon whom the sun never set, were no small potatoes. Mickey in particular had his own dynamic. Appearing as a teenager in his first Yankees camp in 1951, his power had been compared to Babe Ruth from the left side and Jimmie Foxx (then still an iconic power symbol) from the right. Mantle and Willie Mays, the two mighty center fielders of the age, were constantly being measured one against the other (the debate remains ongoing). But there was no comparing DiMaggio to anyone, or anyone to DiMaggio.

The jewel in the crown is of course that hitting streak, and then add to it that other, postcareer, page-one episode that shot him up to an even higher, baseball-transcending realm— that Marilyn marriage, with all its glamour, controversy, and tragedy, with fillips of Sinatra and not one but two Kennedys thrown in. (He believed that the singer and the president and the attorney general had exploited the confused and vulnerable actress, the latter two perhaps helping set her on her suicide track. If he could glare at a teammate who hadn't hustled, try imagining the quality of the venom he felt for those men.)

I looked at the two abandoned Hall of Famers in the dugout corner. Ford appeared disinterested; Mantle, however, was watching with a studious, perhaps uncomprehending, curiosity the crowd that had left to seek a share of the nimbus, a crowd whose dinnertime story would no doubt be, I gabbed with Ford and Mantle today, but I stood next to *DiMaggio*!

I wished I knew what Mantle was thinking. What did players of such stratospheric stature think of one another? One assumes that DiMaggio, a man of unyielding pride, saw no one above, only below. Mantle, as mighty a player as there had ever been, had to know that he was not Joe, that charisma was not mystique. When the unknown Mantle made what has become a storybook appearance in that 1951 spring camp, he said that DiMaggio hardly spoke to him, even though the youngster had all the trappings of heir apparent. "He was like a senator," Mickey said, reaching for some epitome of stately distinction. The small-town Oklahoman, who the year before had experienced the giddy camaraderie of Class-C ball, would have been unprepared for a lot and DiMaggio in particular. Whether he ever came to understand what "the senator" represented is questionable.

Mantle's moody contemplation of DiMaggio put in mind something that former Yankees manager Bob Shawkey told me about another spring training, the one in 1930, his single year as skipper. Ruth was in the batting cage, Shawkey said, blasting one monstrous shot after another. Gehrig was sitting on the bench watching, motionless, his eyes rising and following each Ruthian detonation as it shot off into never-explored realms. "His face never changed expression," Shawkey said. "I was taken by his fascination with Ruth and couldn't help watching him, a little smile on my face. When he noticed me, he looked at me and then turned quickly away, as if he had been caught thinking about something he didn't want anybody to know about."

Looking trim and game-ready in his Yankees uniform, the encircled DiMaggio was nodding politely to those who greeted him, somehow resembling a candidate whose mind was already on the next town. He stared directly into the eyes of those who spoke to him, though I did not think this was interest as much as an alertness, as if anticipating hearing something he didn't want to.

"He looks good, doesn't he?" a smiling man next to me said. To whoever moved up close he said the same thing.

Earlier in the day, sitting in the Mets cafeteria, I had run an interview with onetime DiMaggio teammate Eddie Lopat for a book I was writing on World Series heroes, of whom the former left-hander was one. Lopat, a most congenial man, was then a scout in the employ of the Montreal Expos.

"Will you introduce me to DiMaggio later?" I asked when we were through.

He shook his head. "He doesn't like that."

"I just want to say hello."

"Do it yourself," Lopat said. "He won't bite you."

"What's he like?"

"Joe? He's all right."

"Did you get along with him?" I asked.

"Why shouldn't I have? All the ball games he won for me."

That was a way of looking at it, I thought, and from a ballplayer's perspective probably the best way.

"He's supposed to be kind of shy," I said.

"Joe's not shy," Lopat said. "He has instincts for people."

"You mean he's always on guard."

"Maybe. Maybe it's something like that. But we always got along."

Don't even try to interview him, several writers of my acquaintance counseled me about DiMaggio. He'll say yes. He's very cordial. He'll tell you to write to him in care of the Yankees. Then you'll never hear a word, one way or the other.

"He looks good, doesn't he?" the smiling man was still saying. As part of his magic the old Yankee Clipper had grown more distinguished-looking as he grew older.

Ritter and I were standing about ten feet away from him. The crowd around him had thinned; his admirers had inhaled his presence and were probably becoming self-conscious about standing near him without saying anything. As they drifted by they all readily agreed with the smiling man that Joe looked good.

Pittsburgh Pirates left-hander John Candelaria, a bona fide ace, approached with camera in hand and quietly asked Joe, "Would you mind?" Joe obliged. Someone snapped the picture and Candelaria walked away, holding the camera like a treasure.

"What do you think?" I asked Ritter.

"Fuck 'im," Larry said. "Let's talk to him."

Eddie Lopat had just come up to Joe, who greeted him warmly. Then Joe frowned at him.

"Why aren't you in uniform?" he asked.

"I'm workin', Joe," Lopat said quickly, explaining his position with the Expos and the need to be in the stands for the first pitch.

Then, noticing me standing there, Lopat said, "This is a friend of mine, Joe," and slipped away.

DiMaggio fixed me with a cool stare and nodded. I told him I was glad to meet him. He nodded again, studying me carefully. The pleasure, evidently, was all mine. He waited for me to say something, no doubt anticipating something he had already heard thousands of times before.

I would imagine it was a product of too much boyhood awe, but I found it wasn't easy standing next to Joe DiMaggio on a ball field and not feeling the occasion, the adult version of the awe—not intimidation but, let's say, inhibition. After all, he was more than that hitting streak, more than "the perfect player": there were those ultra-baseball aspects:

married to Marilyn Monroe (herself by then long apotheo-sized), divorced after eleven months and thereafter holding high a large and famous torch for her, and then to have that ex-wife hammered (allegedly) by two world-famous and sub-sequently martyrized brothers. So you see the problem—it wasn't baseball clouding up my mind, it was the idea of that delectable blonde and those two brothers and their disparate and fatally ordained histories, and this man, and his place among them.

Yes, standing next to Joe DiMaggio could be very com-plicated because what was so sensitively private for him was all too three-dimensional for the rest of us. You could imagine him guessing at what you were thinking, and most of the time he was right and you couldn't help feeling found out.

Ritter, as he often did on these occasions, carried with him a copy of *The Glory of Their Times*. He was a shameless collector of autographs. That copy of his book was a trove of notable signatures, and he was out to add one more. The canny Ritter knew his man. He had the book open to an at-tractive, smiling photo of old-time outfielder Lefty O'Doul. O'Doul (by then deceased), one of the sharpest hitters of his time, and a charming *bon vivant*, had been a fellow San Franciscan of DiMaggio's and someone Joe had looked up to and admired.

"Would you sign this, Joe?" Larry asked, showing the O'Doul photo and handing over a pen.

"He looks pretty good there," Joe said, taking the book in hand.

"Lefty introduced us in San Francisco," Larry said.

"Who are you?" Joe asked, running his signature across the photo.

"I wrote this book."

DiMaggio closed the book and looked at the title. There was a glimmer of recognition; this book was known to baseball people everywhere, icons included.

"I'd be happy to send you a copy," Larry said.

"That would be nice," Joe said. "Send it to my sister in San Francisco." Then, as if he had given away too much, he amended and said, "No, send it in care of the Yankees. They'll pass it on."

We had watched him from deep in the Stadium's center-field bleachers, Stanley and I, in 1941 and 1942, and I could remember an illusion of nearness, probably out of wishing for so much. But now, a mere arm's length away, he seemed utterly remote, as though fixed within by some guardian stillness.

The book Ritter and I had collaborated on, *The 100 Greatest Baseball Players of All Time*, was heavily illustrated. An editor at *The Sporting News* had called me soon after the book's publication and asked if I would lend him one of the DiMaggio pictures, saying Joe had seen it and pronounced it the best of him ever taken. The editor intended to have a portrait made from it, to be presented to Joe.

I mentioned the book to Joe and my status as co-author.

"The 100 Greatest Players?" he said.

I don't know what possessed me, but I said, "We managed to squeeze you in."

He looked at me uncertainly, his eyes narrowing just a fraction.

"It was between you and Mike Kreevich," I said, referring to a steady but unspectacular Chicago White Sox outfielder of the 1930s.

At that he looked aside for a moment and laughed. But then, quickly—and interestingly—as if not to allow the slightest disparagement for a fellow professional, he said, "Mike was a good ballplayer."

"It actually was a very hard book to put together," I said.

"I would imagine so," he said.

"We had a few arguments along the way," Ritter said.

"A hundred is a good number," Joe said. "It sounds official."

"We caught a lot of flak," I said. "People take these things to heart."

"I know they do," he said.

"If you had to pick a number one," Ritter said, "who would it be?"

"I wouldn't know where to begin," Joe said.

That could have been diplomacy. I wondered how deep his interest in the game was. California-born and -bred, he had grown up half a continent away from major league baseball. Had he had heroes growing up, or did becoming the hero of heroes obliterate that sort of thing? Lefty Grove had idolized Walter Johnson, Bob Feller's hero was Rogers Hornsby, the St. Louis–bred Pete Reiser's favorite was New York Giant Mel Ott, and down in San Diego Ted Williams grew up admiring another Giant, Bill Terry. Did the young DiMaggio have a hero? Maybe, but I don't know. I didn't ask him. It may have sounded to him like the beginning of an interview and quite possibly the end of the conversation. We had drawn a modicum of interest and wanted to keep it going.

From the grandstand, upper and lower, shouts of *Joe, Joe, Joe* were flying on the air. He was deaf to them, as practiced at ignoring the cry of his name as they all were, all the stars, as though their hearing were equipped with a special filtering system. Now and then when someone of especially exuberant sonic power roared out the name, Joe would stare at us, as if to say, *See how it is?*

"You should write a book like that, Joe," Ritter said. "Picking the greatest players."

"I'm not a writer," DiMaggio said.

"You've seen most of them," Ritter said.

DiMaggio nodded. He had a way of lifting his eyebrows slightly, furrowing his forehead, when he thought no reply was necessary.

And then, amid the hail of *Joes* coming down from the grandstand, I heard a wholly unexpected, and disconcerting, sound—my own name. Shea Stadium was a mere few miles from Maspeth, and it seemed that some of the old schoolyard boys were there and to their amazement and excitement had spotted a most unlikely person talking to Joe DiMaggio. I was standing with my back to the grandstand and couldn't see who it was, but they weren't too far off, and they were animated and insistent: *Honig! Don! Hey, Donnie!* Like calling to a stray pup to see which name he might answer to.

Ritter, saying something to Joe, passed me a brief glance. He probably thought it was funny. It probably was. But it was also a dilemma, or so I found it. What was I supposed to do—emulate the revered icon I was standing next to and ignore them, or turn and wave? Would that have been gauche? But there was a protocol here, right? It was all very familiar to Joe, wasn't it? He'd been going through this for most of his life; it was easy for him to remain unstirred in these situations because the supplicants no doubt expected it. The way they continued shouting down to his poised indifference meant they had accepted being ignored, that it was part of their gestalt relationship with him. They were settling for being heard, without their idol losing one jot of their esteem and adoration.

But I wasn't Joe DiMaggio. I hadn't even gone to *school* fifty-six days in a row. But there I was, standing out in God's bright sunshine on the pampered green grass of Shea Stadium, talking to him, and by a marvelous stroke of luck being seen by old and no doubt envying friends. What a grand thing it would have been to turn around and, grinning like an idiot, wave to them, acknowledging them and bygone days, letting them know I'd made it and to go forth and spread the word, that yes, it was me, me and Joe, best buddies, discussing the great players and, for all anyone knew, Jack and Bobby and Marilyn too.

But I didn't wave. I didn't turn around. I stood like a totem pole, feeling my name bouncing off the back of my head. It was an act of self-control, I think, and not by conscious decision, because on what basis do you decide something when you're in a situation that is new and absolutely unique to you? Like a totem pole. It was that protocol—DiMaggio's, not mine. He sets the dials. So you stand there, pretending not to hear the outcries of your own name, and for that moment you've been pulled into his orbit, comporting yourself like him, even beginning to feel something like genteel arrogance, that you could very easily adapt yourself to this sort of thing.

They soon stopped calling out to me. They'd go back to Maspeth later and tell their tale, but I didn't think they'd get much sympathy. *He was talking to Joe D.? What the hell did he need you for?*

DiMaggio continued showing an interest in our *100 Greatest Players*. He asked if Phil Rizzuto was in the book. We told him no. (By asking the question he evidently felt Rizzuto belonged, but made no comment on the omission.) What about Yogi Berra? Yes. It was puzzling: he talked about the book as if he were unfamiliar with it; yet we knew he had commented on the "favorite" photograph.

"We had to leave some personal favorites out of the book," Ritter said.

Joe didn't ask who those might be.

"On what grounds did you pick your men?" he asked.

"If a man was dominant in his era," Ritter said, "we felt he belonged."

"Did you rank them in order?"

"No," Ritter said. "That would have got us into worse trouble. And anyway, you can't rank pitchers against position players."

"That's right," Joe said. "Pitchers are different."

"We have Feller in there," I said.

"Bob was the best," Joe said.

"You always hit him pretty well," I said.

He seemed to ponder it, or ponder something anyway. I wondered if he thought I might be trying to slip an interview past him. It made me realize how self-conscious I was talking to this man. It was because of those forbidden areas, of course, and because my mind kept circling back to them, to that blonde and those two brothers. (If you think he wasn't deadly serious about this, I was told by an editor that Joe had been offered several million dollars to tell his Marilyn story and had turned it down. Privacy, loyalty, scruples, possessiveness, whatever it was—all of them, probably—she was not for sale. In a tell-all culture, this was quite remarkable.)

"Well," he said in response to my Feller comment, "I knew he was always trying his best against me, so I did the same against him."

"Which was tougher to hit," I asked, "the curve or the fastball?"

"They were both tough," he said.

"Some people," I said, "claimed Bob was faster than Walter Johnson."

"I wouldn't know about that," he said.

But, Christ, I thought, he must have *heard* something about it, somewhere along the line. He had come into the league the same year as Feller, 1936, as one of the "Golden Rookies." He must have heard judgments, one way or the other. That fastball, after all, was the talk of baseball. Had he heard and forgotten, or had he never cared, thought it of little interest?

"I was there when Feller no-hit you guys at the Stadium," Ritter said.

"Right after the war," Joe said.

"Everybody was wondering if Bob still had it."

"He had plenty that day," Joe said.

We had been watched from a short distance by a small knot of people who had seemed unwilling to intrude upon a DiMaggio conversation. Now they began coming forward, pilgrims and acolytes and maybe even someone whom he was actually glad to see. We were soon moved aside. There was no handshake, no goodbye, no "nice meeting you." We simply melted out of the orbit and retreated to the corner of the Mets dugout where Mantle and Ford had earlier been. Those luminaries were out on the field now, having gathered a new coterie of admirers around them.

Ritter looked at me with an incredulous smile.

"*Squeezed him in?*" he said.

"He laughed, didn't he?"

"You made Joe DiMaggio laugh."

"You notice how he stares right at you when you're talking to him? Like he's waiting for you to say the wrong thing."

"That means he's got it on his mind all the time," Ritter said, "at least when he's talking to a stranger."

"How does this guy make new friends?"

"I'll bet he doesn't," Ritter said.

We tried to reason out why he had taken an interest in the book and why he had pretended not to know about it. For the former, we had no answer; for the latter, we felt he didn't want us to know that he had in any way been breached.

"He doesn't like to give much away," Ritter said. "He's very guarded."

"I sneaked in my Bob Feller questions. He didn't seem to mind."

"Why didn't you wave to your fans?" Ritter asked teasingly.

"Jesus, what was I supposed to do? They must think I'm a real shit."

"No, no. You took your cue from Joe. You behaved like a star."

"You think they were impressed?"

"Absolutely. You can't go waving your arms around while you're talking to Joe DiMaggio."

"I didn't know you saw that Feller no-hitter."

"That's because I didn't. I made it up. I didn't know what the hell to say to him."

"Do you think he ever gets bored being Joe DiMaggio?"

"No," Ritter said. "I think he loves it. He's got the perfect personality for it."

I asked him if he was really going to send Joe a copy of *The Glory of Their Times*. He said he was.

"You'll never hear from him," I said.

"Probably not," he said.

He didn't.

You must understand that it wasn't the first time I'd heard my name shouted out on a big-league field. No, sir. Those sounds had first been made audible years before, in a young boy's wishful imagination. I had heard the countless cheers and roars while walking dreamily on my boyhood streets or while lying at night in the narrow bedroom upstairs from the German delicatessen on Grand Avenue. When you fantasize like that you close your eyes even to the dark, the better to see yourself in your sunlit heroism and the better to hear the exultant acclaim pouring from the packed grandstands.

Nor did what I'd heard while standing in Joe DiMaggio's magnetic field bring either wry smile or wistful memory. The original yips and yells, the ones from 1941 or thereabouts, had been too deeply felt, almost canonical, free from the leavenings of reality. This was a fact of my life that took almost six decades to reveal itself to me.

Through siren call or by impulse, I found myself returning to Maspeth after decades of absence. It was past midnight when I got there, late in that betwixt and between month of November, when fall has been tucked away and winter is yet to labor forth. I had been in uptown Manhattan visiting friends, and because of the long drive back home to Connecticut awaiting me I had been nursing my intake, so there was nothing maudlin about it. I simply found myself turning from the West Side Highway and my usual course home and heading downtown, then east. I entered the long bright womb of the Midtown Tunnel, passed under the East River tides, and emerged into the Queens night, slipping back in time and toward my ground of memories.

I followed the Long Island Expressway, which had divided Maspeth in half in the 1950s, and after a ten- or fifteen-minute drive through light traffic exited at Maurice Avenue and rolled slowly into a quiet, familiar surrounding which was just as memory had locked it in. (I think these sentimental reentries are best made at night; darkness seems willing to conspire with whatever it is you're looking for.)

At Grand Avenue I turned left, drove a few blocks, and parked across the street from the four-room apartment upstairs from the still-present delicatessen. There I quieted the car and sat and awaited my ghosts. Three windows looked down on an avenue which itself seemed much smaller and narrower than remembered, as though it had once widened itself to accommodate my musing tides. Foundation, nurturing nest, hall of dreams, point of departure, and now a mute beckoning, as though urging some completion.

There was no ancestral grandeur, of course. My niche of fantasies looked no different from the other six or seven apartments that sat in alignment above other stores. But it was still there, where a boy had lain abed, his closed eyes watching his older self hurling thunderbolt strikeouts or hitting decisive home runs, and hearing the grandstand shouts vocalizing a future of flawless design, for what was there then to stand in the way of it?

Gazing up at my old bedroom window I found a bit of whimsy irresistible: Did whoever was asleep behind those drawn blinds perhaps have any of my books, and if so what might they think knowing that some had been written right there, in that room? (The writer's desire to connect is indeed willful.)

Leaving the car, I crossed the street and walked to the corner where my Uncle Herman's grocery store had been and where on my way home from school I would often find my father standing outside in his long white apron, waiting to ask how it had gone. *Did you learn anything today? No. Did you forget anything? No. Then you broke even.* Ghosts. And why not? As long as we keep them to ourselves.

I don't think I was looking for anything specific; the collective backward was too crowded for that. It was a sentimental curiosity, the kind of wistful mood of remembrance that rises from an accumulation of years, an instinctive desire to bind the beginning with the end.

I turned the corner and found the plain, unremarkable length of Seventy-first Street unchanged: hedge-fronted two-family clapboards on one side, the nearly block-long school on the other with its high fence of narrow spikes across which trooping young players would drag their wooden bats in a steady rat-a-tat.

One thing had changed, however, and I found it stunning and disheartening: one of the schoolyard's concrete diamonds and most of the other were gone, crushed into oblivion under ponderous additions built onto the school. I paused and with saddened disbelief gazed through the tall wire-mesh fence at this obliteration. It was no easier to assimilate than had been the dismantling of Ebbets Field; if the site of Pete Reiser's dashing heroics had been smothered under apartment houses, then so was that of my adolescent line drives, buried here under tiers of classrooms. It seemed that formal education, at which I had thumbed my nose in the name of greater things, had been rather heartless in retaliating.

I wandered through the back streets, memories lifting and vanishing like swirls of smoke. Old friends, forever unaged; certain things for no great reason remembered. But then from the miasma of images one shadow emerged and remained hauntingly constant. It was the figure of the boy who had walked here those years ago plotting and designing his future, which was now my past. I became keenly aware of him, as though a field of energy was still active. I hadn't entirely taken him with me. I felt his wandering reveries, saw what he was seeing, heard what he was hearing. For him it was all yet to happen, was still here, gathering, untried, with all the purity of innocence.

I wandered the old streets, following his shadow as he arranged his place in the future, as he listened to his coming accolades which had come echoing back to me as I stood with DiMaggio on Shea Stadium's big-league grass. I wanted to tell him that he had been right, his name had indeed been shouted out just as he was yearning for it to be, though with some adjustments as to exactly why. Here and there, of course, I had let him down, but I felt that if he knew what I knew now, he would be pleased. It hadn't gone too far wrong. In many ways, some unexpected perhaps, he would be vindicated. I wished I could have reached out in the darkness and tapped him on the shoulder and told him that.

Twenty-Two

⩘   IN PERSONALITY DiMaggio seemed to reign over his realm as if by decree; Ted Williams dominated his as though he had seized it by force. And it might indeed be said that he had done just that, since his conquest of his chosen ground had originated with an ambition that was more challenge than ambition. The ambition must have sounded charmingly ingenuous to those who first heard it, for in order to become what he meant to be, all he had to do was dislodge Babe Ruth, who at the time the youngster was resolving his life's goal was America's most thunderous walloper and one of the world's resonating names. Williams's ambition was as big as they came in a baseball-soaked America, because it wasn't simply a matter of achieving something monumental. Along the way he was going to have to outdo what had already been done, and been done beyond all previous imagining. But with a raw, impetuous talent already wide awake inside him, the skinny San Diego boy was deadly serious about it all.

It's right there, the first sentence of the second paragraph of his autobiography, *My Turn at Bat*: "I wanted to be the greatest hitter who ever lived." You can't say it better than that. Probably every kid who ever swung a bat said, or at least wished, the same thing. But there was room for only one at the top, and the boy from San Diego resolved to be that one. Pete Reiser said that if you slowed down on just one play it was the beginning of the end for you. We can assume it was in this spirit that Williams stepped into the batter's box, every time, and faced every pitch. He never looked less than *involved* at the plate. Among other things, there was an integrity in that.

It wasn't just .400, it was how, and it was who. He did it with a snap and a verve and a passion for perfection, stylizing it with the game's most flawless swing. The beachboy good looks and the zesty persona didn't hurt. (How might we regard Ernest Hemingway if he had written those books and looked like Woody Allen?) Like Ruth, he united stardom and charisma, and like Ruth he aroused the pride and admiration of his peers. He was a man who came to home plate with something more than the obvious purpose in mind, and they watched him with fascination. Some of them uttered the heretical: Williams was as good a hitter as Ruth, maybe better. DiMaggio impressed them, of course; they could turn clinical when they talked about Joe. The difference was, unless asked, they seldom spoke of him, whereas Ted's name was invariably raised, as though the game's soul and spirit lay closer with him. DiMaggio was the cumulative experience, over and over again those radiant, symmetrical talents stunning you this way or that. Williams was the single drumbeat, and it was the sound of baseball's epitomizing moment.

The voice on the telephone belonged to George Sullivan, the Red Sox PR man. He wanted to know if I was interested in coming up to Fenway Park for the team's Old-Timers Day celebration.

"Will Williams be there?" I asked.

George laughed. "I don't think we could have it without him."

"Will you introduce me?"

"Come on up and take your chances," he said.

It was a beautiful sun-yellow sky-blue day in late May 1984 as I sped along the Massachusetts Turnpike toward Boston. I was not without some wistful sense of participation of my own, for wasn't I by now one of the old-timers? Hadn't I come to the bigs at around the same time as Ted? How long ago? Well, from the time I had first set eyes on Ted Williams—forty-three years. Not yet ten years old, shepherded by my older brother (who left home with my mother's injunction: "Don't lose him in the crowd"), I had sat in those open, sunbaked Yankee Stadium bleachers, where the closest thing to us was Joe DiMaggio's backside and even that was a couple of hundred feet away. We tried to see as many Red Sox games as we could because of Jimmie Foxx, whose name was then a metaphor for power. But as the season went on we could feel and hear increasingly the stirrings of anticipation when that slender, twitchily aggressive young Red Socker came to the plate with his bristling self-confidence.

"He's gunning for .400," Stanley said (and of course for more than that, which we didn't know at the time).

In 1942 all he had to do was leave the dugout and kneel in the on-deck circle with his fretful impatience for the stir to sweep through the Stadium. The self-anointing feat was in the books now: on the final day of the '41 season he had hit like a fury through the front and back of a doubleheader in giving baseball one of its sublime numbers, .406. So in 1942 we weren't just watching him at bat but now were drawn to the clear, irresistible view of him when he stood in isolation in that yawn of a left field. Unlike DiMaggio, who was always that picture of predatory concentration in center field, Williams looked restless, preoccupied. He intrigued me. Of course. I was ten years old and he was a .400 hitter, a .400 *hitter*, who hadn't rolled bunts or jabbed line drives here and there to earn his chair. This young man swung every time with all his force and might. A .400 hitter with Ruthian power.

Ruth himself had never attained .400, not even in that Wild West of a 1920–1930 decade when .400 was broken eight times and Cobb could hit .401 and not come close to leading. But baseball had restored its balance, leveling off most of that can't-miss hitting and shutting down the .400 emporiums. Or so it seemed. Until that lanky young man in left field had done it, and with punch (not to mention the last-day theatrics: he was at .400 on the button on the morning of that final day but insisted on going ahead and playing the double-header, in which he went six-for-eight. We spoke earlier of the mighty fastballers being unstoppable when going after personal goals. Why expect less of the greatest of hitters?). And of course the young man had done it against a considerably less vivacious ball than the one used in the '20s. How could you not look at, and wonder about, him?

I had spoken to Williams on the telephone in 1975, trying to coax him into an interview for a book I then had under way. He was living in Islamorada, down in the Florida Keys. I was in Miami. He said he was familiar with *Baseball When the Grass Was Real* and would be happy to get together. There was a problem, however, and he told me frankly what it was: "I'm impulsive and unpredictable." He said that if he woke up in the morning and had the urge to get into his boat and spend the day fishing, that's what he would do, irrespective of any appointments he had made. That's why he hated to set them up. "I break too many of them," he said, "and then I feel like hell." He offered to do it over the phone. I told him it wouldn't be good that way. We talked baseball for a little while, and that was that. When I hung up I told myself I had just turned down an interview with Ted Williams. I decided it wouldn't be a good idea to think about it too much.

When he came out of the dugout on that May 1984 afternoon at Fenway, Williams looked irritably embarrassed by the crowd's noisy, affectionate reception. He raised one arm and swung it through the air, then appeared to try and lose himself among the players who had preceded him onto the field. They included such Red Sox stars of the past as shortstop Johnny Pesky, southpaw Mel Parnell, relief pitcher Dick Radatz, outfielder Jimmy Piersall, pitchers Luis Tiant, Tex Hughson, Gary Bell, and Earl Wilson, and others.

The tall and lanky figure of the early 1940s had filled out to full size, broad through chest and shoulders and unbecomingly heavy in the midsection. But he was still Ted Williams, .400 hitter (the prefix was now "the last" .400 hitter, with that "last" becoming more and more sublime), war hero, man of flinty independence. The aura was palpable. You looked at him and you thought, *Big*: the man, the belly, the voice, the personality. He could have been the captain of a trawler or the foreman in a logging camp. It was commonly said that if you closed your eyes and listened to him you heard John Wayne. And that was right on the money. He not only had Wayne's timbre but the same way of sounding impatient with his own words, as if the preference was for action. Nor was it studied, you could be sure; this man was as original as Adam. And anyway, "John Wayne" didn't really exist, any more than "Cary Grant" or any of them. If there was a John Wayne he was right now in a Red Sox uniform, wearing number nine, loud and overweight and utterly undiminished. You don't stop becoming "the greatest hitter that ever lived," nor does what drove you to that pinnacle ever abate.

He reigned among his fellow ballplayers as a rough-hewn, egalitarian monarch, asking them about themselves, their families, genuinely interested. He cared. You could see it in those famous, much-written-about, once-upon-a-time 20-10 eyes. ("The reason I saw things," he said in that edgy, candid autobiography—brought off with the skilled help of John Underwood—"was that I was so intense. . . . I was *intent* on seeing them.") Those eyes caught every homecoming ex–Red Sox player, and he hailed them all. Among themselves he was referred to as "Number Nine" or "The Big Guy."

Confronting another "big guy," the behemoth, former intimidating reliever Dick Radatz, he asked, "What are you owning up to now?"

"Around three hundred," Radatz said.

Williams whistled and clapped him soundly on the shoulder, as though three hundred pounds was a wonderful thing to be.

He was the central attraction, not just for the fans but for the players, and he knew it. It appeared to make him irascibly self-conscious at times—victim of an optical paparazzi—a feeling he seemed trying to burn off with activity, with loud greetings and bantering. He gave the high-spirited Tiant a hug. He asked George Sullivan if Carl Yastrzemski was there. Told no, he made a sour face and muttered, "He should've come." (There were stories of a spring training row between the two.)

One old, light-hitting former teammate called out to him, "Hey, Four Hundred, lend me fifty points?"

"How you gonna pay 'em back?" Ted riposted.

If there can be said to be a difference in Old-Timers Day styles, there was a difference between those of DiMaggio and Williams. It was, of course, a matter of personality, and a little more. Joe came out and more or less stood in one place, engaging in quiet conversation with those around him. You didn't touch him, nor did he reach out to you. He sometimes gave the impression of wishing he were elsewhere. Ted was vocal, busy, commanding, exuding his manful camaraderie, throwing his arms around his friends, accepting the mild jibes about his poundage. Ted and Joe, a Huck and a Hamlet in spiked shoes, each in his way impervious to time's mandates.

Ted was the city's living monument, as Boston as any Lowell, Cabot, or Kennedy. A monument that could turn utterly charming when it wished, as it did when he was approached by an attractive young woman journalist. He was smiling, flirtatious but never improper, answering her questions patiently, without condescension. I had recently heard a tale about the Williams charm, how captivating it could be, the tale told to me by a Boston attorney.

The attorney was active in Ted's favorite charity, the Jimmy Fund, which contributed to research into children's cancer. (Williams was more selflessly active in this cause than he ever wanted people to know.) Ted and the attorney, an elderly man, had become quite close. The attorney had a friend, a woman who idolized Ted. Her name was Rosemary. She was Irish Catholic, extremely devout, in her fifties, a spinster living at home with her parents.

"She was a wonderful woman," the attorney said. "Why she never became a nun, I don't know, because her life was like that. The only thing outside of God, the church, and her parents she cared about was Ted Williams. She knew about my friendship with him, and one day she—very shyly—said she would like to meet him. So I called Ted. He was living at the Shelton Hotel then—this was in the early fifties, I think. I knew he'd say no, no, no. But I also knew I'd finally get him to say yes. And he did. Ted always liked to say no before he said yes. You had to understand him.

"So we drove over to the Shelton. You can imagine how excited she was. This was a longtime dream coming true. I was delighted for her. We got to the Shelton and went up to his room. You never knew which Ted you were going to get, the sulky one or whatever. But this time he turned on the charm, and when Ted Williams wanted to charm you, you were charmed for life.

"We sat and talked for about ten minutes, and then there was a knock on the door. Ted jumps up and answers it. We hear a woman's voice and then Ted whispering, 'No, not now.' He closes the door and comes back. Five minutes later, another knock. Same thing: 'Not now.' Well, in the course of thirty or forty minutes it happened about four times. After the third time he started to get agitated. And after the fourth time he really slams the door and comes back and roars out, 'Women! From the Mother of God on down, all they're interested in is one thing.'

"Well," the attorney said, "I look over at Rosemary and she's got her teeth in her lower lip, giving me the most doleful look. Now Ted is slouching there in a sulk and I'm figuring it's time to get the hell out of there. So we made our goodbyes and cleared out.

"I'm driving Rosemary home, and for the first ten minutes or so it's dead silence. I'm thinking that this was probably the worst, the most disillusioning experience of her life. Then she starts shaking her head, and says, 'Isn't it terrible how those awful girls torment that poor boy?' I was astounded.

'*From the Mother of God on down*'? Believe me, there isn't another man in the world who could have gotten away with that. You want to talk about charm?"

George Sullivan introduced me to Ted. I received a full, powerful handshake.

"I'd like to talk to you for a few minutes, Ted," I said.

"Catch me later," he said, moving on.

"Does he mean it?" I asked George.

"He always means it," he said. "But you have to catch him. Wait until after he hits."

There were two old-timers I had set my sights on. Ted, of course, was one, for all the reasons you can imagine; the other was a purely nostalgic quest. On the field was my long-ago seatmate on the East Coast Champion heading to Melbourne, Florida, in April 1948. Frank Malzone had made it all right, coming to the big leagues with the Red Sox in 1955 and playing nowhere but third base for them until 1965, a total of 1,335 games. (I tell you, you could see it from the first day. It was there.) He played a year with the California Angels, leaving the game with a .274 lifetime; like Elbie Fletcher, one of those solid men that make the game go. He was still in the Red Sox's employ, as a "super scout," his job during the season to remain a team ahead of the Sox, scouting that team to give Boston what advantage he could.

To my eye he had changed little across thirty-six years (or is that pure conceit?—if they hadn't changed, it made sense that neither had we).

We shook hands. I introduced myself, reminding him of when and where.

"Jeez, it's a long time ago," he said, in apology, I took it, for not remembering me.

I showed him a snapshot I had dug out of my files and brought along. It was of our old quarters, the Bahama Beach Club. There was Frank—he had wandered into view just as I was taking the picture.

"That was a nice place," he said, studying the old photo.

We talked about the Milford team. Out of the whole squad, all those boys who had swarmed the Melbourne diamonds, only Frank and one other, a hard-hitting infielder named Ray Jablonski, had made significant dents in the big leagues.

I reminded him again: we had sat together on the train going south. Once more he looked me over. I think he was trying to remember. I think he wanted to. But no.

"It's a long time ago," he said again.

We shook hands and parted. He took a few steps, then turned around and pointed a finger at me.

"Right-handed pitcher," he said.

"How the hell did you remember that?" I asked.

He shrugged. Baseball people. Baseball memories.

There probably wasn't a person in the sold-out Fenway Park who didn't know all about Ted—.406, the farewell home run, the lost years, all of it—but I wondered how many knew the story of the frail old man being helped carefully and slowly out of the dugout. They announced his name over the PA system and there was applause, whether knowledgeable or merely polite it was hard to say. It no doubt had been louder seventy-two years before, when young Joe Wood had dazzled these grounds and the city of Boston and the whole Universe of Baseball as he incised his 34-5 record into Red Sox history, and then icing the greatest season ever for a Red Sox pitcher with three World Series wins and a championship. Twenty-two years old then, with style and dashing good looks. Seventy-two years ago (the year Fenway Park opened). Pull out your calculator; it made him ninety-four on that shining afternoon (he died a year later, having outlived his fastball by nearly three-quarters of a century). Everyone had retreated to the dugout, leaving the field to Smoky Joe, the onetime teammate of Cy Young. Ted was applauding with the others, watching the near-last of the old man, who was trying one final restep into the familiar.

"They say he could really throw," Ted said, to no one in particular.

Earlier I'd had lunch with Smoky Joe and his son Bob (an adoring and idolizing son he was, too) in the Fenway dining room. I was renewing an acquaintance made some years before, when I'd spoken with Mr. Wood for a book I then had under way. Bob told his father who I was (speaking up a bit; there was a hearing problem now), but I think the greater part of the old man's mind was by now at rest. He stared at me as if through a haze, with vacant curiosity, knowing I was there but not sure where, just somewhere, somewhere within his ninety years of stock and store. Bob several times mentioned the book, and each time his father nodded, taking it on faith more than memory.

"They're going to ride him around in a golf cart," Bob said. "It's really a special occasion."

"Is he up to it?" I said.

"He's fine. He's a tough customer," Bob said. Again he asked his father if he remembered me. It had been five or six years since I'd been to New Haven to see the only thirty-game winner I'd ever met. He had been remarkably vigorous then but had, it appeared, since taken on a rush of debilitating time. And then, as if my face had for a moment peeped through the clouds, the old man said, "How have you been?"

"Very busy, Mr. Wood," I said.

"You remember, don't you, Dad?" Bob said. "He wrote *The October Heroes.*"

"I remember," Joe Wood said, with that touch of irritation the elderly will show when they suspect they're being doubted.

When he reached the infield grass they helped the frail old man into the golf cart, where he sat down. He was wearing a slightly too-large Red Sox cap. He was holding a baseball in his gnarled, arthritic-looking right hand, the hand that had, they said (and "they" know, don't they?) fired that ball as fast as Walter. Then began his slow odyssey around a small tract of land patched into a wondrous long ago, where he had ruled as mightily as any sceptered king. The crowd was on its feet, applauding Joe Wood around the infield. As though the cheers were some sort of time-melting elixir, the old man came to his feet, raising the baseball into the air, as if to remind them that he whipped that thing past Cobb and Nap Lajoie and Shoeless Joe and matched strikeouts with Walter.

"He was only twenty-three when he hurt his arm," Bob Wood said. (I knew that. He was lamenting.) We were standing in front of the dugout, watching the relic of a once young, flashy fastballer hearing it all again for that one last time. "They say he was as good as Walter Johnson," Bob said wistfully. "And Johnson even said it: 'Nobody throws harder than Smoky Joe Wood.' Look at the teams the Red Sox had coming along—they won three World Series over the next few years. Do you know how many games he could have won?" The son confessed to sitting up nights writing down the won-lost records that might have been, the way latter-day romantics guess at the blanked-out careers of Pete Reiser and Herb Score and try to fill in Feller's and Williams's "lost years." "I could see him winning three hundred games in ten years," Bob said.

"Does he ever talk about it?" I asked.

Bob pushed out his lower lip and shook his head. "No," he said. "He always says that's the way it was. But I wish I knew what he really thought."

Yes, what he thought, and what he was thinking now. I watched as the golf cart with its ghostly passenger standing with his raised baseball and his slightly too-large Red Sox cap moved around the infield grass, to cheers that must have sounded distantly surflike to his diminished hearing. He was circling the mound that had been his old summit of fame, where he had beaten Christy Mathewson and the Giants in the final game of the 1912 World Series. Given my predispositions, I was trying to imagine the monumental Matty out there throwing his fadeaway and the most beautiful curve, Joe Wood said, that he had ever seen. Baseball remains in perpetual cycle, from past to present and around again; a cycle of reappearing, never-ending memories, handed off from one generation to the next like heirlooms.

The golf cart circled past the place where one damp April afternoon in 1913 young Smoky Joe Wood had gone after a ground ball and lost his footing and fallen and injured that right arm and become a reverse lightning bolt, leaving behind a shadow for meditation, a player who never grew old. I don't think that patch of grass meant a thing to him anymore, whether remembered or not. He just stood in that golf cart, looking around at the crowd and holding a baseball up in the air and proudly bearing his years. The man who had beaten Mathewson, right there, on that mound.

When Joe Wood's trip around the infield was over and he was being helped away, the batting cage was rolled into place at home plate. Part of the Old-Timers Day tradition is having the men of yesterday step in for a few nostalgic rips. And they are quite serious about it, too. No matter how many years retired, for these few handfuls of pitches a big leaguer stepping into the cage is once more a big leaguer. Whether the crowd gets much out of this, I'm not sure. But this day there was going to be a special attraction in that batting cage, and anticipation of it was high: Ted Williams was going to hit. They were going to see it one more time, once more for those who remembered and for those who would never forget. Here, at a moment marking a high noon of past and present at once, the cycle was going to return him and pause, returning history to the sunlit immediate.

Williams had continued moving restlessly about, going from one old Red Socker to another. But the sound of baseballs being whacked in the cage seized his attention. Unsurprisingly—these had been his arias and siren calls since childhood. He took up a position behind the cage and, as the other players joked and needled the batter, watched with great interest. What he was still looking for, God knew, but his eyes were fixed, watching each swing, some of them labored, some rusty, all determinedly exerted, and all of inexplicable fascination to him.

Each batter was announced over the PA system, as was each change of pitcher. Luis Tiant, always extremely popular in Boston, drew a loud cheer when he took the mound and began entertaining the fans with some of his old, crowd-pleasing whirling dervish deliveries. Watching from behind the cage, Tiant's onetime batterymate, catcher Bob Montgomery, said, "He pitched the greatest game I ever saw. The fourth game of the 1975 World Series. He beat Cincinnati and threw 163 pitches." Montgomery looked around and repeated the pitch total, in verbal italics.

Throwing considerably fewer pitches today, Tiant left the mound, lifting up and waving his cap to an ovation. He was followed to the hill by Mel Parnell. In 1949 this highly skilled left-hander won twenty-five games for Boston. He was sixty-two years old now. He threw four pitches. None reached home plate. The ball left his hand and dropped ten or so feet from the plate and then rolled along. After the fourth pitch Parnell walked off the mound, folding over his glove and stuffing it into his back pocket, staring at the ground.

"That's sad," Williams muttered, watching him.

Williams returned to the dugout, selected a bat, and turned and strode toward the cage, his obvious purpose picked up by the home-plate crowd and soon spread through a ballpark suddenly filled with town criers: *Ted is going to hit!*

"Can he still do it?" I asked George Sullivan.

"Ted would never allow himself to look bad," he said.

Ted was grinding the bat handle in his hands. His face was set; there was no bantering now. It was as if the clock had rewound itself back to the beginning, back to when he was the skinny kid in San Diego setting out to prove something, when it all still lay ahead, the swings and the pitches, the years and the miles.

The crowd of players and media and whoever else had been ritually standing around the cage, in tribute melted away, leaving Ted solitary at the plate, in clear view to all.

All had melted away, that is, except for one. I looked around and found myself standing alone at the side of the cage as Williams was setting himself in the box. I don't normally try to make a spectacle of myself, nor was I trying this time. It simply happened. So everyone in Fenway Park was staring at Ted Williams and, through no fault of their own, at D. Honig, author and batting-cage barnacle. I didn't want to move. I felt that through a lifetime's lunacy, fidelity, and passion I had earned the right to remain there. Allowing the crowd its unobstructed view of Williams, I got down on one knee (resembling, no doubt, genuflection, which, again no doubt, probably looked appropriate, given what was about to happen), took hold of the cage wires, and watched. For a few moments I felt extremely self-conscious—more than 35,000 people were focused on Williams, and who was this guy kneeling there? (Zoom-lensed photographers were no doubt at work, and I would guess that somewhere in the files of the Boston newspapers are pictures of Williams at the plate and, if the angle is right, some nondescript character at his devotions.) But that feeling of exposure soon left me as Ted Williams began uncoiling on batting-practice fastballs and doing what no man has ever done better.

He was knocking the ball around with authority; pitch after pitch came in and went right out. That quick lash of a swing seemed improbable snapping out of that bulky body, making solid, nail-hammering contact. Most of his shots were dispatched to right field or through the right side, followed by another precise resetting of that stance, that taut, focused anticipation. Ted Williams in a batting cage versus his original challenge—a pitched ball—was a patently serious and unrelenting man. His sixty-five busy years were irrelevant. Whatever was left of what had been the most flawless coordinates in baseball history were being summoned and bunched and unleashed. There was nothing wistful or good-old-days about it. He was at bat. Line drives were leaving his bat with prime-time authority. Ground balls were shooting through to right field on one or two maniacal hops, reminding me of what one old-timer had said of Gehrig: "He didn't hit ground balls; he hit line drives that bounced." Former teammate Billy Goodman had said: "When you were on first base and Ted was up, you had to be awfully careful. The way he scalded the ball he could take your head off with a line drive."

Whack! Whack! Whack! There were long, very high drives out to right field, toward the Red Sox bullpen, an old Williams landing ground ("Williamsburg," they once called it). But no matter how squarely hit, none went out, falling just short of the barrier. Well, sixty-five years old; something had to give. Interestingly, he never glanced away to track any of them, the focus remaining always the next pitch.

After each swing he leaned slightly back, drew a breath, then came forward again, snapped the bat, waited, saw, then strode and whipped at the ball one more time. The intensity never for a moment left him. There was no compromise, not even decades after having attained his goal, attacking each pitch as though the competition was still on, the crown not yet quite his.

I was witnessing a kind of ferocity, the kind that evolves when passion unites with desire. It was controlled, certainly, and surely aesthetic in its context, but it was more than simply the satisfaction of drilling a baseball. (After all, a dozen or more other batters had been in the cage, and there had been nothing approaching this single-mindedness.) What, I wondered, must it have been like to pitch to him when he had been younger and quicker and absolutely lethal, when he was still in the midst of his ascent to the summit? Gene Conley had given me some idea. A rare two-sport man, Conley had pitched winning ball for several big-league teams in the 1950s as well as playing basketball for the Boston Celtics.

He had faced Ted in an exhibition game. "You talk about a guy putting you back on your heels on the mound," Conley said. "He dug in, and he looked so *big* up there and the bat looked so light in his hands, and he didn't swish it around, he *snapped* it back and forth." Williams looked *big* up there? To Gene Conley, who stood six feet eight plus the height of the mound, Williams looked big.

When left-hander Bobby Shantz, good enough to be voted Most Valuable Player in 1952, came into the league he asked how he should pitch Ted. "They said he has no weakness," Shantz said, "won't swing at a bad ball, has the best eyes in the business, and can kill you with one swing. He won't hit at anything bad, but don't give him anything good. In other words, Good luck, kiddo."

Deep into his private world, Williams never relented. Pitch after pitch came and went, the impacts sharp and definitive. Still fussy as ever about the strike zone, he let the occasional ball go by, like a man rigidly adhering to religious convictions. Now and then there were bursts of applause, a few cheers, but for the most part the ballpark was quiet, as if the onlookers did not want to miss the sound of each bat-and-ball contact. It was twenty-four years since that famous last at bat in 1960, when he had closed the book with a home run that seemed as much an act of will as anything else. A parting gift, from the gods to Ted, from Ted to us.

I looked over my shoulder for a moment. In the visiting team's dugout the day's opposition, the Kansas City Royals, were to a man on the top step—the estimable George Brett among them—watching with quiet interest. Unusual for a roster of big leaguers to come out to watch a sixty-five-year-old man in the batting cage? Most unusual. But today was not usual. (In his heyday, of course, it was almost *de rigueur* for everyone on the field to pause in their activities and watch when Ted stepped into the cage.)

When you are dealing with Ted Williams all reveries are allowable; they are the lineal continuities of the awestruck boy in the Yankee Stadium bleachers watching him turn loose at the plate or fidget in left field. And so I told myself that this could be the last time he was going to do this, that what had begun a continent and a lifetime ago was ending here, each crack of the bat pounding another sealing bolt into that history. And there I was, having completed a journey of my own, right there in the boiler room with all its steams and thumps, watching the pistons snap and the dials turning toward conclusion.

Once, as he was setting himself, he glanced over and for a moment's fraction we were eye to eye; then he went back to work, swing after swing, each as gravely calculated as the one before. He was drawing deeper breaths now, pausing an extra second or two before hoisting that bat and tightening his fingers around it, each time looking as though he were building for one last mighty and conclusive sweep of it.

It appeared now that he was putting greater effort into those swings. His face was more tightly drawn, as though an anger was stirring inside him. At that incoming baseball? No, I don't think it was that; I think it was something more. The anger—or maybe it was frustration or resentment—was being provoked by a wholly different sensation. He was tiring. Given what resurgence had been firing through him, this was subversive and galling. This had never been a part of it. He was emitting short, barely audible grunts with each swing now. It had been about ten minutes, maybe more.

"Next hitter," he called out.

No one in the dugout budged. They were no less enchanted by the scene than anyone else.

A few more shots, some of them dropping into left-center.

"Next hitter," he called out again, irritably now.

Still no one budged. The bat continued crossing the plate, with less verve than before, but still the ball darted, climbed. No one wanted it to end, not in 1960, not today.

Never moving his eyes from the pitcher, the old lion roared the call again.

"Next hitter, goddammit!"

This time it was a command. There was stirring in the dugout. I looked over and saw Frank Malzone walking reluctantly forward, bat in hand, a most unwilling next hitter.

"Good luck, Frank," I said facetiously, straightening up and moving away from the cage.

"Some act to follow, huh?" he said with a wry grin as Williams left the cage and Fenway Park became a tempest of cheers.

Williams took a seat in the dugout, leaned back, and pushed his cap up from his forehead. He was clearly tired. I walked over and sat down next to him.

"Can we talk now, Ted?" I asked.

"If you've got something to talk about," he said.

Some fifteen or twenty feet away his old teammate Johnny Pesky was standing on the field looking over at him. Williams saw him and winked. As if he had been waiting for that, Pesky winked back and then turned away.

I wanted to say to him that he had looked good in there, but that would have been a hell of a thing to say to Ted Williams, wouldn't it? I mentioned the phone conversation we'd had those years before and the substance of it, the book I was writing. He didn't remember it, of course, but he'd no doubt had many similar ones, because he repeated what he had said then: "I don't like to set up appointments. I break too many of them, and then I feel guilty."

A clubhouse attendant brought him a damp towel, and Ted began wiping himself around his face and neck. He took several deep breaths; there was a weariness in the exhalations.

"What was the book about?" he asked.

"The old days," I said.

He nodded to the old days. I asked him if he knew much about baseball history.

"Not a hell of a lot," he said.

"But you know about the great hitters."

"Well, sure. Ruth, Cobb, Hornsby, Joe Jackson. I knew their records." For what he had in mind, he would have had to. "I got to know them all personally, except Jackson. Cobb used to give me batting tips."

"Did they help?"

"They were great for Cobb, but not for me." He turned to me with a look of mild curiosity. "That was you at the cage, wasn't it?"

"That was me."

"You were lucky."

"Best seat in the house," I said.

"That's not it," he said. "You had your fingers on the wire. If I'd have ticked one it could have broken them."

I was going to ask why he hadn't warned me, but he turned to look at the cage, attracted by the sound of Frank Malzone's bat making contact. But I think I knew why he hadn't warned me. Vic Raschi, the formidable Yankees right-hander who had practiced intimidation on the mound, told me he had always tried to stare a hitter down, to break their concentration. It had invariably worked, he said. Except for one man. Guess who?

he asked. I guessed. "You couldn't break his concentration at home plate with a hot poker," Raschi said. "He never let up. He was the most intense player I ever saw."

"What did you used to think about when you were up at the plate?" I asked Williams.

"I was watching," he said. In other words—I surmised—the thought was in the intent.

"For what?"

"Just watching."

"Were you playing mind games with the pitcher?"

"No," he said somewhat impatiently.

"Do you think the pitchers were afraid of you?"

"I don't know why they should have been—they were getting me out two out of three times."

But we both knew that wasn't efficient enough.

Dick Gernert, former power-hitting first baseman, was in the cage now, making some solid contact. Williams was watching every swing, following the flight of the fly balls.

"You meant business in that cage, didn't you?" I said.

"What's the point otherwise?" he said offhandedly.

I was going to comment on how hard he had been hitting them, but I realized that, as with DiMaggio, this was not a man you flattered. Nevertheless there was something I remembered and couldn't help mentioning. It was an at bat rather late in his career, at Yankee Stadium, against right-hander Bob Turley—"Bullet Bob"—at the time one of the game's premier fastballers. He'd had Ted 0-2 and gone right after him with a blazer.

"I don't think I ever saw a ball hit harder," I said, after setting the scene for him. (He was listening to this with great care.) It began as a line drive, low enough for the first baseman—Joe Collins, I think—to go up in the air for, and then it began to climb, like something launched with booster rockets inside it. It ended up in the second deck.

"I was ready for it," he said.

"You remember it?"

"Turley had a terrific fastball."

"But to come in like that oh-and-two?"

"Why screw around when you can throw like that?"

"He figured he'd slip one past you."

"Probably," he said.

"You were guessing with him?"

"I wasn't guessing," he said, again with slight impatience. "I was watching him."

"What did you see?"

He shrugged.

"Do you remember all your home runs?" I asked.

"No," he said. "Unless people start talking about them."

In other words, they weren't remembered, but neither were they forgotten. You had to rub one to make it appear.

"Do you get that from a lot of people," I asked, "some guy coming up to you and saying he saw you hit a home run in 1949 or whenever?"

He nodded. "I hear that now and then."

"Do you get tired of hearing it?"

"You know, you really shouldn't. But you can. It depends on what mood you're in."

"You could be a moody guy," I said.

"How do you know?" he asked.

"People told me."

"Well, I guess maybe. Sometimes."

"Did you ever have somebody tell you he saw you go oh-for-four?"

"Why the hell would anybody want to tell me that?" he asked querulously.

"I figured by now you must've met every kind of screwball."

"Probably have," he said.

Players and nonplayers were coming by to exchange a few words. Ted signed some full-color glossies of himself, barely glancing at his much younger self that was sometimes smiling, sometimes not. The young Williams had been extremely handsome, while smiling, engagingly so. Add a .400 batting average and you could understand those women knocking one after the other on his door. (According to one of his old teammates, Ted had been an accommodating magnet rather than an active chaser.)

A young man in a Red Sox uniform was sitting by himself farther along the dugout bench, gazing out at the field with what appeared to be a decided lack of interest. Young though he was, he had the comportment of a veteran. "That's Roger Clemens," George Sullivan had told me earlier. "They just brought him up from Pawtucket. If he's half as good as we think he is, we've got something." Nobody was paying much attention to the boy, which seemed just fine with him.

"Do you ever think what your record might have looked like," I asked, "if you hadn't missed all that time in the service?" (Three years in World War II, the better part of two more after being recalled for the Korean War.)

"I don't have to," he said. "People are always telling me about it. They make it sound better than it probably would have been."

"Another three or four batting titles, two hundred more home runs."

"Well, maybe," he said without interest. "Who knows?"

"They think about Feller too. What he might have done."

"Bob Feller," he said, nostalgically, it sounded.

"Was he the best you ever faced?"

"He had the most stuff. By far."

He was still watching the batting cage, where the solitary whacks continued to ongoing banter from a surrounding knot of bat-holding former players. (The current Red Sox squad had for the most part kept to the clubhouse.)

"Did you ever say to anybody," I asked, "that you were the greatest hitter who ever lived?"

"I said I wanted to *be* that," he said, defensively, I thought.

"That was a hell of an ambition. I mean, with Ruth, Cobb, and Hornsby already in the books."

"It was a goal," he said watching the cage.

That was how he described it in his book—a goal. A man has to have goals, he had written—"for a day, for a lifetime . . ." All athletes have goals, from the Olympic sprinter who measures his by nanoseconds to the man who must achieve his day by day and swing by swing over decades.

"Nobody starts off shooting for second best, do they?" I said.

"I don't know why they would want to do that."

It wouldn't have been unreasonable, I thought, with Babe Ruth at the top.

"When all was said and done," I said, "did you think you'd made it?"

"That's for others to say. If I say it, it doesn't mean much, does it?"

"No."

"You writing a book here?" he asked. I had been scribbling some notes.

"How often do I get the chance to talk to you?"

"So you're letting it fly, huh?"

"Do you mind?"

He shook his head indifferently.

I didn't know how long he was going to sit there, or when we might be interrupted. So I tried it again.

"How about believing it yourself?" I asked.

"Believing what?" he asked.

"That you were the greatest hitter. I mean, without bullshitting yourself."

"I don't bullshit myself," he said irritably.

"If enough people told me I was a great writer," I said, "I would come to believe it."

"Not if you didn't believe it first yourself," he said. "That's how you get there."

He'd circled around it, come close. But he wasn't going to come out and say it.

"Jimmy Dykes told me you were the best hitter he ever saw," I said. "He said not Ruth, not Cobb, not Joe Jackson, but Teddy Williams. He called you 'Teddy.'"

He grunted a chuckle.

"Ted Lyons said the same thing," I said. The former Chicago White Sox right-hander had faced Ruth for a dozen years and later pitched to the young Williams. "He said you were the best."

He sat thoughtfully for a few moments, then said, "You know, Tris Speaker said the same thing to me once. He said, 'Ted, I've seen them all from Ty Cobb on out, and you're the best.'" It was like he was sharing a confidence. He sounded ingenuous; there was neither boast nor vanity in his voice. He was passing along the judgments of others, the ones who had "seen them all," the ones whose judgments were as conclusive and indisputable as a jury's.

I told him that in one of my books I had stated unequivocally that he was the greatest hitter ever.

"That's good," he said noncommittally.

"Am I out on a limb?"

He laughed at that, still watching those swings in the cage.

"Do you think that someday somebody will take it away from you?"

"Sure they will," he said. "Some day."

"As long as they swing at strikes."

"Good strikes," he said.

"Is that the secret?"

"Christ," he said, "that shouldn't be any secret."

I was in no hurry driving home that night. The traffic on the Mass Pike was light, the roadside foliage rushing aside in the darkness, leaving my mind free to roam through what the day had been. I thought of Williams in the batting cage, with that swing materializing from out of history, crossing the plate for a moment of flashing sunlight, then back into history. I would be telling people about it over the next few days, how a sixty-five-year-old man had been able to transform himself and once more enchant a crowded ballpark. There would be none of *Listen, for a man his age to . . .* It had been the real thing, that bat loaded with real bullets, firing scalding line drives. I had been right there, hadn't I, feeling those vibrations from the past?

You take them all—the venerable Fenway, Smoky Joe Wood, Ted Williams—drop them into the mind of a baseball fool, who will churn them around and find the alchemy he wants, and out of the fantasy will come the quickening essence reborn. I had not seen a frail old man that afternoon but a young, flashy thirty-game winner, and I had seen a .400 hitter resurrected. And don't forget, Christy Mathewson (of whom "everybody had heard") had stood right there on that mound, throwing his fadeaway, in 1912. Christy Mathewson. I'd seen him too. Yes I had. Seen them all. You have to know how to look.

Twenty-Three

⚜ IN HIS retirement years Babe Herman, Brooklyn's thunderous slugger of the 1920s and 1930s (he still holds many of the franchise's heavy-hitting records), spent a lot of time traveling around the world with his wife.

"We were on a cruise in the South Pacific," Herman said, "and one of the ports of call was the Fiji Islands. One night we were sitting on the veranda of this restaurant having an after-dinner drink and looking out at the Pacific. There was a full moon, and it was a gorgeous night. And then some guy—very elegant looking, probably in his seventies—sits right down at our table and says to me, 'Mr. Herman, I saw you play once.' This is in the Fiji Islands."

Herman, a gentleman all the way, acknowledged the intruder politely.

"The guy says it was in 1937, when I was with Detroit. He says I came up as a pinch-hitter and whacked a double into right-center. He's telling me about this thirty or thirty-five years after the fact. Now, the thing is, I only played in about a dozen or so games with Detroit. Here's a guy who saw one of them, remembered it, and is telling me about it."

"In the Fiji Islands."

"That's right."

I thought of my Kemp Wicker game and those glutinous memories.

"Maybe it was his first game," I said. "You never really forget them."

"I don't know," Herman said. "He didn't say."

I asked if he'd had many similar experiences in his travels.

He had. "I've been picked out in London, Paris, Rome, places like that," he said. "And not only there, where you might expect it, but I've sat and talked baseball in Bangkok, New Zealand, India. And believe me, I've never started the conversation."

"I guess," I said, "they want to hear about those famous stories."

There was no doubting the reference, and he laughed good-naturedly. Despite his colossal years with the Dodgers, Babe Herman is permanently fixed in baseball lore as the man who one sunny day in Ebbets Field was hit on the head by a fly ball and who had, in that same blissful venue, tripled into a triple play. But these gems of folklore, he patiently explained, had never happened. The fly ball, he said, had actually bounced off the dome of his late-inning replacement, whose insertion into the game had gone unannounced and unnoticed, leaving Herman with the notch for his resumé. The other business was merely *doubling* into a *double* play, which is messy and complicated enough but still lacks the cachet of the popular story.

Herman was a cultured man, a philatelist, a grower of prizewinning orchids, a devotee of grand opera (his son, Robert, had been administrative assistant at New York's

Metropolitan Opera). I asked if his somewhat ragtag image bothered him.

"Not a bit," he said. "People enjoy telling those stories. It doesn't matter if they're true or not. And it helps keep my name going. Maybe some of them might get curious about me and look up my record."

"They'd be surprised," I said.

He gave me a sly smile.

While we were on the theme of cherished diamond tales and their resemblance to reality, Herman shared an insider's knowledge of the most famous one of all. In 1941, during the filming of *Pride of the Yankees*, Hollywood's fanciful biography of Lou Gehrig, Herman, then playing in the Pacific Coast League, was asked to stand in for Gary Cooper—playing Gehrig—when Cooper was supposed to tag a long one. Herman also stepped in for Babe Ruth (playing himself in the movie) when Ruth, nearly fifty years old then, was unable to lift the ball into the air to director Sam Wood's satisfaction.

"Talk about famous stories," Herman said, "that's the biggest one, isn't it? The Babe calling his shot in the '32 series. Well, one day during the making of that film I was standing around the set talking to Ruth when who walks in but Charlie Root, the guy who was on the mound when it happened." (Root was also then still active, pitching in the Pacific Coast League.) "I introduced them," Herman said, "and they shook hands. After some idle talk back and forth, Root, who never liked that story, suddenly said to Ruth, kind of sternly, 'Hey, you never pointed out to center field that time, did you?' Ruth laughed and said, 'Of course not, but it made a hell of a story, didn't it?' After some more talk Ruth walked away. Charlie looked at me and said, 'It won't make a damned bit of difference.'"

No, it wouldn't. It was too late for that. It remains the story too good not to be true.

Big stories, little stories. Baseball produces them all, from Babe Herman talking about Babe Ruth to, well, a little old lady and a TV repairman.

In 1984, a year or so before she died, my mother, then living in eastern Pennsylvania, called me at my Connecticut home. After the usual exchange of pleasantries, she said, "Some crazy guy asked me about the Phillies."

"Well," I said, "given where you live, they're your team."

"I don't have a team," she said, as firmly above it all as she had ever been.

"He probably thought you were a fan."

"Me?" she said, her tone expressing how ludicrous that was.

It seemed she had just had a TV repairman in to service her balky set, and he had asked her how she thought the Phillies would do that season. She told him she was not a baseball fan, nor had she ever been one.

I was familiar with her small apartment, and I knew that, proud mother that she was, on the small coffee table adjacent to the TV set she kept a stack of my baseball books (at that time numbering about fifteen). The repairman had no doubt spotted them and assumed he had stumbled upon one of the game's scholars. I pointed this out to her.

"He must have thought you knew your stuff," I told him, "with all those books."

"Oh," she said pensively.

"And you told him you weren't a fan."

After some moments of silence, which I interpreted as thoughtful, she said, "Well, at least I knew the Phillies were a team."

You have to be alert; you never know from which direction or unlikely person the next bit of baseball amusement may come. From one's own little daughter, for instance.

When she was around six years old, Catherine, wide-eyed and innocent as a kitten, said something to me I am certain no one on solid ground or rolling sea had ever said before or ever will again. She came home from school one day bright with news she was certain would make her father proud.

"I'm a Yankees fan," she announced.

This to an old Brooklyn Dodgers man still bearing the scars of Yankees hammerings in World Series after World Series, who had grown up under barrages of unanswerable Yankees taunts and boasts.

"Why?" I asked her gravely.

"I like Reggie," she said.

"Well, Reggie is a good player, but . . ."

I could see she sensed something was amiss. A child's face, at that age of purity, is a roadmap of inner paths and trails.

"I'll tell you the truth, Cathy," I said as gently as possible, "but I sort of like the Red Sox."

Now the dismay was obvious. She had done something to disappoint the center of her universe. But she was a resourceful child.

"Well," she said, "the Yankees are my favorite team, but the Red Sox are my second favorite team."

Ask yourself, outside of a windowless room with rubber walls, have you ever heard those words uttered?

It is a truly bountiful place, this America of ours. Where other locations on our planet twirl about with but four seasons, we have a fifth, a commanding and versatile fifth, superimposed upon all the others with their peeping buds and yellow summers and colorful leaves and whirling snows. We call it the Baseball Season, a timeless time that arches over the full calendar, evoking and embracing hope and optimism, action and excitement, fantasy and reality, memory and reminiscence. Faithfully cyclical, there really is no end to it.

Bear the above in mind as I tell you how tightly—and indeed perversely—focused are some of the hardy souls who celebrate this season. It was a winter's night and I was sitting with some of these celebrants. We were mellow with whiskey, and the cigar smoke was thick enough to hold rain. Given the time of year, the talk had been, naturally, about trades and free agents, about the upcoming Hall of Fame voting, and how many days to pitchers and catchers. Then somehow, the talk found its way to global warming. Opinions were expressed, dire scenarios depicted. Greenland might come sidling up to Manhattan. The oceans would rise. Dolphins would catapult from the waters of Lexington Avenue. We were facing, it was warned, twelve months of summer.

Twelve months of summer. Irresistibly the conversation veered back to its original base. Twelve months of summer. Twelve months of baseball. Foreseen was one grand three-hundred-game season every year, renewing after the World Series. What could be more appropriate than Opening Day on January 1?

A three-hundred-game season. The statistics would be sumptuous. Sluggers routinely banging out more than a hundred home runs. The dinosaur known as the forty-game winner would rise from extinction and stalk the land once more. Fan fatigue? Never. As always, too much would be just enough.

Twelve months of summer. Think of the possibilities. Think of all the stories.